REPRESENTING HISTORY, CLASS, AND GENDER IN SPAIN AND LATIN AMERICA

ALSO BY CAROLINA ROCHA

Masculinities in Contemporary Argentine Popular Cinema (2012)

New Trends in Argentine and Brazilian Cinema (2011), coedited with Cacilda Rêgo

Violence in Contemporary Argentine Literature and Film (2010), coedited with Elizabeth Montes Garcés

Argentinean Cultural Production during the Neoliberal Years (1989–2001) (2007), coedited with Hugo Hortiguera

Representing History, Class, and Gender in Spain and Latin America

Children and Adolescents in Film

Edited by Carolina Rocha and Georgia Seminet

REPRESENTING HISTORY, CLASS, AND GENDER IN SPAIN AND LATIN AMERICA
Copyright © Carolina Rocha and Georgia Seminet, 2012.

Softcover reprint of the hardcover 1st edition 2012 978-1-137-03086-3
All rights reserved.

First published in 2012 by PALGRAVE MACMILLAN® in the United States
—a division of St. Martin's Press LLC, 175 Fifth Avenue, New York, NY 10010.

Where this book is distributed in the UK, Europe and the rest of the world, this is by Palgrave Macmillan, a division of Macmillan Publishers Limited, registered in England, company number 785998, of Houndmills, Basingstoke, Hampshire RG21 6XS.

Palgrave Macmillan is the global academic imprint of the above companies and has companies and representatives throughout the world.

Palgrave® and Macmillan® are registered trademarks in the United States, the United Kingdom, Europe and other countries.

ISBN 978-1-349-44061-0   ISBN 978-1-137-03087-0 (eBook)
DOI 10.1057/9781137030870

Library of Congress Cataloging-in-Publication Data is available from the Library of Congress.

A catalogue record of the book is available from the British Library.

Design by Scribe Inc.

First edition: August 2012

To Evangelina
—Carolina Rocha

To my parents and brother
—Georgia Seminet

Contents

Acknowledgments ix

Introduction 1
Carolina Rocha and Georgia Seminet

I Memory and Trauma

1 Surviving Childhood: The Nepantla Generation
  as Portrayed in *On the Empty Balcony* by Jomí García Ascot 33
  Julia Tuñón

2 Fairies, Maquis, and Children without Schools:
  Romantic Childhood and Civil War in *Pan's Labyrinth* 49
  Antonio Gómez L-Quiñones

3 A Child's Voice, A Country's Silence:
  Ethnicity, Class, and Gender in *El silencio de Neto* 63
  Georgia Seminet

4 Children's Views of State-Sponsored Violence in Latin America:
  Machuca and *The Year My Parents Went on Vacation* 83
  Carolina Rocha

5 Enabling, Enacting, and Envisioning Societal Complicity:
  Daniel Bustamante's *Andrés no quiere dormir la siesta* 101
  Janis Breckenridge

II Childhood and Paths to Citizenship

6 Innocence Interrupted: Neoliberalism and the
  End of Childhood in Recent Mexican Cinema 117
  Ignacio M. Sánchez Prado

7 From Buñuel to Eimbcke: Orphanhood in
  Recent Mexican Cinema 135
  Dan Russek

8 Through "Their" Eyes: Internal and External Focalizing Agents
   in the Representation of Children and Violence
   in Iberian and Latin American Film   151
   Eduardo Ledesma

9 Roads to Emancipation: Sentimental Education in *Viva Cuba*   171
   Rosana Díaz-Zambrana

III Gender Identity

10 Constructing Ethical Attention in Lucía Puenzo's *XXY*:
   Cinematic Strategy, Intersubjectivity, and Intersexuality   189
   Jeffrey Zamostny

11 Cinematic Portrayals of Teen Girls in Brazil's Urban Peripheries:
   Realist and Subjectivist Approaches to Adolescent Dreams
   and Fantasy in *Sonhos roubados* and *Nina*   205
   Jack Draper

12 No Longer Young: Childhood, Family, and Trauma
   in *Las mantenidas sin sueños*   223
   Beatriz Urraca

Notes on Contributors   239

Index   243

Acknowledgments

The impetus for this project was provided by the Latin American Studies Association (LASA) Montreal conference in 2008, which allowed the coeditors a venue to think about children and young protagonists in film. We are grateful to the contributors for their dedication to meeting deadlines and their collaboration throughout the process. We also want to thank Cristina Carrasco, Caryn Connelly, Sophie Dufays, Regina Faunes, Yvonne Gavela, Erin Hogan, Juliet Lynd, Aldona Pobutsky, Anna Profitt, Liz Rangel, Ana Ros, and Sarah Thomas who are also working on this topic and have provided us with insight along the way. We are especially indebted to Rachel Merriman for her professional work on the index. Contributors Janis Breckenridge, Jack Draper, Beatriz Urraca and Jeff Zamostny generously took the time to help out during the editorial process. Naomi Lindstrom, Philippe Seminet, Sylvia Carullo, Cacilda Rêgo, and David Uskovich have provided insight and critical commentary through their thorough reading of the volume. We are indebted to them, as well as to Melissa Raslevich, who provided us with historical data from LASA. Finally, we would like to thank the anonymous readers who provided us with valuable comments on the manuscript and our assistant editor at Palgrave, Sara Doskow, who promptly supported us throughout the process.

Our family and friends can attest to the hours we have put into the volume, and for their support and patience Georgia Seminet would like to thank the Silversteins, the Smiths, the Seminets, the Zacharys, and most of all Philippe, Chloé, and Camille for helping Seminet keep her feet on the ground. For her part, Carolina Rocha is very grateful for her family's understanding while she embarked on yet another project. Thanks to Camila, Clara and Armando. Rocha is grateful to, Paulina Piselli, who helped in obtaining films.

The coeditors are also indebted to their institutions. Georgia Seminet would like to thank the College of Humanities at St. Edward's University for their enthusiastic support of her ongoing research projects. She is also indebted to the College of Liberal Arts and colleagues in the Department of Modern Languages at the University of Texas–Arlington. Seminet would also like to thank her students during the fall of 2010, who proffered exceptional help in the editorial process and deserve to be named:

Adriana Cabeza, Ana Dávila, Laura Díaz, Moyasser Elqutob, Christina García, Anel Herrera, Lauren Jaynes, Ruby Manuel, Hugo Montalván, Donna Montoya, Katherine Monzón, Johana Orellana, Danielle Purcell, María Saldaña, Ana Saldívar, and Jorge Vásquez. She is also grateful to her students from the spring of 2011, who helped cultivate ideas and theories regarding the child and adolescent in film.

Carolina Rocha is grateful for the support of the Graduate School of Southern Illinois University and the support of her colleagues: Jennifer Miller, Tom Lavallee, and Joaquín Florido Berrocal, as well as Deidre Johnson for her patience and continuous help. Special thanks are in order for students Joshua Castillo and Kristina Becker, who were her research assistants.

Introduction

Carolina Rocha and Georgia Seminet

Pizza, birra, faso (*Pizza, Beer, and Cigarettes*; Adrián Caetano and Bruno Stagnaro 1998) follows a group of adolescents as they roam the streets of Buenos Aires, dodging the police and stealing to survive. Made with a tight budget, the film was not popular among viewers, though it was well received by critics for its original depiction of contemporary Argentine youth (Falicov 119).[1] *Central do Brasil* (*Central Station*; Walter Salles 1998), an inspirational drama of the same year, which follows the young Josué (Vinícius de Oliveira) on a trek from São Paulo to the Brazilian northeast in search of his long-lost father, was very popular at the box office and received numerous awards in film festivals. *Amores perros* (*Love's a Bitch*; Alejandro González Iñárritu 2000) focuses on the lives of several young characters in Mexico City. The film garnered over fifty prizes and was nominated for Best Foreign Language Film at the Academy Awards. In recent years, youths have also been cast to offer a unique vision of historical events such as José Luis Cuerda's very successful film *La lengua de las mariposas* (*Butterfly Tongues*; 1999), which portrays a young boy as he grows up during the Spanish Civil War, forced to witness the ugly realities of that fratricidal conflict. Finally, *El laberinto del fauno* (*Pan's Labyrinth*; Guillermo del Toro 2006) blended the tropes of the traditional fairy tale with the historical context of the Spanish Civil War.[2] A smashing success, *Pan's Labyrinth* received three Academy Awards out of the six for which it was nominated. This brief overview touches on only a handful of films in which children and adolescents are used as the agent through which the desires and fears of adults are manifested, prompting the questions: Why do so many recent films feature youth as a site of cultural angst? Who is the intended audience for these films, and what happens when adults view children and adolescents on screen? In some cases, the actors' charisma and youth is used to dramatize the representation of the victims of civil violence as innocent and ideologically pure. In others, children, and in particular adolescents, are the aggressors whose anger, and often delinquency, represent an indictment of the world bequeathed to them by their parents.

Spanning film and cultural studies, with a particular emphasis on history as well as the cultural construction of class and gender *Representing History, Class and Gender in Spain and Latin America: Children and Adolescents in Film* is the first book-length study of its kind to analyze the representation of children and adolescents in films from Latin America and Spain. The chapters in this volume examine the representation of children and adolescents as protagonists, victims, and witnesses within societies polarized by political divisions. In this increasingly postnational era, children and adolescents are appropriated to mediate issues of identity and difference, history, class and gender, as well as their place in discourses that question the construct of family and nation.

The study of children's and adolescents' representation in cinematic productions from Spain and Latin America has been pioneered by scholars such as Marsha Kinder, Tzvi Tal, Santiago Fouz-Hernández, Matthew Marr, and Laura Podalsky, all of whom have authored articles and book chapters examining the role of youth in film. However, the dearth of book-length studies on Spanish and/or Latin American film is indicative of a critical gap in the scholarship further highlighted by the increasing number of books on the topic from English-speaking countries (Doherty 2002; Gateward and Pomerance 2002; Shary 2002; Lebeau 2008; Lury 2010).[3] Consequently, this book is the first study to explore the representation of children and adolescents in film. As a debut anthology, the scope is intentionally broad, covering cinematic productions from Spain as well as a variety of Latin American countries in order to draw attention to the salient features of films screening young characters.

The essays in this collection address such questions: How are child and teen characters represented in Spanish and Latin American films that deal with political violence and repression? Are the traditional values of family and state exalted or questioned through the voice and gaze of these young protagonists? What does the representation of children contribute to debates on ethics and morality within societies that have endured violence, intolerance, and injustice? In societies that have been undermined by exile and migration, are changing family structures perceptible through the representation of children and adolescents? In what contexts are young protagonists employed to portray the breakdown of traditional gender assumptions? Finally, how do children and adolescents face the multiple challenges represented by poverty, violence, high unemployment, and the reduction of state support for education and welfare during globalization?

As suggested by the previous questions, the essays gathered here do not focus on films produced *by* or *for* children.[4] Rather, children and adolescents appear on screen as narrative devices or focalizers in plots written by adults. Sharon Roberts, who has studied children in museum exhibits, explains that "children's culture is appropriated by adults and turned into the commodity of 'childhood,' in which the child's world becomes framed in an adult perspective" (154). Roberts's statement is also pertinent to childhood films because as young characters move the story forward, they are usually objectified as vehicles of adult anxieties over the nature of civic society. Hence, following the description of Stinne Krogh Poulsen, some of these films could be dubbed "childhood films" as a way to recognize that though they are *about* childhood, they have not been produced *for* young viewers. It is also worth noting, as Laura Podalsky points out, that films can produce new emotions rather than simply representing existing ones (*Disaffected Youth* 4–7). Thus another possibility is that films featuring young characters have been framed intentionally by adult directors in order to unsettle adults' typical assumptions about children and their worldviews. Beyond simply representing adult anxieties, they may actually attempt to produce, play with, or reshape these anxieties.[5]

So what is meant by *child* and *childhood*? The definitions intersect and integrate legal, social, and biological perspectives, thus their exact meaning is slippery. For the purpose of this book, we have worked under a set of general assumptions. In particular, children who are 12 years old and younger are defined as preadolescents, and are also generally understood to be prepubescent or on the threshold of puberty. When referring to children in the age group 13 to 18, we use the more specific term teenager, teen, or adolescent to signify that they have reached the onset of puberty, which lasts until the next period—adulthood. Therefore, the word *childhood* refers to that period of life from birth to 18 years of age; but while adolescents are often referred to as children, the reverse is not as common. To be clear, in this volume the terms *teenager(s)*, *teen(s)*, or *adolescent(s)* are employed to refer exclusively to children ages 13 or older; whereas *child(ren)* and *childhood* refer to the preadolescent phase. However, the terms *child(ren)* and *childhood* are also used in general contexts to represent the age range from infant to the end of adolescence. Obviously, age parameters can muddy the issue, as puberty does not automatically begin at age 12, nor does adulthood necessarily begin at age 18. Perhaps the clearest and simplest definition is offered by the United Nations Children's Fund (UNICEF) for whom the term *childhood* is very broadly defined to cover the span of life from infancy through puberty up to the threshold of adulthood, which they stipulate as anyone 18 years of age or older.[6]

The primary goal of this volume is to analyze the representation of history, culture, and society vis-à-vis the child focalizer in film, meaning young children and adolescents 18 years old and younger. Therefore, it is important to delineate the function of the child and adolescent perspective in film. Focalization includes the dual roles of both the focalizer and the focalized. The former term indicates the perspective, or point of view, from which something is being seen, and the latter is the object being seen or focused on. Celestino Deleyto points out that "in film [...] there can appear, simultaneously, several focalizers, external and internal, on different points of the frame (or outside)" (167). Therefore, at times the viewer follows the perspective of the child, while at others the child is being observed. This fragmentation of focalization "on different points of the frame" creates a space in which ideological content is constructed by careful selection of the position of the focalizer/focalized. Consequently, it is the representation of the child's point of view, either as the focalizer or as the focalized, that determines the ideological content, which in turn reflects the concerns of the adults who both produce and watch films. As Karen Lury writes, "The child figure does not, or cannot, provide authority on the facts of war, yet the representation of its experience as visceral, as of and on the body, demonstrates how the interweaving of history, memory and witness can be powerfully affective" (7). Her insight reminds us that the child focalizer/focalized dramatizes the effect of portraying history and memory and leads adults to view their own ideas and actions as belonging to an "Other." Thus, in an inversion of roles, children and adolescents, who normally comprise a relatively powerless "age minority" in society, are utilized to scrutinize the actions of adults.[7]

The essays in this volume reveal an interesting distinction between the representation of children and adolescents in film. First, preadolescent children are much more frequently cast in filmic narratives constructed on historical memory and trauma. In these films, child protagonists revisit a period of their childhood that took place during a traumatic national event such as the Spanish Civil War or the periods of repressive military governments in Central and South America. The desire to understand the past and justify the lives of the victims of state violence has inspired a number of films that revisit the past through the gaze of the child. Given the intense interest in childhood on the part of the film industry, Vicky Lebeau's recent work showing that cinematic history and the depiction of childhood are closely intertwined, is particularly relevant to this volume. She asserts, "If, as Lesley Caldwell has suggested, the 'myth of childhood actively shapes our epoch and ways of thinking,' then early cinema brings into renewed focus the visual dimension of that myth, or myths: our modern commitments to the idea of the child are inseparable from its representation in visual form" (10).

In light of this revelation, it is not surprising to see that young children, hypothetically untainted by ideology, are cast to revisit history. Although depictions of the bad or monstrous child abound,[8] it also continues to be the case that children are associated with innocence, curiosity, and dependence on adults. For their part, teens are often characterized by rebelliousness against adult rule, the loss of innocence, sexual awakening, and self-conscious behavior. Given these qualities, teens have become ideal vehicles through which a scathing critique is leveled on adults and adult society. Thus, as opposed to the typical representation of preadolescent children in film, teens are a less likely choice of protagonist for revisiting the past. Instead, teen focalizers are used to analyze and question society, therefore calling attention to anxieties about the future.

The teenage protagonists of many of these films move through puberty toward adulthood and citizenship, demonstrating the limitations of contemporary cultures that have been informed by traditional, patriarchal values. As adolescents are exposed to, and contribute to, changing attitudes toward sexuality, drug use, and child-parent relationships, traditional assumptions underlying cultural values and standards are questioned through their representation on screen. Nonetheless, adolescents in Spanish and Latin American films are mostly cast for adults' cinematic viewing. Unlike the development of US cinema in which the "teenpic" drama of the 1950s was created to appeal to young cinemagoers (Doherty 14), the genre did not arise in Spain and Latin America. In those countries, teenagers of that time period did not comprise a lucrative market for exploitation since they were not as likely to have the discretionary income or the mobility (owning cars) of their US counterparts.[9]

It is crucial to note that the use of children and adolescents in film is imbued with an ideological subtext that transcends the interest of a youth audience. The reason lies in the fact that the "myth of childhood" is constantly evolving to accommodate the changing boundaries of social mores and political realities, within both the local and global contexts. Henry Jenkins, Comparative Media Studies scholar, has succinctly articulated the importance of ideology as it relates to children's culture, "Children's culture is not 'innocent' of adult political, economic, moral or sexual concerns. Rather, the creation of children's culture represents the central arena through which we construct our fantasies about the future and a battleground through which we struggle to express competing ideological agendas." The recent cinema of both Spain and Latin America exemplifies Jenkin's definition in that it has appropriated children's and adolescents' culture as a medium for revoicing and reenvisioning "competing ideological agendas" that had been squelched by military dictatorships whose regimes were repressive, violent, and bent on the annihilation of dissent or difference within tightly controlled societies. The historical context of violence and repression characterizing the recent histories of these regions is revisited repeatedly in many of the films included in this volume, indicating an ongoing need to question the past. However, with one exception, the films studied here were produced from the 1990s up to the present. In fact, the utilization of children and adolescents is far from being a recent development in the cinemas of Spain and Latin America. In the following section, we will point out some of the most well-known precedents for the films analyzed in this volume.

Precedents and an Ongoing Trend

Los olvidados (*The Young and the Damned*; 1950), *Crónica de un niño solo* (*Chronicle of a Boy Alone*; 1965), *El espíritu de la colmena* (*The Spirit of the Beehive*; 1973), *Pixote: A lei do mais fraco* (*Pixote: The Law of the Weakest*; 1981) and *Alsino y el cóndor* (*Alsino and the Condor*; 1982) constitute landmark films in Spanish and Latin American cinemas in which children and adolescents are featured. These productions have established a history of the child in film and have set precedents whose legacies continue to be visible not only in Spanish and Latin American cinema but also around the world.[10] For example, the portrayal of destitute orphans as seen in *Los olvidados*, *Crónica de un niño solo*, and *Pixote* remains an urgent theme in Latin America, where a lack of social infrastructure and economic support has led to thousands of children living in the urban streets, surviving by their wits and/or begging and stealing. In *El espíritu*, the scathing critique of the metaphor nation = family highlighted the shortcomings of the *national father* (the dictator, Francisco Franco) by undermining the regime's legitimacy and obliquely exposing government repression as well as grave social problems that could not be addressed openly. A more detailed look at these earlier landmark films reveals their importance in the genealogy of the representation of children and adolescents in film.

Los olvidados was shot by Spanish filmmaker Luis Buñuel (1900–1983), who was exiled in Mexico during the Spanish Civil War. The film is set in a period characterized by a push for national development and modernization in which street children were an embarrassment to the nation.[11] Using techniques of social realism, *Los olvidados* captures the effects of marked inequalities as portrayed by a group of Mexican adolescents. The film's social message focuses on a concern for poor children living in the streets of Mexico and is very critical of the adults who are ostensibly responsible for their well-being.[12] Ironically, the state school for boys featured in the film symbolizes the potential magnanimity and good intentions of the modern patriarchal state, though it ultimately fails to rehabilitate Pedro. The school's—and also society's—failure reveals a cynical attitude toward the government's ability (and willingness) to address social problems in the increasingly industrialized and modernized Mexico City.

Crónica de un niño solo was Argentine filmmaker Leonardo Favio's *opera prima*.[13] Shot in black and white, this film narrates the story of Polín, an orphaned child who is sent to a reformatory where he suffers the abuses of the adults who are in charge of the children. For María de los Ángeles Carbonetti, the film's aesthetic and theme is greatly influenced by Buñuel's *Los olvidados*. Nonetheless, Favio not only shows the predicament of a vulnerable child but also uses internal focalization to express the young protagonist's feelings (Raggio 29). He also provides a nuanced representation of Polín as both a victim and a traitor (Farina 45). This ambiguity in the boy's character has led Carbonetti to read *Crónica de un niño* as a film that foretold authoritarianism, perceptible in the depiction of the reformatory's correctional officers. If this is the case, then Polín serves as a metonym for Argentine society since the film was made at a time when Argentine political life was constrained: Peronism was forbidden and the military was threatening to take over. Thus Argentine society (like Polín) is simultaneously controlled and given the possibility of fleeing—albeit briefly—from oppression. The topic of subjugation under authoritarianism is also present in another landmark film.

Director Victor Erice's *El espíritu de la colmena* consciously undermined the official history of a homogenized and modern version of Spain that Franco's regime strove to create through cinema. Amid restrictive social and political conditions, *El espíritu de la colmena* presented a story of initiation depicting the development and maturation of a young girl (Elena 102). The film also challenged the image of the patriarch by encoding in the narrative "an obsessive love/hate relationship between an austere father and a stunted child" (Kinder 1997, 61), popularizing a trope that was used to implicitly critique the Franco regime during the years of censorship and repression. *El espíritu de la colmena* constituted a pioneering vision of Spain during the Franco years through the eyes of a child, mirroring Erice's contention that cinema is the ideal medium through which to portray "innocence or the purity of the gaze" (Elena 106). Critics have also pointed out Erice's novel handling of silence (and dialogue) to enrich and challenge the perceptions of the visual.[14]

Subsequently, *El espíritu de la colmena* had a major influence on a generation of films as there were no less than seven productions (including *El espíritu*) between 1973 and 1980 with child focalizers, or that privileged childhood, through flashbacks: *La prima Angélica* (*Cousin Angélica*; Carlos Saura 1973) and *Cría cuervos* (*Cría*; Saura 1975); *El nido* (*The Nest*; Jaime de Armiñán 1980); *A un dios desconocido* (*To an Unknown God*; Jaime Chávarri 1977); *Camada negra* (*Black Litter*; Manuel Gutiérrez Aragón and José Luis Borau 1977); and *Furtivos* (*Poachers*; Borau 1975) (Kinder 59). Kinder names these directors "children of Franco" and characterizes them as a "generation of filmmakers [. . .] forced always to define themselves and their films in opposition to Franco, both before and after his death in 1975" (57–58). As a consequence, their films echoed the theme of infantilized adults made manifest not only in the artistic praxis of the filmmakers, but also in the "representation on screen—of the precocious children who are both murderous monsters and poignant victims, and the stunted childlike adults who are obsessed with distorted visions of the past, both placed in the social context of a divided family that is fraught with sexual deviations and that functions as a microcosm for the corrupt state" (59). Clearly these films represent an ideological critique of the adult world focalized through the eyes of children that also shapes *Pixote*.

Pixote (Héctor Babenco) is another crucial film showing the lives of children. According to Robert Stam, João Luiz Vieira, and Ismael Xavier, the film belongs to "an international genre, the street urchin film," which shares important commonalities with Buñuel's *Los olvidados* (412). The film revolves around a group of orphaned children who represent Brazil's large homeless population. The film, censored by the military authorities, immediately generated public debates both in Brazil and abroad about the status of poor children in a society that, according to the slogan adopted by the dictatorship authorities was "um país que vai pra frente" (a country moving forward).[15]

In the early 1980s, Miguel Littin, a Chilean filmmaker in exile, directed *Alsino y el cóndor*.[16] Alsino, a young Nicaraguan boy, witnesses the abuses of his country's civil war exacerbated by American participation. In his article, "*Alsino y el cóndor* hacia una crítica del espectador latinoamericano y nicaraguense," Daniel Chávez notes that this film, the first fictional Nicaraguan film, uses cinematic techniques to prompt the spectator to identify with Alsino. This constitutes an important strategy on Littin's part according to Chávez because of the difficulty in presenting political violence. The presentation of violence through the eyes of young protagonists provides an opportunity for the victims (spectators) to come to terms with

Nicaragua's traumatic past. *Alsino y el cóndor* constitutes one of the first Latin American films to provide a youth perspective on civil war. Building on the themes of these productions, a more recent crop of films continues to privilege the unresolved ideological conflicts of the past while maintaining the tradition of filmic narrations in which childhood is portrayed as a site of social and cultural critique. By the mid- to late 1980s, diminished state censorship in many of the countries allowed for film production to represent the violence of the recent past. In Argentina, *La noche de los lápices* (*Night of the Pencils*; Héctor Olivera 1986) was based on the true story of a group of student representatives who fought for reduced bus tickets and, as a result of their "rebelliousness," were savagely repressed by military authorities. Parallel to this, a slow but steady stream of films depicting children's culture begins to make an impression on moviegoers in Spain and Latin America. The current boom in both regions can be traced back to such films as *Las bicicletas son para el verano* (*Bicycles Are for the Summer*; Jaime Chávarri 1984) that narrates the frustrations and deprivations of a wealthy family trying to deal with the consequences of the Spanish Civil War from the perspective of the young son. *Réquiem por un campesino español* (*Requiem for a Spanish Peasant*; Francesc Betriu 1985) also revisits the Spanish Civil War through the tragic death of its young protagonist played by Antonio Banderas. In Latin America, Victor Gaviria's *La vendedora de rosas* (*The Rose Seller;* 1988) relates the life of Mónica, a poor girl in Colombia. In an essay on the film, critic Francisco Peña references the stylistic similarities that *La vendedora* shares with Italian neorealism in its representation of the underclass and applauds Gaviria's incorporation of the Latin American cinematographic testimonial as a way of drawing attention to one of Colombia's most disadvantaged and destitute sectors of society —street children.

More recently, the drudgery of poverty and shocking violence has continued to echo in Latin American films such as the Spanish-Mexican film *Perfume de violetas: Nadie te oye* (*Violet Perfume: Nobody Is Listening*; Maryse Sistach 2001) in which gender and impoverishment are portrayed as obstacles to the aspirations of the two young female protagonists. The two friends, who live in one of the poor neighborhoods of Mexico City, become victims of the violence against women, machismo, and deprivation that entrap them. The Brazilian film *Cidade de Deus* (*City of God*; Fernando Meirelles 2002) follows the lives of male teens in their poor and drug-ridden neighborhood of Rio de Janeiro. Joshua Marston's *María llena eres de gracia* (*Maria Full of Grace*; 2004) tells the tale of a teenager who, in an ill-advised decision, becomes a "mule" for drug traffickers bringing cocaine into the United States. Seeking a way to escape a monotonous life that bodes little hope for the future, the teenage girl's decision sets in motion a chain of terrifying and deadly consequences. More recently, Cary Fukunaga's *Sin nombre* (*Without Name*; 2009) also ponders the effects of poverty on children and teens in Mexico and Central America who turn to either drugs and crime or migration as a way out of despair. Migration also becomes a theme in the Costa Rican–French production *El camino* (*The Path*; Ishtar Yasín Gutiérrez 2007), which traces the at times dark and at times humorous journey of two children as they leave their grandfather and set out from their Nicaraguan village to find their mother who left them eight years earlier in search of work in Costa Rica.[17]

Adolescents have also been screened in Latin American films to characterize the transitional period from the 1990s to the new century when globalization has intensified due to neoliberal policies that have been implemented in the region. In this period, the rite of passage, a central feature of adolescence, and the volatility it implies, mirrors the insecurity and instability of many Latin American societies as they veer away from stolid paternalist states to uncertain free-market economies. Thus the transition from adolescent to adult in the films serves as a metonymy for the experiences of society as a whole. This is the case of *Pizza, birra, faso* in which the young characters engage in petty crime amid an atmosphere of parental neglect and *Y tu mamá también* (*And Your Mother Too*; 2001), which utilizes techniques of mass popular culture like the road movie to illustrate the transition faced by young male protagonists as they temporarily evade and then rejoin society. In other films, such as in the Mexican film *Amar te duele* (*Love Hurts*; Fernando Sariñana 2002), the challenges faced by youths of different social backgrounds are depicted so as to challenge current social policies.[18]

Latin American productions engaging children and adolescents in a manner critical of the authoritarian past have continued unabated up to the present moment. In light of this, it is worth mentioning a selection of the many films not treated in this volume, such as the Argentine films *Valentín* (Alejandro Agresti 2002) and *Kamchatka* (Marcelo Piñeyro 2002), and Fabrizio Aguilar's *Paloma de papel* (*Paper Dove*; 2003). The year 2005 brought *Cautiva* (*Captive*; Gastón Biraben), portraying a teenager who suddenly discovers that her real parents were among the disappeared during Argentina's Dirty War, and the Mexican production *Voces inocentes* (*Innocent Voices*; Luis Mandoki 2005), relating the appalling use of child soldiers during El Salvador's bloody civil conflict (1980–92). From 2007, we have the US-Argentine production *3 Américas* (Cristina Aurora Kotz Cornejo 2007). Both *3 Américas* and an earlier Chilean film,

Gringuito (Sergio Castilla 1998), narrate children's return to their parents' native countries (for different reasons) after the fall of the dictatorships that had necessitated their exile.[19]

In Spanish cinema, the civil war continues to capture the imagination of directors and audiences alike, as there are numerous films that portray the Franco dictatorship through the eyes of children and adolescents. Films from the 1990s include *Urte ilunak/Los años oscuros* (*The Dark Years*; Arantxa Lazkano 1992), focusing on the postwar years and showcasing a young female protagonist (Bárbara Goenaga); and the internationally acclaimed *La lengua de las mariposas*, which uses a young boy to narrate the impact on everyday life of the Spanish Civil War. The trend depicting the war years and the Franco dictatorship is echoed in other films such as *El viaje de Carol* (*Carol's Journey*; Imanol Uribe 2002), which repeats the trope described earlier by Kinder of a childhood cut short by Fascist violence in the aftermath of the civil war. A similar theme can also be found in the 2001 ghost story *El espinazo del diablo* (*The Devil's Backbone*; Guillermo del Toro 2001), featuring child protagonists pitted against a cruel character that represents the nationalist ideology of the period. Characterized as a transnational film par excellence, *El espinazo* takes place in an orphanage that acts as a "microcosm for the conflict taking place outside" (Lázaro-Reboll 4).[20]

There is also a group of Spanish films from the 1990s that have turned away from the themes of the civil war and its aftermath toward topics that reflect the concerns of society during globalization. Films questioning the evolving meaning of Spanish identity or the lack of a future for Spanish youths in the stagnant economy of the 1990s become prevalent and have also drawn attention to the influence of transnational financing on the portrayal of national themes. The Spanish-French production *La teta i la lluna* (*The Tit and the Moon*; Bigas Luna 1994), according to Kinder, "is posed as a tale of nostalgia foregrounding the process of looking back from a moment of contemporary crisis to the presumed security of an 'age of innocence'" (1997, 202). If *La teta* emphasizes a "refigured" Spanish national identity, as Kinder argues, the film *Secretos del corazón* (*Secrets of the Heart*; Monxto Armendáriz 1997), functions more on a personal level in which ten-year-old Javi's inquisitiveness will reveal secrets about his own identity and help him to "grow up" (Barnier 11). Set in the early 1960s, *Secretos* was the winner of four Goya awards and nominated for an Academy Award for the Best Foreign Language film of 1998. *Barrio* (*The Neighborhood*; Fernando León de Aranoa 1998), a film in the neorealist tradition, depicts the angst of its three adolescent male protagonists. *Barrio* is exemplary of Núria Triana-Toribio's statement that in Spanish cinema since the 1990s, "films rewarded with prizes tend to 'mirror' and denounce social ills" (157). *Cine social* is also alive and well in films such as *Mensaka* (Salvador García Ruiz 1998), which follows a group of adolescents (and young adults as some of the characters are older than 18) as they attempt to balance the exhilaration of their rock band's budding fame with their chaotic lives. In an essay focusing on the youngest member of the group, Laura, Matthew Marr shows how her portrayal as a "brazen version of female youth subjectivity" typifies "social relevance to the Spanish cultural milieu of the 1990s" (2). Finally *La pistola de mi hermano* (My Brother's Gun; Ray Loriga 1997) features the story of a 17-year-old boy whose hasty decision to shoot a security guard leads him, and his suicidal girlfriend, to further calamity. *La pistola* is also a clear commentary on social themes as they pertain to Spanish teenagers of the period. For example, critic Jonathan Holland has noted that the film's dialogue was "meant to suggest the emptiness of teenage lives" (n/p). Furthermore, Kathryn Everly has noted that "Loriga has developed and expanded Gen X themes of disgruntled youth, family tension, and popular culture" (170).[21]

There are many possible reasons for the current interest in children and teen protagonists. First of all, since the late eighties, the box-office popularity of films depicting childhood coincides with society's increased preoccupation for the safety and well-being of children.[22] For example, the work of Henry Giroux exemplifies a body of writing dedicated to defining and denouncing the threats to children and adolescents posed by postmodern culture, neoliberal, and globalized societies.[23] Another important example can be found in the work of geographer Owain Jones, who notes that recent poststructuralist appraisals have stimulated new directions in research on childhood. Jones, however, is wary of the poststructuralists' attempts at "decolonizing" childhood, because they become just another imposition on the "mysteries of childhood" (202). In order to understand children's otherness, Jones recommends analyzing children's play, referring to their "creative production and witnessing (rather than representation)" (210).[24] Conscious of the potential manipulation and appropriation of youth, some filmmakers have sought to share the creative process with their young actors. Of particular interest in this respect are the films *Viva Cuba* (Juan Carlos Cremata Malberti and Iraida Malberti Cabrera 2005), created specifically, though not exclusively, for children and in which the director encouraged creative contributions from his young stars; and *Rodrigo D: No futuro* (Victor Gaviria 1990) in which the director recruited nonprofessional teens to portray the gritty reality of their lives in the poor sections of Bogotá. However, in most films, children and teens are not used solely for the sake of exploring their *otherness*. The films are geared toward an adult audience, whose purpose is to recover and preserve the "unofficial" memories of horrific and violent events.

Second, the boom coincides with a turn toward democratic political systems and the subsequent emergence of a young generation of filmmakers eager to represent their own conceptions of the past and/or critique of the present. A number of these films were box-office hits and won awards in several film festivals, thus attesting to the fact that representing children and adolescents on screen appeals to a broad audience. This generation of directors displays a profound concern for contemporary social issues possibly due to the fact that several of these directors were either young adults or coming-of-age during the intensification of globalization and the imposition of neoliberal economic policies. A case in point is Spaniard Achero Mañas (born 1966), who directed *El Bola* (2000), and countryman David Trueba (born 1969), whose opera prima was *La buena vida* (*The Good Life*; 1996).[25] Other young directors include, for instance, Mexican Alejandro González Iñárritu (born 1963), who directed *Amores perros*, and Alfonso Cuarón (born 1961), director of *Y tu mamá también*. Both films portray the coming-of-age of young males in contemporary Mexican society. Adrián Caetano (born 1969), who codirected *Pizza, birra, faso*, recently returned to focusing on young protagonists in *Francia* (2009), which follows Mariana as she witnesses her young parents' struggles to have stable romantic relationships and become responsible providers for her. Mexican director Guillermo del Toro (born 1964) has added to the contributions of his generation with, among others, *El laberinto del Fauno*, an aestheticization of childhood depicted as a period in life populated by fantastic and imaginary elements set in Spain following Franco's victory.

Third, the proliferation of Latin American women filmmakers has also spurred the interest in the plights of young characters. Some examples are Argentine Vera Fogwill (born 1972), director of *Las mantenidas sin sueños* (*Kept and Dreamless*; 2005); Lucrecia Martel (born 1966), director of *La ciénaga* (*The Swamp*; 2001) and *La niña santa* (*The Holy Girl*; 2004); and Lucia Puenzo (born 1976), director of *El niño pez* (*The Fish Child*; 2009).[26] Also included is Brazilian Sandra Kogut (born 1965), who directed *Mutum* (2007), which follows the life of a boy raised in the Brazilian Northeast. In these films, dysfunctional family dynamics affect the young protagonists' childhood and development. In addition, Puenzo in *XXY* (2007) and Julia Solomonoff (born 1968) in *El último verano de la Boyita* (*The Last Summer of La Boyita*; 2009) have explored genetic anomalies affecting the gender of the young characters. Celina Murga (born 1973) explores social differences and parental absence in *Una semana solos* (*A Week Alone*; 2007). Finally, the Peruvian-Spanish production by Claudia Llosa (born 1976), *Madeinusa* (2004), portrays the unique cultural traditions of an isolated Peruvian village. The film exposes themes of race and class divisions, as well as the grim fate of women in a traditional, indigenous culture of rural Peru.

The influence of these emerging directors, born in the 1960s and 1970s, is visible not only in new topics and cinematic styles but also in the way they recognize the heterogeneity of contemporary societies. Cases in point are young Argentine-Jewish filmmakers Ariel Winograd (born 1977), director of *Cara de queso, mi primer ghetto* (*Cheese Head*; 2006); Gabriel Lichtmann (born 1974), *Judíos en el espacio* (*Jews in Space*; 2005); and Brazilian-Jewish Cao Hamburger (1962), who directed *O ano em que meus pais saíram de férias* (*The Year My Parents Went on Vacation*; 2006).[27] Many of these films are operas primas loosely based on the directors' childhood memories. Laura Podalsky claims that "many of these recent Latin American films depart from the older models by privileging the perspective of working-class and lower-middle-class subjects and, in so doing, harshly indict societies riddled by mundane acts of violence, exploitation, and emotional brutality" (*Politics of Affect*, 109). These productions, particularly those that feature adolescent roles, show us how contemporary social conditions negatively affect teenagers' transition to adulthood, and the angst-ridden filmic representations of their lives unnerve society's hopes for a prosperous future.

Fourth, the social and economic conditions of globalization constitute another reason for this trend, as directors perceive it as altering traditional ways of life and national identity.[28] This has led film scholar Gonzalo Aguilar to state that portraits of disoriented youth are a consequence of globalization (197). While globalization gives them more access to commodities, it also renders their insertion as productive citizens into the global market as a problematic scenario at a time when countries are either unable or reluctant to support their aspirations (whether in education or meaningful careers) due to uneven development and shrinking national economies. Even though Brazil represents an exception since it is enjoying an economic boom, the sharp differences between social classes and the competition for a college degree—only possible if students perform well on an entrance exam—still pose challenges to young people as seen in *Linha de passe* (*Offside*; Walter Salles and Daniela Thomas 2008) and the documentary *Only When I Dance* by British director Beadle Finzi

(2009), which details the pressure of two lower-class teenagers to perform in international ballet competitions and flee an anonymous life in Brazil.

Fifth, though childhood is often used to focalize the historical and collective memories of particular nations, the universal appeal of children on screen may very well be related to the need (economic and moral) to go beyond the national audience with narratives that will have global appeal. In fact, globalization has also motivated the dissemination of many of these films mentioned here. Of particular importance is the appearance of Film Movement "a full-service North American distributor of critically acclaimed award-winning independent and foreign films" (Film Movement). Among the directors who are alumni of Film Movement, we can point to Juan Carlos Cremata Malberti (*Viva Cuba*), Fernando Eimbcke (*Lake Tahoe* and *Temporada de patos*), Pedro Gonzalez Rubio (*Alamar*), Achero Mañas (*El Bola*), and Lucía Puenzo (*XXY*). The distribution of foreign films, many of them focused on children and adolescents, is gradually changing consumers' tastes in the United States, as public libraries are one of the subscribers to Film Movement.

Finally, it is worth mentioning the current interest in the interdisciplinary study of children and youth culture around the world.[29] Writing in the early 2000s, Tobias Hecht, in his introduction to *Minor Omissions*, mentioned the lack of interest in childhood as a topic of research in Latin America as reflected in the number of panels at the annual Latin American Studies Association Conference (LASA): "Of the more than three thousand papers presented at recent LASA meetings, scarcely a handful concern any aspect of childhood" (5). However, only a few years later a track was created to group scholarship on this topic. The first LASA conference to include the track "Children and Youth" was in 2006. By the time of LASA 2010 in Toronto, there were 17 sessions in this track.[30] Spain has also witnessed the publication of several books about childhood, particularly in relation to memory such as *La dulce España: Memoria de un niño partido en dos* (2000), *Marcelo: Los otros niños de la guerra* (2004), and the examination of literary works in Maria Nikolajeva's *Aspects and Issues in the History of Children's Literature* (1995).

Hybrid Genres

The films in this volume are all constructed around children's culture. Therefore, it is valid to ask whether or not they represent an existing genre or constitute a new genre, and are there commonalities among them that can be identified and explained? The short answer is that they represent a hybrid of existing genres and share particular, identifiable features; however, they do not constitute any single cinematic genre. On the one hand, we can certainly point to commonalities among the films. First, though the protagonists may be young the narratives proffer life lessons for adults and oblige us to critique our own behavior. Second, these films necessitate an understanding of the social and historical context of the film in order to fully grasp the ideological implications of the narratives. Third, many subvert "official history" with a personal story recalled by the young protagonist who is more often than not an innocent male from the middle class of his respective country.[31] Furthermore, the use of allegory is pervasive in the films that revisit history. One of the main reasons for representing childhood memories is to preserve the historical memory of those vanquished in the military dictatorships of Latin America and Spain. Excellent examples are *Kamchatka*, *Butterfly Tongues*, *The Year My Parents Went on Vacation*, and *Machuca*. The representation of youth in these films as the repository of cultural memory and the guardians of hope for the future has become a staple of films seeking to give voice to those who were unjustly murdered, tortured, or disappeared by dictatorial regimes.

A different set of common features is noted in the films whose protagonists are teens. Adolescents are more often cast to project the future, rather than revisit the past, by introducing topics of emerging social import. Films that showcase teens tend to privilege the themes of drug use, sexuality, and the construction of gender, as well as urban violence and corruption. Though males also star in a majority of these films, there are some notable exceptions. For example, the Argentine film *XXY* delves into the difficulties of coming-of-age for a transgendered teenager. The Brazilian films *Sonhos roubados* (Sandra Werneck 2010) and *Nina* (Heitor Dhalia 2004) present the complications for young girls' coming-of-age in a society that provides little hope for those who have scant social or parental support. The same could be said of the Spanish film *Mensaka*, which has been dubbed an example of "angry girl" feminism (Marr 132).[32]

The films studied here undoubtedly share similar features and derive from similar sociohistorical contexts. A cursory review of the films analyzed in this volume attests to the variety of genres that inform the representation of children and adolescents. Here are some examples: road movie (*Viva Cuba*); coming-of-age (*El silencio de Neto*, *Machuca*, *Andrés no quiere dormir las siesta*, etc.); fairy tales and horror (*Pan's Labyrinth*, *Nina*); teen films (*Lake Tahoe*, *Temporada de patos*);[33] gangsters, drugs, and poverty (*Rodrigo D: No futuro*, *Sonhos roubados*); and family violence (*El Bola* and *Las mantenidas sin sueños*) and state violence (*The Year My Parents Went on Vacation*, *Machuca*).

This volume is divided in three parts. Essays in the first part are concerned with the specificities of a national, cultural tradition under the stress of violent, patriarchal, and repressive regimes, whether in Spain or Latin America. The themes examined in this section most often explore childhood as an allegory for the nation, a site where a panorama of difference—sexual, ethnic, class, and political—must negotiate a complex, and often hostile, social landscape. Section one opens with Julia Tuñón's analysis of Jomí García Ascot's *En el balcón vacío* (*On the Empty Balcony*; 1962). This essay is an example of the earlier films that preceded the more recent trend defined earlier. However, as a cult film, it never garnered the popularity of films such as *Los olvidados*, *El espíritu de la colmena*, or *Pixote*. Tuñón's contribution lingers on the traumatic effects of the Spanish Civil War. Her essay highlights the limits of representation in portraying the disruption and trauma suffered by children who were part of the massive migration of children that occurred during and after the defeat of the Second Spanish Republic in 1939. In his study of *Pan's Labyrinth*, Antonio Gómez L-Quiñones points out in "Fairies, Maquis, and Children Without Schools: Romantic Childhood and Civil War in *Pan's Labyrinth*" that since the mid-1990s the Spanish Civil War has inspired a series of films in which both children and children's point of view have played an essential narrative role. Gómez shows how *Pan's Labyrinth* works as an ideological symptom of a very particular reconfiguration of the Spanish Civil War for democratic Spain's cultural market and complex political rearrangements. In "A Child's Voice, A Country's Silence: Ethnicity, Class, and Gender in *El silencio de Neto*," Georgia Seminet deals with the Guatemalan-US film *El silencio de Neto* (*The Silence of Neto*; Luis Argueta 1996), which follows the exacerbation of political polarization during the cold war in Guatemala. Set immediately before and during the overthrow of President Jacobo Árbenz in 1954, the intimate and personal strife characterizing the family of the 12-year-old protagonist, Neto Yepes, is allegorically linked to the ideological conflict and discord plaguing the nation. His successful coming-of-age amid a divided family, and a divided nation, gives the film an optimistic ending that is ironic given the political context in Guatemala at the time in which the film is set. Carolina Rocha's contribution, "Children's Views of State-Sponsored Violence in Latin America: *Machuca* and *The Year My Parents Went on Vacation*," focuses on the analysis of two very popular contemporary films, *Machuca* (Andrés Wood 2004) and *The Year My Parents Went on Vacation* (Cao Hamburger 2006), in which male children are used as witnesses and survivors of the most recent dictatorships in Chile (1973–90) and Brazil (1964–84), respectively. Rocha proposes that despite these similarities, these films do not use the same cinematic formula given that they correspond to the politics of memory in both countries. Finally, Janis Breckenridge's "Enabling, Enacting and Envisioning Societal Complicity: Daniel Bustamante's *Andrés no quiere dormir la siesta* (2009)," examines the use of a child focalizer to depict the monstrous effects of societal acquiescence, indifference, and complicity on a generation growing up during Argentina's last military dictatorship.

Essays from part II showcase films that revolve around the coming-of-age struggles during globalization. These essays foreground themes of sexuality, unemployment, migration, poverty, consumer culture, and the disintegration of the social fabric under the onslaught of drug violence. Gaze and voice in these films originates in urban settings that have little to offer their teenage citizens. The filmic narratives in this section debate difference and the coming-of-age process from a globally informed viewpoint rather than an exclusively national one. Exemplary of this trend is Ignacio Sánchez Prado's essay, "Innocence Interrupted: Neoliberalism and the End of Childhood in Recent Mexican Cinema" analyzing two recent Mexican films, Alan Coton's *Soba* (2004) and Jonás Cuarón's *Año uña* (*Year of the Nail*; 2009). These two films present drastically different narratives of the end of innocence. In Cuarón's film, a middle-class Mexican boy falls in love with a slightly older American exchange student, while Coton tells us the story of a working-class girl brutally raped by two policemen. Sánchez Prado argues that the end of childhood as the threshold to citizenship in both films can be understood as "the end of innocence." The trope thus articulates the entrance into neoliberal citizenship in gendered and class-marked scenarios that lead to differences in the degree of violence represented. In "From Buñuel to Eimbcke: Orphanhood in Recent Mexican Cinema," Dan Russek continues the indictment of the effects of neoliberalism on the Mexican middle class in his essay examining the figure of the orphan in *Temporada de patos* (*Duck Season*; 2004) and *Lake Tahoe* (2008) by Fernando Eimbcke. Russek's essay takes as its point of departure the role played by orphanhood in Luis Buñuel's *Los olvidados*. Orphanhood is understood as a trope that signifies the helplessness and existential void caused by the absence of an authority figure. The essay analyzes how Eimbcke reinterprets the Buñuelesque tropes of poverty, urban violence, and marginality iconized in *Los olvidados* in order to portray the life of middle-class adolescents in Mexico at the dawn of the twenty-first century. Eduardo Ledesma, in "Through 'Their' Eyes: Internal and External Focalizing Agents in the Representation of Children and Violence in Iberian and Latin American Film" compares the films *Rodrigo D: No futuro* and *El Bola*, underscoring the ethical dilemmas posed by the filmic representation of adolescents and children in situations of violence and poverty and the political stakes involved. Finally, in "Roads to Emancipation: Sentimental Education in *Viva Cuba*," analyzed by Rosana Díaz-Zambrana, we find the only film in the volume that was made specifically for a child audience. Appropriately, the essay examines how children's evolution and development are intertwined with the episodic structure of the road trip. Díaz-Zambrana argues that the transformation that the children undergo does not lie in their indoctrination into institutional and familial structures per se, but mainly in their emotional awakening. The thresholds they breach during their journey through the Cuban countryside trigger their subsequent sentimental education. This facilitates the beginning of another stage of maturity and disillusionment that occurs when they are reunited with their respective families at the end of their voyage.

Lastly, the essays in part III deal with the complexities of gender construction within the context of societies that can also be seen as coming-of-age in the interstices of a violent past and an uncertain future. As these adolescents struggle to define and understand their own identity, their disturbing narratives once again call into question the wisdom of adult society. Adolescent sexuality and gender construction are a potent topic in the hands of directors who explore these themes in combination with those of violence, drug use, and social and family disintegration. The open questioning of heteronormativity as a standard for citizenship or family membership is seen in *XXY*, which stands apart from a long line of other fictional and philosophical works concerned with intersex characters. In contrast to works that use "the hermaphrodite" as a trope for an original unity of the sexes, decadence, an exotic rarity, or degeneration, the film focuses on the lived experience of a concrete, intersex individual raised as a girl. By tracing five days in the life of 15-year-old Alex and her family on a sparsely populated Uruguayan island, Puenzo constructs a complex vision of an intersex character portrayed not as a metaphor but as a material being in relation with others. In "Constructing Ethical Attention in Lucía Puenzo's *XXY*: Cinematic Strategy, Intersubjectivity, and Intersexuality," Jeff Zamostny traces how Puenzo implements narrative and cinematic strategies both to draw ethical attention to the ideals defended by the intersex cause and to illustrate the intense struggles faced by individuals who put the ideals of intersex activism into practice in their daily lives. Jack Draper's essay, "Cinematic Portrayals of Teen Girls in Brazil's Urban Peripheries," on the recent Brazilian films sustains that Sandra Werneck's *Sonhos roubados* takes a realist perspective on the everyday lives of three teen girls living in the favelas of Rio de Janeiro. Werneck portrays many serious problems related to urban poverty: child abuse, the drug trade and related violence, and prostitution. However, she makes a special effort to demonstrate that her protagonists, amid this lawless landscape of dangerous obstacles, continue to pursue the dreams they have for a more normal life and to try to care for their nascent families as well. Heitor Dhalia's *Nina*—described by the director as a loose adaptation of Fyodor Dostoevsky's *Crime and Punishment*—takes a much more subjective approach. The film takes us into the mind of the protagonist Nina, exploring this teenage girl's passion for her goth- and manga-inspired art as well as her often tenuous grip on reality. Draper's essay places these two films in the broader context of Brazilian cinema to suggest that Dhalia's approach can serve to problematize some of the common assumptions and propositions of realist cinema and its portrayal of youth in the urban peripheries. In "No Longer Young: Childhood, Family, and Trauma in *Las mantenidas sin sueños*," Beatriz Urraca complicates the female coming-of-age trope by focusing on a film whose female protagonist is unwilling to accept her budding puberty. Urraca analyzes the narrative and filmic strategies employed in encoding the subjectivity of the child protagonist in a recent Argentine film, Vera Fogwill and Martín Desalvo's *Las mantenidas sin sueños* (2005). By focusing on the examination of the child's articulation of traumatic, self-altering events and her socialization in a family of maladjusted female or feminized characters, Urraca argues that the film devolves into an untimely coming-of-age narrative in which the child's struggle to define her identity is marked by a futile process of resistance against her own body.

The films analyzed in this study focus on history, class, and gender, as well as various aspects of contemporary Spain and Latin America. Taken together, these essays aim to expand our knowledge of cinematic representations of children and adolescents in Spanish and Latin American productions, problematizing both the gaze and voice of these young protagonists and what we, as spectators, see through their eyes.

NOTES

1. The production garnered a place in Argentine film history as one of the first films of the New Argentine Cinema.
2. There are clear parallels between the social and historical context of the traditional fairy tale genre and *Pan's Labyrinth*. In his study of fairy tales, Jack Zipes points out that "both the oral and literary forms of the fairy tale are grounded in history: they emanate from specific struggles to humanize bestial and barbaric forces, which have terrorized our minds and communities

in concrete ways, threatening to destroy free will and human compassion. The fairy tale sets out to conquer this concrete terror through metaphors" (1). Viewers will notice del Toro's use of the traditional structural elements of the fairy tale to represent a particular moment in Spanish history.

3. In his article on the representation of youth subjectivity in the film *Mensaka* (Salvador García Ruiz 1998), Matthew Marr, referring specifically to Spanish films, also notes this critical gap (131).
4. The one exception to this rule is *Viva Cuba*. None of the other films mentioned in the introduction were produced specifically for children.
5. Thank you to Jack Draper for this observation.
6. From the United Nations Fact Sheet, Article 1 (Definition of the Child), "The Convention defines a 'child' as a person below the age of 18, unless the laws of a particular country set the legal age for adulthood younger. The Committee on the Rights of the Child, the monitoring body for the Convention, has encouraged States to review the age of majority if it is set below 18 and to increase the level of protection for all children under 18."
7. Timothy Shary makes the point that children and adolescents are a minority group, and thus they are relatively powerless when confronting adults (2).
8. Kathy Merlock Jackson, in her study of children in American films, distinguishes between the good and bad child. In Spain and Latin America, the bad child has often been a victim of parental and social neglect. Like American films, Spanish and Latin American films depicting adolescents often focus on juvenile delinquency and teensploitation (Shary 14–21).
9. Laura Podalsky finds "signs that Latin American producers are trying to nurture the equivalent of the 18–24 year old niche market in the US" (2011 103).
10. These three films are included in Ian Wojcik-Andrews's *Children's Films: History, Ideology, Pedagogy, Theory*. Also, in a recent article, Alberto Elena links Erice's film to Abbas Kiarostami's cinematography (2009).
11. For a discussion of the sensitivity of Latin American leaders to this issue, please see Donna Guy's essay in *Minor Omissions*. The presence of orphans and abandoned children in the streets of Latin America was embarrassing for leaders who projected images of progress and modernization in their rhetoric.
12. Nara Milanich presents an interesting historical study on the views of illegitimacy and illegitimate children in Latin America.
13. The film garnered two awards in Argentina: one for the best film and another one at the FIPRESCI.
14. For more on the tension between sound and image, see Xon de Ros's article "Innocence Lost."
15. For more on this, see Luis Alberto Pereira Junior's article.
16. The film was nominated for an Academy Award as Best Foreign Language Film. It was a Cuban, Mexican, and Costa Rican coproduction with a multinational cast.
17. The migration of Central American and Mexican children and youth have also attracted the attention of US filmmakers. One example is the poignant Which

Way Home (Rebecca Cammisa 2009), which was nominated for an Academy Award.
18. For a judicious analysis of *Amar te duele*, please see María Luisa Ruiz's article.
19. There are also films that move away from the topics of poverty and the authoritarian past. For example, the Uruguayan film *25 Watts* (Juan Pablo Rebella and Pablo Stoll 2001) blends dark humor and social critique in portraying teenage youths in Montevideo. The Mexican-US production *La misma luna* (*Under the Same Moon*; Patricia Riggen 2007) provides a happy ending to the story of a young boy who crosses the US-Mexico border alone in search of his mother who had been working in California and whom he has not seen for years. *Alamar* (Pedro González Rubio 2010), a unique film from Mexico, showcases the beauty and harmony of nature in the portrayal of a young boy and his father as they commune in a small fishing village in Mexico.
20. While not depicting Francoism directly, Javier Fesser's *Camino* (The Way; 2008) portrays a dying child who is a member of a strict Catholic family belonging to Opus Dei. The denunciation of Opus Dei as a pitiless, patriarchal, and authoritarian hierarchy becomes an anachronistic metaphor for the indifference of the Franco regime, which treated the opposition as recalcitrant children and punished them accordingly.
21. *Los chicos* (*The Boys*; 1959), a much earlier Spanish film by the Italian director Marco Ferreri, ponders a similar theme during the Franco years. *Los chicos* is a portrayal of the cultural angst experienced by teenagers in Madrid in the 1950s. Popular at the time of its release, it provides an interesting point of comparison for these later Spanish films depicting adolescent anxiety in an urban setting.
22. Also on this topic, see Joel Best's *Threatened Children*.
23. For an excellent source on the related topic of the ideal childhood in crisis, see Anne Higgonet's *Pictures of Innocence*.
24. Emma Wilson has also taken an approach to the study of children in European (especially French) films, focusing on the otherness of childhood, and children's subjectivity. In an article on French women filmmakers, she states that they "have rendered children subjects in their cinema and freed them from the idealizing or angelising gaze of erotic or indeed of maternal attention" (169).
25. The list of a younger generation of directors is meant to be exemplary and not exhaustive. Other examples will become apparent in the contributions to this volume.
26. Ana Peluffo calls this approach "feminocentric" (213).
27. For more on this, see Carolina Rocha's "Jewish Cinematic Self-Representations in Contemporary Argentine and Brazilian Films."
28. Transnational productions have led many scholars to scrutinize how historical and cultural memories are being recreated in transnational productions that reflect the "deterritorializing dynamics" of modernity (Perriam, Santaolalla, and Evans 6). For example, Ann Davies points out that regarding Spanish film studies "there is traffic between Spain and Latin America, particularly Mexico" (7). Chris Perriam, Isabel Santaolalla, and Peter Evans edited a volume of the *Hispanic Research Journal* devoted to the topic of the Transnational in Iberian

and Latin American Cinemas in which they trace in broad strokes the advantages and disadvantages of transnational productions and their varying takes on national identity.
29. One such book is the volume edited by Louise Holt, *Geographies of Children, Youth and Families*.
30. Thank you to Melissa Ralesvich for providing us with this information.
31. There are exceptions to this statement, particularly in films screening girls.
32. Matthew Marr discusses the theorization of "angry girl" feminism and also provides an overview of the representation of gender in Spanish films from the 1990s.
33. The reference to postmodern teen films can be found in Podalsky in Shary and Siebel (89).

Works Cited

A un dios desconocido. Dir. Jaime Chávarri. Perf. Héctor Alterio, Xabier Elorriaga, Angela Molina. Elías Querejeta Producciones Cinematográficas, 1977. Film.
Aguilar, Gonzalo. *New Argentine Film: Other Worlds*. New York: Palgrave Macmillan, 2008.
Alamar. Dir. Pedro González Rubio. Perf. Jorge Machado, Roberta Palombini, Natan Machado Palombini. Mantarraya Producciones, Xkalakarma, 2009. Film.
Alsino y el cóndor. Dir. Miguel Littin. Perf. Dean Stockwell, Alan Esquivel, Carmen Bunster. CRFC, Instituto Cubano del Arte e Industrias Cinematográficos, Latin-American Film Releasing Corporation, 1983. Film.
Amar te duele. Dir. Fernando Sariñana. Perf. Luis Fernando Peña, Martha Higareda, Ximena Sariñana. Altavista Films, Videocine, 2002. Film.
Amores perros. Dir. Alejandro González Iñárritu. Perf. Emilio Echevarría, Gael García Bernal, Goya Toledo, Alvaro Guerrero, Vanessa Bauche, Jorge Salinas, Marco Pérez. Altavista Films, Zeta Films, 2000. Film.
Andrés no quiere dormir la siesta. Dir. Daniel Bustamente. Perf. Norma Aleandro, Conrado Valenzuela, Fabio Aste, Juan Manuel Tenuta. El Ansia, San Luis Cine, 2009. Film.
Ano em que meus pais sairam de férias, O. Dir. Cao Hamburger. Perf. Michel Joelsas, Germano Haiut, Paulo Autran, Daniela Piepszyk, 2006. Film.
Año uña. Dir. Jonás Cuarón. Perf. Eireann Harper, Diego Cataño. Esperanto Filmoj, 2009. Film.
Barnier, Martin. "The Sound of Fear in Recent Spanish Film." *MSMI* 4.2 (Autumn 2010): 197–211.
Barrio. Dir. Fernando León de Aranoa. Perf. Críspulo Cabezas, Timy Benito, Eloi Yebra. Elías Querejeta Producciones Cinematográficas, MGN Filmes, Sociedad General de Televisión, 1998. Film.
Best, Joel. *Threatened Children: Rhetoric and Concern about Child-Victims*. Chicago: U of Chicago P, 1990.

Bicicletas son para el verano, Las. Dir. Jaime Chávarri. Perf. Ampara Soler Leal, Agustín González, Victoria Abril. Impala, In-Cine Compañía Industrial Cinematográfica, Jet Films, 1984. Film.

Bola, El. Dir. Achero Mañas. Perf. Juan José Ballesta, Pablo Galán, Alberto Jiménez. Canal+ España, Televisión Española (TVE), Tesela Producciones Cinematográficas, 2000. Film.

Buena vida, La. Dir. David Trueba. Perf. Fernando Ramallo, Lucía Jiménez, Luis Cuenca. Academy, Fernando Trueba Producciones Cinematográficas S.A., Kaplan S.A., 1996. Film.

Camada negra. Dir. Manuel Gutiérrez Aragón and José Luis Borau. Perf. José Luis Alonso, María Luisa Ponte, Angela Molina, Manuel Fadón. El Imán Cine y Televisión, 1977. Film.

Camino, El. Dir. Ishtar Yasín Gutiérrez. Perf. Sherlin Paola Velásquez, Juan Borda, Morena Guadalupe Espinoza. Producciones Astarté, 2007. Film.

Cara de queso, mi primer ghetto. Dir. Ariel Winograd. Perf. Sebastián Montagna, Martín Piroyanski, Federicco Luppi, Daniel Hendler. Haddock Films, Tres Planos Cine, 2006. Film.

Carbonetti, María de los Angeles. "El huevo de la serpiente: *Crónica de un niño solo* de Leonardo Favio." *Anclajes* 4.4 (2000): 39–55.

Cautiva. Dir. Gastón Biraben. Perf. Barbara Lombardo, Hugo Arana, Susana Campos, Osvaldo Santoro. Cacerolazo Producciones, 2004. Film.

Central do Brazil. Dir. Walter Salles. Perf. Fernanda Montenegro, Vinícius de Oliveira, Matheus Nachtergaele, Marília Pêra. BEI Comunicações, 1998. Film.

Chávez, Daniel. "*Alsino y el cóndor*, hacia una crítica del espectador latinoamericano y nicaragüense." *Chasqui* 37.2 (2008): 28–49.

Ciénaga, La. Dir. Lucrecia Martel. Perf. Graciela Borges, Mercedes Morán, Leonora Balcarce, Sofia Bertolotto. 4kFilms, Wanda Vision, 2001. Film.

Cría cuervos. Dir. Carlos Saura. Perf. Geraldine Chaplin, Ana Torrent. Elías Querejeta Producciones Cinematográficas, 1976. Film.

Crónica de un niño solo. Dir. Leonardo Favio. Perf. Diego Puente, Tino Pascali, Cacho Espíndola, Victoriano Moreira, 1965. Film.

Davies, Ann. Introduction. *Spain on Screen: Developments in Contemporary Spanish Cinema.* Ed. Ann Davies. New York: Palgrave Macmillan, 2011. 1–18.

De Armiñan, Jaime. *La dulce España: Memoria de un niño partido en dos.* Barcelona: Tusquets, 2000.

De Ros, Xon. "Innocence Lost: Sight and Sound in *El espíritu de la colmena*." *Sound on Vision: Studies on Spanish Cinema*, Special Issue *Bulletin of Hispanic Studies*. Ed. Robin Fiddian and Ian Michael lxxxiv, 1 (1999): 27-37.

Deleyto, Celestino. "Focalisation in Film Narrative." *Atlantis* 13.1–2 (Nov. 1991): 159–77.

Doherty, Thomas. *Adolescents and Teenpics: The Juvenilization of American Movies in the 1950s.* Philadelphia: Temple UP, 2002.

Elena, Alberto. "*Dream of Light*: Erice, Kiarostami and the History of Cinema." *Studies in Hispanic Cinemas* 6.2 (2009): 99–110.

En el balcón vacío. Dir. Jomí García Ascot. Perf. Alicia Bergua, Martín Bergua, María Luisa Elio. Ascot, Torre, 1962. Film.

Espinazo del diablo, El. Dir. Guillermo del Toro. Perf. Marisa Paredes Eduardo Noriega, Federico Luppi. El Deseo S.A., Tequila Gang, Anhelo Producciones, 2001. Film.

Espíritu de la colmena, El. Dir. Víctor Erice. Perf. Fernando Fernán Gómez, Teresa Gimpera, Ana Torrent. Elías Querejeta Producciones Cinematográficas, Jacel Desposito, 1973. Film.

Everly, Kathryn. "Television and the Power of Image in *Caídos del cielo* and *La pistola de mi hermano* by Ray Loriga." *Generation X Rocks: Comtemporary Peninsular Fiction, Film and Rock Culture.* Eds. Christine Henseler and Randolph D. Pope. Nashville: Vanderbilt UP, 2007. 170-183

Farina, Alberto. *Leonardo Favio.* Buenos Aires: Centro Editor de América Latina, 1993.

Film Movement. 1 Apr. 2012 <http://www.filmmovement.com/filmclub.asp?>

Fouz-Hernández, Santiago, and Alfredo Martínez-Expósito. *Live Flesh: The Male Body in Contemporary Spanish Cinema.* London: Tauris, 2007.

Francia. Dir. Adrián Cateano. Perf. Milagros Cateano, Natalia Oreiro, Lautaro Delgado, Daniel Valenzuela. 2009. INCAA, La Expresión del Deseo. Film.

Furtivos. Dir. José Luis Borau. Perf. Lola Gaos, Ovidi Montllor, Alicia Sánchez, Ismael Merlo. El Imán Cine y Televisión, 1975. Film.

Gateward, Frances, and Murray Pomerance, eds. *Sugar Spice and Everything Nice: Cinemas of Girlhood.* Detroit: Wayne State UP, 2002.

Giroux, Henry. *Youth in a Suspect Society: Democracy or Disposability?* New York: Palgrave Macmillan, 2009.

Gringuito. Dir. Sergio Castilla. Perf. Sebastián Pérez, Mateo Iribarren, Catalina Guerra. Amor en el Sur Ltda, 1998. Film.

Guy, Donna. "The State, the Family, and Marginal Children in Latin American." *Minor Omissions: Children in Latin American History and Society.* Ed. Tobias Hecht. Madison: U of Wisconsin P, 2002. 139–65.

Hecht, Tobias. "Introduction." *Minor Omissions: Children in Latin American History and Society.* Ed. Tobias Hecht. Madison: U of Wisconsin P, 2002. 3-20.

Higgonet, Anne. *Pictures of Innocence: The History and Crisis of Ideal Childhood.* London: Thames and Hudson, 1998.

Holland, Jonathan. "La pistola de mi hermano." *Variety.* Reed Business Information, 1 Dec. 1997. Web. 14 Oct. 2011. <http://www.variety.com/review/VE1117912594?refcatid=31>.

Holt, Louise, ed. *Geographies of Children, Youth and Families: An International Perspective.* London: Routledge, 2011.

Izquierdo Vallina, Jaime. *Marcelo: Los otros niños de la Guerra.* Madrid: Obrerón, 2004.

James, Allison, and Alan Prout. "A New Paradigm for the Sociology of Childhood? Provenance, Promise and Problems." *Constructing and Re-Constructing Childhood.* Ed. James and Prout. London: Plamer, 1990. 7–35.

Jenkins, Henry. *"Children's Culture."* Massachusetts Institute of Technology, n.d. Web. 2 May 2011. <http://web.mit.edu/cms/People/henry3/children.htm>.

Jones, Owain. "'True Geography Quickly Forgotten, Giving Away to an Adult-Imagined Universe.' Approaching the Otherness of Childhood." *Children's Geographies* 6.2 (May 2008): 195–212.
Judíos en el espacio. Dir. Gabriel Lichtmann. Perf. Gabriela Andermann, Axel Anderson, Luna Paiva, Gerardo Cheno. 2005. Film.
Kamchatka. Dir. Marcelo Piñeyro. Perf. Ricardo Darín, Cecilia Roth, Héctor Alterio, Fernanda Mistral. Alquimia Cinema, Oscar Kramer, Patagonik Film Group, 2002. Film.
Kinder, Marsha, ed. "The Children of Franco in the New Spanish Cinema." *Quarterly Review of Film Studies* 8.2 (Spring 1983): 57–76.
———. *Refiguring Spain: Cinema, Media, Representation*. Durham: Duke UP, 1997.
La pistola de mi hermano. Dir. Ray Loriga. Perf. Daniel González, Nico Bidasolo, Andrés Gertródix. Enrique Cerezo Producciones Cinematográficas, 1997. Film.
Laberinto del fauno, El. Dir. Guillermo del Toro. Perf. Ivana Baquero, Sergi López, Maribel Verdú, Doug Jones. Estudios Picasso, Tequila Gang, Esperanto Filmoj, 2006. Film.
Lake Tahoe. Dir. Fernando Eimbcke. Perf. Diego Cataño, Hector Herrera, Daniela Valentine. Cine Pantera, Fidecine, Instituto Mexicano de Cinematografía, 2008.
Lázaro-Reboll, Antonio. "The Transnational Reception of *El espinazo del diablo* (Guillermo del Toro 2001)." *Hispanic Research Journal* 8.1 (Feb. 2001): 39–51.
Lebeau, Vicky. *Childhood and Cinema*. London: Reaktion, 2008.
Lengua de las mariposas, La. Dir. José Luis Cuerda. Perf. Fernando Fernán Gómez, Manuel Lozano Uxía Blanco. Canal+ España, Los Producciones del Escorpión, Sociedad General de Televisión, 1999. Film.
Linha de passe. Dir. Walter Salles, Daniella Thomas. Perf. Sandra Corveloni, João Baldasserini, Vinícius Oliveira. Media Rights Capital, Pathé Pictures International, Videofilmes Produçoes Artisticas, 2008. Film.
Lopate, Phillip. "Images of Children in Films." *Green Mountains Review* 8.1 (1995): 90–96.
Lury, Karen. *The Child in Film: Tears, Fears and Fairy Tales*. Piscataway: Rutgers UP, 2010.
Machuca. Dir. Andrés Wood. Perf. Matías Quer, Ariel Mateluna, Manuela Martelli, Federico Luppi. 2004. Film.
Madeinusa. Dir. Claudia Llosa. Perf. Magaly Solier, Carlos J. de la Torre, Yiliana Chong. Oberón Cinematográfica, Vela Producciones, Wanda Visión S.A., 2004. Film.
Mantenidas sin sueños, Las. Dir. Martín de Salvo, Vera Fogwill. Perf. Vera Fogwill, Lucia Snieg, Mirta Busnelli. Avalon Productions, Hubert Bals Fund, Instituto Nacional de Cine y Artes Visuales, 2005. Film.
María llena eres de gracia. Dir. Joshua Marston. Perf. Catalina Sandino Moreno, Guilied Lopez, Orlando Tobón. HBO Films, Fine Line Features, Journeyman Pictures, 2004. Film.
Marr, Matthew. "Generation X and Its Discontents: The Girl Aggressor and Youth Subjectivity in the Cinematic Adaptation of *Mensaka*." *Revista de Estudios Hispánicos* 42 (2008): 133–55.

Mensaka. Dir. Salvador García Ruiz. Perf. Gustavo Salmerón, Tristán Ulloa, Adrià Collado. Tornasol Films, 1998. Film.
Milanich, Nara. "Historical Perspectives on Illegitimacy and Illegitimates in Latin America." *Minor Omissions: Children in Latin American History and Society*. Ed. Tobias Hecht. Madison: U of Wisconsin P, 2002. 72–101.
Mutum. Dir. Sanra Kohut. Perf. Thiago da Silva Mariz, Wallison Felipe Leal Barroso, Izadora Fernandez, João Miguel. Ravina Filmes, Gloria Films, 2007.
Nido, El. Dir. Jaime de Armiñán. Perf. Héctor Alterio, Ana Torrent. A Punto P.C., 1980. Film.
Nikolajeva, María. *Aspects and Issues in the History of Children's Literature*. Westport: Greenwood, 1995.
Niña santa, La. Dir. Lucrecia Martel. Perf. Merces Morán, Alejandro Urdapilleta, Carlos Belloso, María Alche. La Pasionaria Producciones, R & C Produzioni, 2004. Film.
Nina. Dir. Heitor Dhalia. Perf. Guta Stresser, Milhem Cortaz, Anderson Faganello. Branca Filmes, Fábrica Brasileira de Imagens, Gullane Filmes, 2004. Film.
Niño pez, El. Dir. Lucía Puenzo. Perf. Inés Efrón, Nariela Vitale, Pep Munné, Diego Velázquez. MK2 Producciones, Wanda Vision, 2009. Film.
Noche de los lápices, La. Dir. Héctor Olivera. Perf. Alejo García Pinto, Vita Escardó, Pablo Novak, Leonardo Sbaraglia. Aries Cinematográfica Argentina, 1986. Film.
Olvidados, Los. Dir. Luis Buñuel. Perf. Estela Inda, Miguel Inclán, Alfonso Mejía, Roberto Cobo. Ultramar Films, 1950. Film.
Only When I Dance. Dir. Beadie Finzi. Perf. Irlan santos da Silva, Isabela Coracy Alves, Nascimento Santos, Mariza Estrella. Tigerlilly Films, 2009. Film.
Paloma de papel. Dir. Fabrizio Aguilar. Perf. Antonio Callirgos, Eduardo Cesti and Aristóteles Picho. Luna llena Films, 2003. Film.
Peluffo, Ana. "Staging Class, Gender and Ethnicity in Lucrecia's Martel's *La ciénaga* (The Swamp)." *New Trends in Argentine and Brazilian Cinema*. Ed. Cacila Rêgo and Carolina Rocha. Bristol: Intellect, 2011. 211–224.
Peña, Francisco. "*La vendedora de rosas* de Victor Gaviria." *Cine Visiones* 26 Dec. 2008. Web. 6 Jan. 2011. <://cinevisiones.blogspot.com/2008/12/vendedora-de-rosas-la-de-vctor-gaviria.html>.
Pereira, Luis Alberto, Jr. "As Representações da Marginalidade Infantil Através da Obra Cinematográfica *Pixote, A Lei Do Mais Fraco*." *Revista Opsis* 9.12 (2009): 23–43. Web. <http://revistas.ufg.br/index.php/Opsis/article/view/9435/6523>.
Perfume de violetas: Nadie te oye. Dir. Maryse Sistach. Perf. Ximena Ayala, Nancy Gutiérrez, Arcelia Ramírez, María Rojo. Centro de Capacitación Cinematográfica, Cnca, Filmoteca de la UNAM, 2001. Film.
Perriam, Chris, Isabel Santaolalla, and Peter Evans. "The Transnational in Iberian and Latin American Cinemas: Editors' Introduction." *Hispanic Research Journal* 8.1 (Feb. 2007): 3–9.
Pizza, birra, faso. Dir. Adrián Cateano and Bruno Stagnaro. Perf. Héctor Anglada, Jorge Sesán, Pamela Jordán, Adrián Yospe. Palo a la Bolsa Cine, 1998. Film.

Podalsky, Laura. *The Politics of Affect and Emotion in Contemporary Latin American Cinema: Argentina, Brazil, Cuba, and Mexico*. New York: Palgrave Macmillan, 2011.

———. "Out of Depth: The Politics of Disaffected Youth and Contemporary Latin American Cinema." *Youth Culture in Global Cinema*. Ed. Timothy Shary and Alexandra Siebel. Austin: U of Texas P, 2007. 109–30.

Poulsen, Stinne Krogh. "History, Memory and Nostalgia in Childhood Films." *Cinemascope* 13.5 (2009). Web. 19 April, 2009. <http://www.cinemascope.it/Issue%2013/PDF/STINNE%20KROGH%20POULSEN.pdf>

Prima Angélica, La. Dir. Carlos Saura. Perf. José Luis López Vázquez, Fernando Delgado, Lina Canalejas, María Clara Fernández de Loaysa. Elías Querejeta Producciones Cinematográficas, 1974. Film.

Raggio, Marcela. *Leonardo Favio: Cine argentino de antihéroes*. Mendoza: Jaguel, 2011.

Réquiem por un campesino español. Dir. Francesc Betriu. Perf. Francisco Algora, Simón Andreu, Antonio Banderas. Nemo Films, Venus Produccion, 1985. Film.

Roberts, Sharon. "Minor Concerns: Representations of Children and Childhood in British Museums." *Museum and Society* 4.3 (Nov. 2006): 152–65.

Rocha, Carolina. "Jewish Cinematic Self-Representations in Contemporary Argentine and Brazilian Films." *Journal of Modern Jewish Studies* 9.1 (2010): 37–48.

Rodrigo D: No futuro. Dir. Víctor Gaviria. Perf. Ramiro Meneses, Carlos Mario Restrepo, Jackson Idrian Gallego. Compañía de Fomento Cinematográfico, FOCINE, Fotoclub-76, 1990. Film.

Ruiz, María Luisa. Me enamoré de ti en un bazar: Gender, Consumption and Identity in *Amar te duele*." *Journal of the Midwest Modern Language Association* 43.1 (2010): 77–96.

Secretos del corazón. Dir. Monxto Armendáriz. Perf. Carmelo Gómez, Charo López, Silvia Munt. Aiete Films S.A., Les Films Ariane, 1997. Film.

Semana solos, Una. Dir. Celina Murga. Perf. Natalia Gómez Alarcón, Ignacio Jiménes, Films, Zeta Films, 2000. Film.

Pixote: A Lei do Mas Fraco. Dir. Héctor Babenco. Perf. Fernado Ramos da Silva, Jorge Julião, Gilberto Moura, Edilson Lino. Embrafilmes, HP Filmes, 1981. Film.

Shary, Timothy and Alexandra Seibel, Eds. *Youth Culture in Global Cinema*. Austin: U of Texas P, 2006.

Shary, Timothy. *Generation Multiplex: The Image of Youth in Contemporary American Cinema*. Austin: U of Texas P, 2002.

Silencio de Neto, El. Dir. Luis Argueta. Perf. Óscar Javier Almengor, Eva Tamargo Lemus, Julio Diaz, Herbert Meneses. Buenos Dias, 1996. Film.

Sin nombre. Dir. Cary Fukunaga. Perf. Paulina Gaitán, Marco Antonio Aguirre, Leonardo Alonso. Scion Films, Canana Films, Creando Films, 2009. Film.

Soba. Dir. Alan Coton. Perf. Claudia Soberón, Dagoberto Gama, Antonio Algarra. 9.5 Grados en la escala de Richter, La Chancla Producciones, 2004. Film.

Sonhos robados. Dir. Sandar Werneck. Perf. Ângelo Antônio, Zezeh Barbosa, M.V. Bill. Cineluz, Estúdios Mega, Labocine, Europa Filmes, 2010. Film.

Stam, Robert, João Luiz Vieira, and Ismael Xavier. "The Shape of Brazilian Cinema in the Postmodern Age." *Brazilian Cinema*. Ed. Robert Stam and Randall Johnson. New York: Columbia UP, 1995. 387–472.
Temporada de patos. Dir. Fernando Eimbcke. Perf. Carolina Politi, Daniel Miranda, Diego Cataño. Cine Pantera, Esperanto Filmoj, Fidecine, 2004. Film.
Teta i la lluna, La. Dir. Bigas Luna. Perf. Biel Duran, Mathilda May, Gérard Darmon. Creativos Asociados de Radio y Televisión, Hugo Films, Lolafilms, 1994. Film.
Triana-Toribio, Núria. *Spanish National Cinema*. London: Routledge, 2003.
Último verano de la Boyita, El. Dir. Julia Solomonoff. Perf. Guadalupe Alonso, Nicolás Treise, Mirrella Pascual, Gabo Correa. Travesia Productions, Domenica Film, El deseo. Film.
UNICEF. "Fact Sheet: A Summary of the Rights under the Convention on the Rights of the Child." Web. 18 Sept. 2011. <http://www.unicef.org/crc/index_30228.html>.
Urte ilunak/Los años oscuros. Dir. Arantxa Lazkano. Perf. Mikel Albisu, Ramón Barea, Txema Blasco. 1992. Film.
Valentín. Dir. Alejandro Agresti. Perf. Rodrigo Noya, Julieta Cardinalli, Carmen Maura, Jean Pierre Noher. Miramax, 2002. Film.
Vendedora de rosas, La. Dir. Victor Gaviria. Perf. Lady Tabares, Marta Correa, Mileider Gil, Diana Murillo. Producciones Filmamento, 1988. Film.
Viaje de Carol, El. Dir. Imanol Uribe. Perf. Clara Lago, Juan José Ballesta, Álvaro de Luna. Aiete Films S.A., Aiete-Ariane Films, Ariane Films, 2002. Film.
Viva Cuba. Dir. Juan Carlos Cremata Malberti and Iraida Malberti Cabrera. Perf. Malú Tarrau Broche, Jorge Milo, Luisa María Jiménez Rodríguez. Quad Productions, DDC Films LLC, TVC Casa Productora, 2005. Film.
Voces inocentes. Dir. Luis Mandoki. Perf. Carlos Padilla, Leonor Varela, Xuna Primus Lawrence Bender Productions, MUVI Films, Organización Santo Domingo, 2005. Film.
Wilson, Emma. "Miniature Lives, Intrusion and Innocence: Women Filming Children." *French Cultural Studies* 18.2 (2007): 169–83.
Wojcik-Andrews, Ian. *Children's Films: History, Ideology, Pedagogy, Theory*. New York: Garland, 2000.
Y tu mama también. Dir. Alfonso Cuarón. Perf. Maribel Verdú, Gael García Bernal, Diego Luna, Ana López Mercado. Anhelo Producciones, Besame Mucho Pictures, Producciones Anhelo, 2001. Film.
Zipes, Jack. *When Dreams Came True: Classical Fairy Tales and Their Tradition*. New York: Routledge, 1999.

PART I

MEMORY AND TRAUMA

CHAPTER 1

SURVIVING CHILDHOOD

THE NEPANTLA GENERATION AS PORTRAYED IN ON THE EMPTY BALCONY BY JOMÍ GARCÍA ASCOT

JULIA TUÑÓN
TRANSLATED BY GEORGIA SEMINET

Childhood is often associated with peace, a world of illusions, and extreme kindness, thus it is thought that children should grow up in a sheltered environment void of any harshness or hardship. The word *infant* derives from the Latin *infans* and refers to an undeveloped logical consciousness and an inability to produce speech. Representative of infans, young children are perceived as dependent and powerless, overly influenced by their emotions and consequently defenseless against their fears. At the same time, they rely on the power of their imagination as a means of comfort. Childhood is a period in which small children mature by learning new skills and social structures, as well as acquiring a civic consciousness passed on through parents and school. In accordance with ideas developed in a previous essay by Julia Tuñón, children in classic Mexican cinema have often been represented as a symbol of purity ("La imagen de los niños" 135–48), but what happens when children live in a chaotic world of war and fear where they lose their homes and no longer have the protection of a sheltered environment? This was the case when thousands of families went into exile during the Spanish Civil War (1936–39) in order to escape the violence and, later, during the postwar period to escape the persecution of republican sympathizers and supporters.[1] Mexico was one of the countries that welcomed Spanish families and children attempting to escape the consequences of the Spanish Civil War and its aftermath. Not surprisingly, the exiles, as well as their children, have left a mark on Mexican cultural production. In this essay, I will analyze how the trauma of displacement and the effects of exile on adults, who were uprooted as children, are presented in the cult film *On the Empty Balcony* (*En el balcón vacío*) by Jomí García Ascot (1962). This film revolves around the incomplete memories of a young Spanish girl exiled in Mexico who as an adult attempts to cope with her ongoing trauma and pain.

Spanish exiles began arriving in Mexico after the defeat of the Second Spanish Republic in 1939. The Mexican government welcomed the exiles, which numbered about 25,000 people, many of whom were children. Twenty years later, a group of these Spanish immigrants filmed *On the Empty Balcony*, which narrates the difficult life of Gabriela, a young girl who experiences the onset of the Spanish Civil War and as a result escapes into exile, first to France and later to Mexico. The film takes stock of Gabriela's inability to integrate the traumatic effects of her childhood experiences into her adult life. The psychological trauma of her suspended childhood continues to torment her as an adult. The film delves stunningly into Gabriela's unresolved and ever-present psychological pain. As a consequence, her anguish accumulates and is represented nonlinearly through a patchwork of barely remembered moments of her childhood. Her mourning for a childhood interrupted by violence, death, exile, and migration has deprived Gabriela of a coherent sense of self in adulthood. The film exemplifies the fact that exile and immigration have impeded Gabriela from completing the task of healthy mourning, which Sigmund Freud defines as "the reaction to the loss of a loved person, or to the loss of some abstraction which has taken the place of one, such as fatherland, liberty, an ideal and so on" (164). Instead, she exhibits some of the traits of melancholia, which Freud describes as "profoundly painful dejection, abrogation of interest in the outside world, loss of the capacity to love, inhibition of all activity, and a lowering of the self-regarding feelings to a degree that finds utterance in self-reproaches and self-reviling" (165).

ON THE EMPTY BALCONY

On the Empty Balcony is an emblematic film on several levels. In part, it is the film manifesto of the Mexican journal *Nuevo cine*,[2] which tried to change the direction of the Mexican film industry so as to adapt it to the canons of the French *Cahiers du Cinéma* as well as the aesthetic ideas of the nouvelle vague. However, the film has been valued for its authenticity and sincerity of its content, and has thus acquired an iconic status as a representation of the nature of the Spanish exile in Mexico and the conflicts associated with their circumstances.

The film was made in forty Sundays spanning 1961 and 1962. This unusual schedule resulted from the director's lack of support—both technical and financial—from the film industry, and he was thus obliged to film on the crew's days off. García used a 16mm Pathé Webo camera with a hand crank and dubbed sound.[3] The project had only cost around MXN$50,000.00 (approximately $400.00) obtained with the help of donations, which is surprising if we consider that the average cost of a Mexican film at that time, as reported by Julia Tuñón, was $100,000 ("Bajo el signo" 51). The technical limits of sound production led to very few scenes in which the characters speak, thus *voice off* is prevalent, adding to the film's unique character. Despite its low budget, the film won the FIPRESCI Prize (International Federation of Film Critics) at the Locarno International Film Festival in 1962 and the Jano de Oro at the Latin American Film Festival of Sestri Levante in 1963. Its duration, barely 64 minutes, made commercial exhibition difficult, but according to the film director this was never their intention.

The plot is based on writings by María Luisa Elío who arrived in Mexico as a child, thus her inclusion in the Nepantla generation. Elío later went on to edit and publish *Cuaderno de apuntes* (Notebook; 1995), an account of her troubled childhood interrupted by a war she did not understand. The theme stems from the experiences of little Gabriela Elizondo as an "outcast from paradise," given that "whoever has their childhood stolen is also kidnapped from paradise," as Elío has described her experience in an interview with Tuñón ("Bajo el signo" 48). Elío also wrote about the return to her childhood home years later in *Tiempo de llorar* (*A Time to Cry*), stating, again to Tuñón, "it is the reality that is fantasy in the film" ("Bajo el signo" 48). Jorge Ayala Blanco points out that the personal drama is inscribed as a collective catastrophe in the manner of *Hiroshima mon amour* (1959) by Alain Resnais. He also recalls that they jokingly called the film *Pamplona mon amour* (21). The stock footage of documentarist Joris Ivens[4] refers the viewer to the objective, external history that anchors reality in opposition to the internal, psychological drama of Gabriela.

The film is divided into two perfectly delineated parts. In the first, Nuri Pereña wonderfully interprets Gabriela; in the second, we witness the conflicts of the adult Gabriela. Though she lives in Mexico City, Gabriela later moves to her native Pamplona in an attempt to recover a childhood stolen by exile and marked by the death of her mother. The credits, with deeply significant paintings by Vicente Rojo in the background,[5] are followed by the sound of music heavily infused with percussion. The dramatic use of the drums is reminiscent of the Drums of Calanda that were widely used by Luis Buñuel in his movies.[6] The dedication reads, "A los españoles muertos en el exilio" (to the Spaniards who died in exile) and is followed by an adult female voice off that informs us, "En aquellos días en que ocurrió aún era yo muy niña. Qué diera yo por ser tan niña ahora, si es que acaso lo he dejado de ser. Y entonces había algo en las calles, algo en las casas que después desapareció con aquella guerra" (In those days, when it happened, I was still very young. What I wouldn't give to be that little girl now, if indeed I am no longer that girl. Back then there was something in the houses that later disappeared with that war). Many of the refugee children in Mexico identified with the two parts of the film since they had undergone similar traumatic experiences in their own childhood, and that as adults, similar to Elío, they were never able to overcome.

The point of view is created through "the voice that remembers." Michel Chion notes that the power of the voice off is very important, as it seems to arise from outside the body and reach everywhere, know everything, like the mother's voice would sound for a baby or an unborn child (57). Its mysteriousness evokes the past: "When a voice tells something from the past, voice off, without body, time seems suspended. The disembodied voice occupies all space; it seems to speak into the ear of the spectator, establishing identification with him or her" (Chion 47).[7] Pascal Bonitzer notes that alongside the "absolutely undetermined" character of a voice off, the image retains an indescribable power that, due to its dominating character, is often seen as masculine (133–34).

Nevertheless, in the case of *On the Empty Balcony*, the voice off is a woman whose voice leads us into a peaceful family scene. The father is reading the newspaper, the mother is sewing, the sister is studying, and Gabriela is calmly dismantling a wristwatch in her room. The camera shows us the home and the four of them listening to the harmonious music of Bach. The third-person perspective focuses on Gabriela sitting at a table, appearing diminutive before the open window. We see her as she notices a man who is being chased by the *Guardia Civil* quietly lowering himself from the roof outside her window. She mentally speaks to him while pretending not to notice, looking elsewhere so as not to betray him. Suddenly, a woman's scream shatters the silence, abruptly putting an end to the order and tranquility. A vertical cut divides Gabriela's face in half before she runs and announces to her parents, "The war just started on the roof!," implying that Gabriela is cognizant of the eruption of war in their midst.

Serge Daney refers to the sound emitted from the mouth, such as yelling or accusations, as *voice out* (which is the opposite of *voice off*) because here the presence of the body allows us to fetishize the moment when sound is produced. It is essentially pornographic in that it parallels the idea of an object being expelled from the body (135). Furthermore, Chion objectifies the scream, describing it as an absolute that organizes everything: "A black hole in which magical and sumptuous things converge—a party, political crime, a sex murder, and the entire film—all will be consumed, dissipated, in the unthinkable and instantaneous scream" (68). Even more important than the modulation of the scream is the moment when it occurs since it happens when the next moment is still unknown. Furthermore, it is worth noting that the impact of the scream is heightened because it is produced from the mouth of a woman. The female figure represents the origins of our humanity and the inevitability of death, which in turn reminds us of the anguish provoked by the limitless and centrifugal forces unleashed by the war. The masculine figure, on the other hand, reminds us of power and the centripetal delimitation of a territory. The screams erupt with force in *On the Empty Balcony* and represent an augur of death; but the gaze is also captured symbolically. We have seen what she sees and the spectator's identification with her increases as the number of close-ups and subjective point-of-view shots increases. The spectator has internalized Gabriela's gaze so the techniques promote identification with the character. Furthermore, they characterize the first part of the film.

Next, following this scene is a series of actions. First, the father leaves the house to go into hiding. While at school, a shady character approaches Gabriela to ask where her father is, but she remains silent. Another man gives her mother a bag of dirty clothes, and Gabriela rifles through the bag, obviously seeing something that the spectators are not able to see in detail. The face of the frightened and bewildered girl, framed in black hair, reminds the viewers of their own fears through the use of a close-up. Gabriela observes and is observed with sympathy by a prisoner, but the next day when she brings cigarettes to the prison for him, she finds out that prison authorities have killed him. In all of these sequences, her gaze and silence emphasize the emotional aspect of the film.

Thereafter, the mother and the two daughters escape from Pamplona and go to Valencia and Barcelona, where little Gabriela learns to fear bombs. Again, she is presented huddled in a corner, tiny in the face of fear. For the second time, a vertical line that literally splits her in two divides her face. She also learns to play in the ruins of the bombed buildings, where she finds a glass cork that will gain symbolism during the film. From Pamplona, the three flee to southern France looking for the father, but instead they learn about his death. At this point, Gabriela comes to understand not only nostalgia but also exile when she hears a melody coming from a neighboring house: "La verbena de la paloma" (The Dove's Verbena).[8]

Moving forward, the subsequent part of the film is undertaken with delicacy and care. The actions that affect the personal life of Gabriela are alternated with Ivens's stock footage, which creates the context of her misfortune. José María Naharro Calderón notes that the first image of Mexico, the country of asylum in which Gabriela reaches adulthood, is a close-up of a cactus with thorns, which suggests that the exiles were rejected by their adoptive country (155). Though the welcome received by the Spanish refugees was ambivalent on the part of the Mexican population in general, all in all it was considered to have been exemplary given that the government willingly opened its doors to the exiles. Thus the shot of the cactus is also ambivalent, and can be interpreted (in the lapse of time not represented in the film) as either the exiles rejecting Mexico or as feeling rejected by Mexico.

Significantly, in the second part of the film, the voice off is predominant with the difference that it now corresponds to the image of an adult woman. The voice off by the adult Gabriela narrates her feelings. Paradoxically, most of her thoughts at this point relate to childhood. During childhood, the voice is of an adult woman, but on the contrary, the voice of adulthood is the voice of a child. Pietsie Feenstra, who has studied the treatment of voice in the film, comments on this oppositional effect by noting that the words and the image of the body refer to mismatched periods of time and are only joined by memory (167). As the film continues, the solitary woman wanders throughout Mexico City, walking slowly along the huge esplanade of the Monument of the Revolution in an establishing shot in which she appears as tiny. Though the camera follows her from a distance, we hear her voice very near, as if in our ear. After a lapse of twenty years, she informs us of her tribulations. When she gets on a bus, the voice off explains that she must decide whether to go to Pamplona in order to recuperate her lost childhood. At this point, the vertical cut through her face appears once more.

We see the elegant blond woman (Gabriela) visiting the cemetery with her sister where they buried their mother. They reminisce on the mishaps of their journey into exile, and once Gabriela is alone she takes the glass cork, salvaged after a bomb raid, from an old box. This is the point in which Gabriela is caught between remembering and forgetting: she cannot remember her father's face specifically because the images escape her, but she cannot forget the circumstances of her childhood. Since in both the film and the novel memory constitutes the primary theme of the narrative, it is easy to understand why critic Emilio García Riera finds that the film conforms closely to Marcel Proust's *In Search of Lost Time* (1994, 9: 24).

Gabriela's Lost Time

To what does Gabriela owe this feeling of uprootedness that she is experiencing as an adult? Why has she lost all sense of space and time? Her experience becomes a metaphor for the lives of those who arrived in Mexico as children and teens. Dolores Pla states that there were 19,960 Spanish refugees, all older than 15, who arrived in Mexico Between 1939 and 1950 ("Un río español" 61). According to data from Mauricio Fresco, Spanish emigration to Mexico amounted to 16,000 men; 4,000 women; and close to 8,000 children within a span of 11 years. Not to mention that the group of children soon increased to 8,750 following new births that subsequently registered as Mexican citizens (53). The young Spanish children had come from a war that imposed great suffering on the population. Although they rarely participated, they heard the threats on the radio; they heard the bomb raids from which they had to take refuge underground or in subway stations. They also experienced the effects in the countless family misfortunes, in the hunger and fear they suffered, and finally, in the effects of the invisible wounds that marked their families. Evidently, the time had come to flee. Some were children and others adolescents but, regardless, they were too young to face the hardships that they were forced to endure. Consequently, the question begging to be asked is, is it even possible for these children to determine whether this was self-exile or a hereditary circumstance?

One of the particular problems faced by the group of Spanish children who went into exile is the construction of their identity. In the early period of exile there was an urgent need to integrate into Mexican society without relinquishing their Spanish identity because they believed they would soon return to their country. The need to strengthen their Spanish identity was centered on cultural norms and manifested in taste, attitudes, dress code, and their acceptance of *Habitus*, according to Bourdieu (ipse dixit)—which helped them distinguish themselves from the Mexican other and privilege their own cultural origins. Among the distinguishing features recognized among the group were austerity and sobriety in daily life.

In the definition of identity, a series of tensions comes into play in which differences are taken to be mutually exclusive, thereby exacerbating the tension that exists between individuals and groups. In the early years, exile was not understood as a permanent state. The children of exiles were in a state of crisis and searched for equilibrium, although contradictorily, a balanced life bored them, as they were accustomed to adrenaline electrifying their experiences. There is a peculiarity in these "children of exile" or "children of war" that has affected them in similar ways, essentially freezing them in a state of childhood. According to Pla, these "borrowed refugees" suffered from violence that they had not provoked ("Los niños del exilio" 164). Pla goes on to comment that "Mexico was their physical environment; their stomping ground and where they rested their feet, but their gaze and their minds were directed toward Spain" ("Los niños del exilio" 164). In this way their parents' exile dominated them.

The stunted childhood seen on film is also expressed verbally by Enrique de Rivas who raises the issue that "our parents ran away from physical and moral destruction with their appendages, which were us. Children, during childhood, are the material extension of their parents. Therefore, as they get older, they are their continuation, with variations and metamorphoses" ("Destierro").

In addition, Gloria Artís, daughter of Catalonian refugees, analyzes not only the children who arrived but also those born in Mexico and considers them an "ethnic group" since not only do their members see themselves as different, but they interact among themselves and are distinguished by others for being different as well (293–333). In particular, Artís refers to them as an ethnic rather than as a racial group because their difference is perpetuated in biological terms as well as in cultural values, including their ambiguous identity based on their, or their parents', past as refugees. The characteristics that the group believes make them different, according to Artís, have much in common with Mexican culture and the differences are less than what the refugees perceive them to be. On the other hand, given that identities are plural, feelings of difference do not exclude them from being Mexican. However, being characterized by social, cultural, and economic differences so sharply defined that they become exclusive can turn the group into a breeding ground for the creation of a different social field.

Nonetheless, those who came as children or adolescents formed a group with its own characteristics, especially in psychological or emotional terms. They have named themselves the Nepantla generation, a Nahuatl word that means "between two worlds," as if they were amphibious and trying to navigate a comfort zone that exists neither in Mexico nor in Spain. Luis Rius calls them "fronterizos" (border dwellers)—a disoriented generation, neither from here nor over there—and argues, "We were too young when we arrived in Mexico to be like our parents, Spaniards; and it was too late for us to become Mexicans [. . .] we are living on the border, like lizards and poets" (qtd. in Aznar Soler, 236), and he felt that he was left as "a Spaniard without real support in Spain, at the time that he was a supported non-Mexican in Mexico" (qtd. in Fagen, 163). According to Tomás Segovia, the difference between the two worlds that existed for the exiles is clear: the education they received at home and at school, and the fact of an idealized and always-present Spain, which isolated many from the dominant Mexican culture. Segovia also describes the culture of the exiles as often being "exclusive and conflictive," as can be seen in the representation of Gabriela's psyche in the film. Another description is that of José Gaos who employs the term *transterrado* (exile). This term refers to the ability of the Spanish refugees in Mexico to adapt to their adopted country by taking advantage of the similarities between the two cultures (18–179). Segovia points to the paradox that although children had not chosen exile, those who experienced its effects most acutely were in fact "children of the exiled, heirs of the exiled, and those who were protected and pampered from exile" (131–32). On the other hand, he considers that these life conditions also provided advantages, including the ability to choose and enjoy diverse realms of influence (131–32). Opinions on exile rotate along this same axis. Faced with the dilemma, José de la Colina says, "I am from exile as I would be from a country" (qtd. in Aub 1992, 271), and though we may be able to observe a certain balance in these experiences, there are also different styles of feeling and/or expressing it. On a more pragmatic note, Justo Somonte says, for example, "My country is the *Marco Polo*; it is *Havana* and the *Covadonga*, and the same friends as always, those of Vives and of the Academy and the JSU" (qtd. in Aub 1992, 271).[9] Enrique Rivas says,

> Para preservarnos en vista de ese regreso, nos transterraron, con las raíces tiernas totalmente al aire, pero al pasarnos de una tierra a otra, como no se trataba de que echásemos raíces exóticas, tuvieron buen cuidado de que el abono fuera el mismo que el del otro lado del océano o lo más parecido, para que resultásemos las mismas plantas que hubiéramos sido de no haber existido la necesidad del refugio. [. . .] Crecimos, pues, en «tiestos» hechos para nosotros, es decir, en ambientes familiares reconstituidos en función principalmente de lo que había que preservar, en colegios hechos para nosotros, con maestros para nosotros, envueltos en una mitología para nosotros, mitología que nacía, como todas, de la observación de las catástrofes naturales: la mitología de una religión de libertad y de ideales nobles.[10]

The construction of any identity involves resolving diverse tensions that exist between the self and the other, reflecting the interaction involved in becoming an individual while continuing to be part of a group. This consciousness is often seen as belligerence in adolescents and is manifested in their relationships with adults. These adolescents were known as "difficult." For them, the need to start a new life and build self-awareness was urgent, as was the need to preserve the life they brought with them. Thus, within the context of the aforementioned descriptions and testaments to the situation of the children of exiled parents, *On the Empty Balcony* can be seen as emblematic of a third position: that of the Nepantla generation.

THE NEPANTLA GENERATION IN FILM

Unearthing personal narratives from the Spanish Civil War has been a particularly complex task given the resistance in Spain to confronting historical memory. To overcome this, in 2007 the socialist government of José Luis Rodríguez Zapatero promulgated the "Law of Historical Memory," the purpose of which was to enforce the rights of those vanquished during the Spanish Civil War. *On the Empty Balcony*, filmed long before the implementation of the Law of Historical Memory, is a cult film representing the experiences of exile and its impact on children.[11] The film portrays various unresolved impasses that continue to affect this group of exiled youths. *On the Empty Balcony* represents the thoughts and obsessions of their generation. The first of these dilemmas refers to space, the second to time, and the third derives from the first two, leading to the question of whether a life in the present is possible for the Nepantla generation.

The primary depiction of space first appears in the home where we are presented with a metaphor of a typical family life encompassing memories of a cozily furnished home inhabited by a harmonious family who enjoys listening to Bach. This is the home of Gabriela's scattered childhood memories, the place where she had begun her childhood. However, when she returns to Pamplona as an adult, she finds an empty house in which sounds echo, and the balcony of her memories has long since disappeared. As the voice off talks about furniture, there is a lag separating the image and the scene that leaves us feeling disoriented, much like Gabriela, whose obvious discomfort lies in the fact that there is no longer a space for her in her childhood home.

The second dilemma concerns time: is Gabriela living in the past or the present? When the adult Gabriela climbs the stairs of her childhood home, she encounters herself as a child in three instances. This child greets Gabriela, but not only does she not recognize her, but she is not aware of her presence. There is a lack of correspondence between her life as an adult woman and the time that has passed. Gabriela experiences a crisis in the empty house because the conflicting events of her childhood and adult life clash. She asks, "Mama, why have I grown so much? Why am I so tall if I am only seven years old? Help me. I do not know why I have grown so much!" Her questions reveal her own misrecognition and explain the appearance of the vertical cut that splits her face: the young

Gabriela who remained, metaphorically, in the house in Pamplona must grapple with the adult she has become, unable to unify the two halves of her exscinded identity. Similarly, in *Tiempo de llorar*, Elío, demonstrating the ambiguity typical of the Nepantla generation, writes, "I have prayed to find my childhood again, and I have returned, and feel that it is still as elusive as before, and that growing old has been in vain" (23). Gabriela's psychological growth has been stunted, thus she has not experienced a normal process of emotional and psychological development.

Elío, writing about her trip to Pamplona in 1970 after the film was shot, explains the juggling act between past and present: "My soul, that had nurtured my life in the present, had been taken away, and without either the past or the present, it was impossible for me to think of the future" (1988, 21). As a result, any possible resolution of the third dilemma is blocked by the dead end represented in the other two: without the present, without an established chronology of her childhood and adolescence, does she live in the present or the past? Does anything exist beyond her feeling of uprootedness? Juan García Ponce, in reference to *On the Empty Balcony*, writes that along with the portrayal of "eternal outcasts in search of lost unity" we are given an image of the human condition in general (qtd. in García Riera, 1994, 11: 124). This may be true, but for the Nepantla generation, this was, and remains, consubstantial. The film expresses this accurately not only in its theme but also in the way it was filmed. De la Colina states that the movie is not about war or exile, but about nostalgia and uprootedness, which are complemented by the film grain and anomalies in the focus and composition that give the film the aura of a memory (1962, 20). Ayala Blanco takes note of the errors in cinematography but agrees that in part the subjective nature of the narration is more fully realized through these errors (299–300). In other words, the technical problems noted in the film's production could be seen as reflecting the emotional problems manifested in the Nepantla generation.

Overall, the fragmented narrative provides access to memories selected for their affective significance. It also includes great leaps through time that appear to be sifted through the same, repeated circumstances, just as is the case with melancholic memory. For example, the discovery of the glass cork is placed on the same emotional level as the death of the father, the stolen fruit in the restaurant, or the first words spoken in French: it is the memory of incomprehensible and disjointed life experiences that ties the anecdote together, not causality or loyalty to the linear development of a story. The slowness of the narration intensifies this puzzle effect of isolated elements loosely joined and without plausible explanation.

Furthermore, the use of *voice off* heightens the effect of the mystery. As Edgar Morin has suggested that every film animates the inanimate; it breaks the physical space to situate it alongside dreams, and gives time a similarly dreamlike flexibility. However, as many critics have commented, this atmosphere overflows and acquires a poetic weight due to the slowness of movement and the use of silence in *On the Empty Balcony*.

Furthermore, the long shots with a documentary-like style that showcase Mexico, the country that welcomed the exiles, are typical of Latin American cinema of the sixties (Sánchez Biosca 27–38). The long shots also provide an aura of memory rather than transmitting information. Mexico has to be shown in the film in order to be explained and understood, while childhood experiences are internal. Thus it is not necessary to show Spain's landscape or the streets of Pamplona. The representation of Mexico is anecdotal and, therefore, it seems that the director wants to say, "Look, this is the country where Gabriela arrived, but never really put her feet on the ground." The appearance of the cut that at certain moments splits Gabriela's face in two—and represents the two spaces of her identity—parallels the play on presence/absence in the treatment of Mexico and Spain. In several key moments, the image of an empty space due to a sudden absence remains fixed before our eyes. This marks the redundancy of a hollow space with silence: when the young Gabriela warns her family that the war has started, the window is left empty with the background in the dark. The only light comes from outside, where the fugitive has just been apprehended, making the image look like a tunnel. The technique is repeated when the prisoner is killed and again when the adult Gabriela returns to the empty house (Sánchez Biosca 27–38). These scenes are metaphors of an absence that mold the woman's sensibility and emphasize her emptiness while representing her childhood in Spain, left behind but never forgotten. Contradictory messages also provide a sense of mystery, of something evanescent that has escaped. There is insistent talk about a balcony that is never seen. On the contrary, we see only a window, thus the constant reference to the balcony introduces an element of perplexity. Likewise, the fact that the adult Gabriela is blond with blue eyes, but the young Gabriela has dark skin and dark eyes, is equally baffling. These gaffes paralyze reflection because they force us to move in another space in which formal logic is bracketed and has given way to the nonsense of sadness.

Sound is another important aspect of the film but it is limited throughout the plot. We hear the sounds of nature, the breathing of the fugitive in hiding, the singing of the birds when they travel to France, but silence reigns in the troubled times. The music is usually diegetic; we hear it when it is part of the story. At times we hear the songs of the Spanish Civil War as background music. The sound of Gabriela's crying subsumes the second part. Given the sparse soundtrack in the film, the sounds that we do hear stand out for their symbolic significance.

When the young girl gazes out on the world, she remains quiet and we see through her eyes and hear what she thinks; the filmic techniques have led us to identify with her character and experience the conflict with the outside world that neither she, nor the spectator, understands. In the second part, the voice of the adult Gabriela talks about childhood while she appears to float through the streets and over the city. Upon her return to Pamplona, her isolation in turn isolates the spectator. States of mind are difficult to portray on the big screen where the visual is a privileged sense. Nevertheless, films must also depend on symbols, and anecdotes must tell the stories. As de la Colina has written, "The cinema is, above all arts, the one that should count the most . . . with the appearance of things . . . No other art needs the existence of an exterior world more than the cinema . . . No other art has resorted more often to the 'animated images' of the catalog of existing things and beings" ("Miradas" 17). This is exemplified by striking images in the first part of the film when we see, for example, the young girl's anxiety as her mother tells her that she can only take one small toy with her. At this point she puts her dolls on the bed, covering them up. Another arresting image is of the mother crying silently with her back to the spectators when she finds out about her husband's death. However, in the second part of the film, while trying to assuage her unresolved pain, Elío, in the role of the adult Gabriela, cries and complains, her catharsis impeding that of the spectator's. Her rhetorical questions paralyze and exclude the spectator and the pain remains without any possible remedy.

On the Empty Balcony is poignant for its theme and for the filmic resources that are masterfully applied to transmit the experience of the exile, even if only partially, and also for its tact and profundity in denoting a sense of alienation as constructed through filmic narrative. The story touches everyone, although it certainly refers specifically to the Nepantla generation in Mexico, formed by the exiles from the Spanish Civil War. The film lays bare the difficulties in representing childhood memories and recuperating childhood. The adult Gabriela and her younger self appear as two different entities due to the traumatic interruption caused by war and exile. Her identity conflicts, and those of her generation, point to the challenges, and even the impossibility, of integrating traumatized childhood memories into an adult identity.

Notes

1. Children were also sent into exile alone, as can be seen in the well-known case of the Children of Russia, who were the children of Republican fighters and sympathizers who were sent to the Soviet Union to escape death and persecution during the period 1937–38. See also the 2001 film directed by Jaime Camino, *Los niños de Rusia* (*The Children of Russia*).
2. Between April 1961 and August 1962, seven numbers of this journal, published in Mexico City, came out representing the ideas expressed in *Manifiesto del grupo Nuevo Cine* in January 1961 and published in no. 1 of *Nuevo Cine*, April 1961.
3. A model produced in Paris, France, from 1946 to 1960 by S. A Pathè.
4. Joris Ivens is a documentary filmmaker and communist. Born George Henri Anton Ivens, November 18, 1898, in Nijmegen, Gelderland, Netherlands. Ivens died June 28, 1989 in Paris, France.
5. Vicente Rojo is a Mexican artist who was born in Barcelona in 1932. He joined his father, a political exile already living in Mexico, in 1949. From that point, Rojo went on to become an important figure in the arts in Mexico.
6. The people of Calanda, Spain, play the drums continuously during Easter week. The drums correspond to Luis Buñuel's childhood memories, and are often present in his films. Buñuel made a film in 1964, *The Drums of Calanda*, documenting the town where his father, Leonardo, had been born.
7. The Spanish version: "Cuando una voz cuenta algo del pasado, *voz off*, sin cuerpo, el tiempo parece suspenderse. La voz sin cuerpo ocupa todo el espacio, parece que le habla a la oreja del espectador y consigue una identificación."
8. "La verbena de la paloma" is a popular zarzuela from 1894, with prototypical characters depicting nineteenth-century Madrid.
9. The Marco Polo and the Havana are cafés, the Covadonga is a soccer team, and Vives is a high school (Instituto Luis Vives). JSU are the initials for Juventud Socialista Unificada (United Socialist Youth).
10. "To preserve us until our return, they turned us upside down, with our tender roots entirely up in the air. Though we went from one land to another, as if it were not alien or unfamiliar, they were careful to ensure that the fertilizer was the same as it was on the other side of the ocean, or as close as possible; that we ended up as the same plants that we would have been before exile. [. . .] We grew, like plants, in pots that were made for us. That is to say, in familiar settings mainly reconstructed on the basis of what needed to be preserved. We grew in schools that were made for us, with teachers for us, who were involved in a mythology for us, myths that were born, like all myths, from the observation of natural disasters: the myths of religious freedom and of noble ideals."
11. Naharro Calderón mentions other films on children and war, such as *The Spirit of the Beehive* (Victor Erice 1973) and *My Cousin Angélica* (Carlos Saura 1974).

Works Cited

Artís, Gloria. "La organización social de los hijos de refugiados en México, D.F." *Inmigrantes y refugiados españoles en México (Siglo XX)*. Ed. Michael Kenny, Virginia García, Carmen Icazuriaga, and Clara Elena Suárez. Mexico: Ediciones de la Casa Chata, 1979.

Aub, Elena. *Historia del ME/59. Una última ilusión*. México: Conaculta-INAH, 1992.

Aznar Soler, Manuel. *El exilio heredado y la poesía de los niños de la guerra en España*. Madrid: Sinsentido, 2003.

Blanco, Jorge Ayala. *La aventura del cine mexicano*. México: Ediciones Era, 1968.

Bonitzer, Pascal. "Sur la voix-off." *La voix au cinéma*. Ed. Michael Chion Paris: De l'Etoile, 1982.

Bourdieu, Pierre. "Algunas propiedades de los campos". En *Sociología y cultura*. México, D.F.: Grijalbo-Consejo Nacional para la Cultura y las Artes, 1990.

Chion, Michael, ed. *La voix au cinéma*. Paris: Editions De l'Etoile, 1982.

Daney, Serge. "Sur les voix off, in, out, through." *Cahiers du Cinéma* (Aug.–Sept. 1977): 135.

De la Colina, José. "Los estrenos: *En el balcón vacio*." Mexico: *Nuevo Cine* 7 (Aug. 1962): 20.

———. "Miradas al cine." *SepSetentas*, 31 (Sept. 1972): 17.

De Rivas, Enrique. "Destierro: Ejecutoria y símbolo." *El exilio literario de 1939: Actas del Congreso Internacional celebrado en la Universidad de La Rioja del 2 al 5 de noviembre de 1999*. Ed. María Teresa González de Garay Fernández and Juan Aguilera Sastre. Logroño, Spain: Universidad de la Rioja, Biblioteca Virtual Cervantes, 1999. Web. N. pag.

Elío, María Luisa. *Cuaderno de apuntes*. México: Conaculta; Ediciones del Equilibrista, 1995.

———. *El tiempo de llorar*. Mexico: Ediciones del Equilibrista, 1988.

Fagen, Patricia. *Transterrados y ciudadano: Los republicanos españoles en México*. México: Fondo de Cultura Económica, 1975.

Feenstra, Pietsie. "L'archetype de l'enfance dans une memoire cinématographique." *Regard/10. Images d'exil: En el balcón vacio, film de Jomi García Ascot (México, 1962)*. Ed. Bénédicte Bertrand and Bernard Sicot. Paris: Universidad de Paris X-Nanterre, 2006. 161–67.

Fresco, Mauricio. *La emigración republicana española: Una victoria de México*. México: Editores Asociados, 1950.

Freud, Sigmund. *General Psychological Theory. Papers on Metapsychology*. New York: Touchstone, 1993.

Gaos, José. "La adaptación de un español a la sociedad hispanoamericana." *Revista de Occidente* 38.4 (May 1966): 18–179.

On the Empty Balcony [*En el balcón vacio*]. Dir. Jomi García Ascot. Perf. Nuria Pereña, María Luisa Elío, and Conchita Genovés. Ascot/Torre, 1961. Film.

García Riera, Emilio. *Historia documental del cine mexicano, 1992–1997*. Vol. 11. México: Universidad de Guadalajara, 1994. 122.

———. *Historia documental del cine mexicano, 1964–1966.* Vol. 9 México: Universidad de Guadalajara, 1994. 24.

———. *Historia documental del cine mexicano.* México: Ediciones Era, 1971.

———, Jomi García Ascot, José de la Colina, Salvador Elizondo, and Carlos Monsiváis. "Manifiesto del grupo *Nuevo Cine.*" *Nuevo Cine* 1.1 (Apr. 1961): 1.

Morin, Edgar. *El cine o el hombre imaginario.* Barcelona: Seix Barral, 1961.

Naharro Calderón, José María. "En el balcón vacío de la memoria y la memoria de *En el balcón vacío.*" *Archivos de la Filmoteca. En el balcón vacio: Película del exilio español.* Valencia: Generalitat Valenciana, 1999. 153–62.

Pla Brugat, Dolores. "Un río español de sangre roja: Los refugiados republicanos en México." *Pan, trabajo y hogar. El exilio republicano español en América Latina.* Ed. Dolores Pla Brugat. México: SEGOB, Instituto Nacional de Migración, Centro de Estudios Migratorios, INAH, 2007. 35–127.

———. "Los niños del exilio español en México." *El exilio de los niños.* Ed. Alicia Alted Vigil, Roger González Martell, and María José Millán. Madrid: Sinsentido, 2003. 162–75.

Sánchez Biosca, Vicente. "Le film comme lieu de mémoire: En el balcón vacío et l'exil mexicain des Espagnols." *Regards/10. Images d'exil: En el balcón vacio, film de Jomi García Ascot (México, 1962).* Ed. Bénédicte Bertrand and Bernard Sicot. Paris: Universidad de Paris X-Nanterre, 2006. 27–38. Web.

Segovia, Tomás. "Notas apartidas de un no exiliado." In Madrid: Publicaciones de la Residencia de Estudiantes (eds.) *Los colegios del exilio en México*, 2005. 131–37.

Tuñón, Julia. "Bajo el signo de Jano: *En el balcón vacío.*" *Regard/10. Images d'exil: En el balcón vacío, film de Jomi García Ascot (México, 1962).* Ed. Bénédicte Bertrand and Bernard Sicot. Paris: Universidad de Paris X-Nanterre, 2006. 39–61. Web.

———. "La imagen de los niños en el cine clásico mexicano: De los presos de La Infancia a *Los olvidados* de Luis Buñuel." *Los niños: Su imagen en la historia.* Ed. María Eugenia Sánchez and Delia Salazar Anaya. México: DEH-INAH, 2006. 135–38.

CHAPTER 2

FAIRIES, MAQUIS, AND CHILDREN WITHOUT SCHOOLS

ROMANTIC CHILDHOOD AND CIVIL WAR IN *PAN'S LABYRINTH*

ANTONIO GÓMEZ L-QUIÑONES
TRANSLATED BY AMBER GODE

FREEDOM AND VICTORIAN DISCIPLINE: SPANISH FASCISM VERSUS THE ROMANTIC CHILD

Among the salient works in recent Spanish cinema about the Spanish Civil War is a group of films that focus on the effects of military conflict on childhood.[1] The latter functions as a trope evocative not only of certain values but also of a particular epistemology that, in *Pan's Labyrinth* (del Toro 2006), is explicitly associated with the fantasy genre and, particularly, the fairy tale. In this film, once the child interprets exterior violence, she creates an image of this violence that amasses some of the ideological concepts with which a significant sector of the democratic Spanish culture sympathizes. This chapter proposes that the gaze of the child has become a privileged locus from which to retell those years, seven decades after the conflict. Recent Spanish cinema seems to find an adequate point of view in the form of the gaze of a child in order to politically and aesthetically represent the war in a satisfying manner.

However, it would be erroneous to refer to childhood or to the gaze of the child as if these were natural realities, and as if their formal characteristics and constitutive elements lacked a history. One of the canonical sources for new childhood sociology is Philippe Ariès's well-known volume, *Centuries of Childhood* (1962). Ariès affirms that the concept of childhood, in as much as it is a specific and distinct life stage, developed between the 1400s and the 1700s, along with the bourgeois notions of family, home, privacy, and individuality. Although both Ariès's historiographical methods and some of his theses have been widely criticized, his work offers a central point that, as Sharon Stephens explains, remains valid for the most recent studies on the topic: "Each culture defines childhood in terms of its own set of meanings and practices" (8).[2] On this matter, it is instructive to remember that it was not until 1950, 11 years after the Universal Declaration of Human Rights by the United Nations (UN), that the UN General Assembly of this body drew up the Declaration of the Rights of the Child. This document includes many of the rights granted to adults and also adds others that recognize the specificity of childhood: an ontological reality that requires special attention, such as love, not legally sanctioned for other life stages (General Assembly of the United Nations 1959, 6). All these facts remind us, in short, that adults, not children, create our understanding of childhood. Adults redefine what it means to be a child, when this condition begins and ends, what the characteristics of this period are (or at least, should be), and what role this plays in the social imaginary of the time. Ludmilla Jordanova refers precisely to this when she concludes that "there can be no authentic voice of childhood speaking to us from the past because the adult world dominates that of the child" (5). As such, deciphering the keys to a particular representation of childhood serves not only to attain a more exact understanding of childhood but also, and most importantly, to understand a culture that projects its dreams and anxieties in that same representation.

From this point of view, it is useful to return to *Pan's Labyrinth* to reflect on the model of childhood that Guillermo del Toro presents. First, this film understands childhood as a social territory that is markedly separate from the adult sphere and, to a certain point, autonomous. Childhood is what adulthood is not and vice versa. As opposed to theories that propound a sort of natural continuity or mutual porosity between both life stages, *Pan's Labyrinth* shows us a child protagonist, Ofelia (Ivana Baquero), focused on unshareable anxieties that she cannot communicate with adults. The structure of the film is, not without reason, organized around the contrast between two worlds—the historic and fantastic, the subterranean and that which happens on the surface, the world of fairies and the world of guerrilla warriors and Franco's soldiers—in short, the world in which only Ofelia participates and the intersubjective world of adults. Both occur in parallel to and, to a large extent, are unconscious of each other. This binary between stages of being human is, as William Corsaro explains in the wake of Philippe Ariès, one of the fundamental aspects of the modern child and, more specifically, of the distinct romantic ideas, which—since the work of Jean-Jacques Rousseau—have determined our perception of childhood (51). Only if the child does not act like a miniature adult and only if the child does not suffer the same internal tensions as the rest of humanity—in short, only if the child is essentially somehow dissimilar—is it possible to assign him or her qualities that, later, are perceived as lacks or losses (such as innocence, integrity, or bounty).[3]

In *Pan's Labyrinth*, the autonomy of childhood is particularly relevant for various reasons. First, Ofelia is the only child character in the narrative. Surrounded by adults, without coconspirators to involve in her adventures with monsters and mythical kings, she alone personifies childhood. Second, Ofelia represents a double innocence because, in addition to being the youngest character, at the beginning of the film she moves to a new home in the mountains, a new geographic context that is completely unknown. The gaze of this child is assigned an added cleanness because they observe a new reality, one unknown until that moment. In these characters, there is something of the tabula rasa, of a quintessential childhood. Third, the very logic of the war, despite its harshness, brings about a respite of almost complete freedom.[4] Ofelia takes part in an exceptional time, the violent years following the Spanish Civil War, in a remote place in northern Spain. In this context, the principle instrument by which a society forms and deforms its children (i.e., school) is suspended, which makes way for something very different: a romantically understood freedom through which an individual imagines and acts with the smallest number of restrictions. He or she also avoids a process of schooling that is necessarily homogenizing. Ofelia functions in *Pan's Labyrinth* as an entity nonnormalized (at least not completely) by institutions designed for the progressive transformation of children into citizens of a specific collective project.

Ofelia's most direct nemesis is her stepfather, Vidal, who faces his relationships with other characters as if they were a process of gears in which accuracy, control, and precision, not emotional or moral values, matter. To educate, from this perspective, means to force a set of behaviors that respond to the expectations of a community of adults, in this case Francoist society. The child becomes a pliable material that adults and the educational system form in their image and likeness. In this context, imagination becomes a problematic faculty because its role in the growth process is necessarily negative. To actually grow would mean to overthrow or tame imagination to prevent it from being the principle that structures the child's behavior. Joe Kelleher explains precisely that one of the symbolic arenas in which successive versions of the romantic and Victorian child have clashed is in that of intellect versus materialism (30). Although the terms used by this critic do not seem to be the most useful for my essay, I do wish to rescue from his argument the basic confrontation between the two philosophies of education. One aspires to impose a speculative and socially agreed-on rationalist epistemology that espouses a principle of reality with which children should comply *tout court*. Rather than to establish methods for understanding and action, the other approach seeks to protect the child as bearer of a creative imagination and of a cognitive purity that adulthood corrupts with its restrictive rationalization of reality.

This is, in my opinion, one of the basic mainstays in *Pan's Labyrinth*'s representation of the Spanish Civil War. Ofelia symbolizes not only the romantic value of childhood but also the political sensibility of one of the two conflicting factions: that of the republican guerrilla fighters. This association could be justified by various arguments. First, Ofelia finds in the Fascist Captain Vidal her main adversary, that opposite pole against which she has to defend her right to her fantastic chimeras. The camera shot that reveals the imaginary nature of Ofelia's adventures is filmed as a subjective shot from the point of view of Captain Vidal. In the final segment of the film, while Ofelia speaks with the fawn, who just asked her to hand over her little brother to sacrifice him, the camera takes up this scene from the perspective of Vidal. What the spectator observes, for the first time, is a girl talking to herself or talking to a void, who was occupied by a marvelous being seconds before. In other words, it is this military man (metonym of the new regime) who literally and symbolically hounds Ofelia and who reveals to the audience the factual inexistence of the world imagined by the girl. Second, this young character never expresses political opinions that could compromise her innocence. However, she does demonstrate solidarity with the Maquis, the anti-Franco guerrilla warriors. Ofelia discovers that one of her stepfather's employees, Mercedes (played by Maribel Verdú), is collaborating with the fugitives, but she immediately promises to faithfully keep the secret. Third, the little information available about Ofelia's parents suggests that they did not consider themselves to have benefited from the end of the war. Although the film does not confirm the political sympathies of the protagonist's biological father, it seems obvious that her family history is not one of a rise in status by way of collaboration with the winning faction. Ofelia's mother, Carmen (played by Ariadna Gil), during a dinner with Captain Vidal's friends mentions that her first husband worked as a tailor before dying in the war. The derogatory reaction of various female guests, as well as the captain's obvious discomfort, allows the supposition that Carmen's social and political background is not shared by the faction reinforced in 1939. Finally, Ofelia shares with the Maquis her marginality and antiestablishmentarianism when confronted with a status quo that neither of them accepts. If childhood has been one of the romantic tropes par excellence, then the previously stylized figures of outlaws have been no less preeminent. The Maquis in the film attempt to challenge the power of Franco's fascism in a fight that they do not believe is finished. For her part, Ofelia represents, in the words of sociologists Allison James, Chris Jenks, and Alan Prout, "a potential challenge to social order by virtue of their [children's] constant promise of liminality" (198). In *Pan's Labyrinth*, children and Maquis are misfits since they jeopardize a certain status quo with their affirmation of alternative possibilities, a political, affective, and/or epistemological "other," which Franco's command perceives as an intolerable threat. In both cases, children and Maquis need to be disciplined by the captain, whose goal is none other than to teach his stepdaughter and the rebels a definitive lesson.[5]

WAR AND FAIRY TALES: SO CLOSE AND YET SO FAR

The most profound connection between Ofelia and the republican partisans, the one that allows an understanding of the former as a synecdoche of the latter, has to do with Ofelia's special epistemological relationship with her new home. Just before arriving at the military encampment where Captain Vidal lives, the film presents Ofelia as a young reader. This could theoretically contradict the natural character of the romantic child since, as Karín Lesnik-Oberstein accurately explains, "The 'child,' in rescuing particular historians and children's literary critics from language and textuality, is made to preserve for them a safe world of an emotion which is spontaneous, caring, and unified" (26). Lesnik-Oberstein affirms that, inspired by thinkers like Michel Foucault, part of the postmodern interest in childhood arises from the desire for something beyond language, beyond the Logos that produces and controls subjects.[6] If this basic principle of the contradiction between textuality and childhood is useful to explain the virtues of Ofelia's deschooling, it does not unravel the subversive effect that a textual genre like the fairy tale has on a little girl (especially when she refuses to grow up in the way that the Francoist society urges her to). This character understands and reorganizes reality using the lens of the epistemology of fairy tales as an exercise in disobedience that, additionally, allows her to reach conclusions very similar to those obtained by the Maquis.

At first, this epistemology does not seem to bring Ofelia closer to a historical reality but instead to increase the distance between them. Just as Elizabeth Wanning Harries appropriately reminds us, "tales are said to be 'timeless' or 'ageless' or 'dateless'; they seem removed from history and change" (3). The narratives about fairies and fauns do not refer to historical periods but instead precisely to a timeless limbo in which immortal lessons and characters prevail, made up of all times and none simultaneously. In *Pan's Labyrinth*, this first impression is reinforced by two facts. First, the camera shot that opens the film shows us the protagonist dying on the ground while a trickle of blood moves backward from her cheek toward her nose. Immediately afterward, the camera performs an abrupt tracking shot toward her eye and, having passed through her pupil, toward a set of castles and fantastical steps. Ofelia's psychological interiority is the space of fairy tales, and its location in the historical world of the Spanish Civil War is made clear enough by the bold movement of the camera with which the film begins. Guillermo del Toro seems to propose with this approach the following dual narrative: on one side, a historical conflict in a known geography with a plot that easily could have a referent in the 1930s; on the other, the ahistorical adventure in an impossible land with a series of characters that have no referent in our zoology (e.g., toads that are several yards long or old men with eyes in the palms of their hands). As such, Ofelia's epistemology seems to be a strategy by which her own psychological interiority protects itself from an excessively severe situation. This interiority serves as a time without time, a locus not subject to determination by historical context. This approach is not novel since, as Carolyn Steedman affirms, one of the most important characteristics of the modern child in his or her romantic form has been the notion of his or her psychological and affective world as a free sphere in which the universe is dehistoricized and to where the child returns in search of protection from a permanently reductive reality (95).

There is a second characteristic that highlights, also from the very opening of the film, the interior and dreamy nature of the adventures in which Ofelia is protagonist. The narrative begins with the previously described camera shot and with a voice-over. This superimposed voice is of great importance because it determines the manner in which the audience receives the whole fantastic plot.[7] Guillermo del Toro uses the clearly well-known rhetoric (equivalent to "once upon a time . . .") of an easily recognizable literary genre. "Cuentan que hace mucho, mucho tiempo . . ." creates in the audience a level of narrative self-reflexivity: that which is told next is explicitly codified in a genre whose contract with the audience we all know in more or less detail. This time so far away is not, in truth, a scientifically remote time. That temporal distance cannot be measured because the said kingdom does not exist or, at least, does not exist on the same ontological plane inhabited by the soldiers who take part in the coup d'état and who govern Spain. That time and that kingdom, in which possibilities that do not belong to human history (like the absence of pain and deceit) develop, are the product of the imagination of an avid reader who approaches the reality of the Spanish Civil War from the perspective of the stories she reads.[8]

Once Ofelia covers all the narrative terrain she could travel in the story that she herself sketches out, this first impression disappears. The fairy tale that organizes her psychological interiority stops presenting itself as an escape mechanism in order to reemerge as a subtext and commentary on the Spanish Civil War. Additionally, at the end of the film, it is clear that the ultimate meaning of the conflict can be reached only from the fairy tale's epistemology. In this story, Ofelia has to pass three tests that show progressive learning. In the first test, Ofelia confronts a huge and fearsome toad from which she needs to extract a key. In the second, she has to open a chest in which she finds a dagger without trying (and this is the important part) the delicacies spread out on a nearby table. Finally, Ofelia has to spill her own blood to prevent her little brother from suffering. All these tests have their base in wisdom. In them, Ofelia learns various virtues: principally control over her own fear, courage, capacity for sacrifice, and extreme generosity, which implies the surrender of her own life so that others do not need to surrender their own. As Julius Heuscher explains, one of the climaxes of the fairy tale genre is the death of the main character, and its underlying significance stems from an ascent of the final step toward cognitive growth and moral improvement (308). The relevant part of this trajectory is that it coincides with the Maquis's project.

The final image of this character, whose body is surrounded by the Maquis admiring her, compiles the political key of the film: Ofelia summarizes the logic of the republican cause, which, despite being condemned to failure, and despite having already failed in one war, persists in doing what is morally right. The Maquis and Ofelia are united not only by their opposition to the small-minded conduct of the captain (emblem of an absolute political and moral evil) but also by their position as defeated. In this defeat itself, however, they paradoxically find recompense. As such, the fairy tale does not separate Ofelia from the historical time but instead it brings her to a series of situations and lessons that she shares with one of the contending factions. In Ofelia's and the loyal republican's ventures, there lies a shared utopian spirit that, as Jack Zipes explains, usually prevails in fairy tales (1999, 4). Like what Zipes suggests in another of his works, in this literary genre, the metaphysical desire for moral fullness, for goodness, and for an unlimited capacity for sacrifice has traditionally been projected (1997, 9). In this narrative family, a wish for purity, for contenders who are fundamentally either good or bad, abounds. While the antagonists systematically exercise their perversity, the protagonists overcome their obstacles to develop a superior state of understanding and virtue. The final result for these protagonists is, as Zipes explains in his essays, a completed identity—that is, learning about one's self, transparence, an accomplished self-understanding, the conquest of an essence that is intimate and identical to oneself. Like in Ofelia's case, this is only possible with the most absolute generosity and unselfishness. This is, as Heuscher in a previously mentioned essay explains, "a one-sided aspect of this 'world of meaningfulness'" (389).

At the end of the narrative, it becomes clear that the film's horizon of expectations represents that of the twenty-first-century context from which it stems instead of that of the characters immersed in the Spanish Civil War. This end can be interpreted from a wider perspective because it ultimately suggests a commentary about the posterior evolution of this historical memory. The image of the newborn in hands of the republican family suggests a state of affairs in which the negotiation of memory is dominated by the material losers of the war. In other words, if the captain's greatest concern is to guarantee who will remember whom and in what way, it seems that his defeat is double. This film prefigures a future where one must add his symbolic death to his physical one: nobody will remember him or, at least, not in the way in which he intended. In conclusion, if the boy for whom Ofelia and the republican Maquis fight the Fascist captain represents a political control of memory (which supersedes blood relation or biological bridges), *Pan's Labyrinth* announces the victory of those who supposedly lose the fight. What is relevant is that, similar to what happened to Ofelia, this victory does not take place on battlefields but instead on a symbolic plane that transcends and exceeds them: the timeless narrative of the fairy tale and the future narrative of memory (in the form of the newborn) controlled by the losers of the war. Both constitute, as such, posthumous triumphs in which the ability and authority to retell what happened are decisive.

Nostalgia for a National Childhood

The death of the child constitutes such a suggestive narrative event because it has served, as Reinhard Kuhn stresses, to fulfill at least three distinct objectives: "To register social protest [. . .], to express a metaphysical revolt [. . .]; or to make a comment on the precarious condition of childhood itself" (193). Of these three tasks, the first two are especially of interest to me because they seem interwoven in *Pan's Labyrinth*. Ofelia's murder encodes the crushing not only of a social protest but also of certain ethic/ moral values (like innocence, exercise of imagination, or romantically understood freedom). In Ofelia's character, both aspects are intertwined, and, as such, in the conclusion of the film, her death comes to represent not only the defeat of a concrete political project but also that of those timeless metaphysical merits. On one hand, Guillermo del Toro suggests that the arrival of Francoism involves the destruction of a pure being. On the other hand, this director seems to historicize the virtues embodied in Ofelia and her particular epistemology of fairy tales. One of the axes of *Pan's Labyrinth* is precisely the close connection between this character and one of the two enemy factions. This connection flows in two directions: del Toro historicizes Ofelia's purity and innocence by associating them with the anti-Fascist Maquis, and he simultaneously dehistoricizes this side by bestowing on it the aura of certain virtues, which are alien to the historical order.

In recent films about the Spanish Civil War, the fact that childhood overlaps with a certain national past gives rise to various consequences. First, it suggests an anthropomorphic evolution for a specific period of a political community. If we judge that the history of a nation has the temporal structure of a human life, a certain past is susceptible to function as a sort of collective childhood. The expulsion from this childhood necessarily entails the loss of an idealized time, of unlimited possibilities, of expansive growth, and of moral naïveté. It is for this reason that Ala Alryyes argues that "children become the loci of vulnerable memory, and, according to organic growth 'theories,' determinants of the future of [. . .] the nation. Children's stories continue to allegorize national victimization and 'hope' well into our days" (208). In order for the process described by Alryyes to be successful, however, a series of requirements must be met. The first is the selection of a past time that the present finds sufficiently remote to be able to idealize but at the same time sufficiently immediate to be able to serve as a sentimental biographical-historical archive. The second is the reinvention of this concrete period in terms of a lost paradise. The end of this period, once identified with childhood, means not only the transition to a new stage (for better or for worse) but also the dissolution of a pure and simple time. Finally, the third requirement is the perception of the present as a time of losses because only in this way does nostalgia acquire significance. In conclusion, one yearns for childhood because during this period there exist (or are projected) qualities that do not exist in adulthood. This brings us to another of the reasons for which the death of a child acquires so much symbolic potential: murder can paradoxically prove to be a solution for safeguarding prior freedom. Kimberley Reynolds and Paul Yates summarize this thesis in the following way: "The textual desire to kill children can be understood as a way of keeping and protecting them; halting the ageing process and preventing children from becoming something less perfect" (167). What is important in all these cases is that death becomes the only logical way out for their inner being. This distrust toward compromise is a logical consequence because (upon interpreting purity, innocence, or freedom in absolute and transhistoric terms) there is no space for negotiation. To negotiate with them would be to destroy them. The task of their possessor is none other than that of a constant and impossible fight to safeguard them. What is interesting in *Pan's Labyrinth* is that this thesis supports the following political reading of Spanish history: Ofelia's death arrives in an irreparable way because, if the Second Spanish Republic and its defense represents a time of innocence, Francoism radically annihilates innocence. The end of the Second Spanish Republic constituted the end of childhood and, consequently, the end of a biographic (and historic), pure, and imaginative time.

At this point, we should reconsider what is at stake in this type of representation, which reinvents the Spanish Civil War not as a collision between two political projects that are more or less legitimate/illegitimate but as the conflict of abstract principles with a prosaic rationalization of the world. In other words, what are the implications of understanding Francoism as essentially a monster whose crime is not of historical proportions but instead of mythical ones? What conclusions can be reached, if one considers the loss of the Spanish Civil War to also constitute the end of national childhood? The first conclusion is that history does not have the temporal structure of a human life, unless we fall into an evolutionist stance. The Second Spanish Republic is implicitly presented as the childhood of our democracy. Second, the beatific states of purity or happy simplicity belong not to the past nor to the present nor to the future because its place is not in *history*. In a passionate essay about the objects of memory, Susan Stewart reminds us that this type of narrative participates in postmodern politics of nostalgia that recreate something that never existed in order to return to a place in which we have never been, with the intention of recuperating a lost object that we never had (23).

In the specific context of the Spanish Civil War and its subsequent cinematographic treatment, Sharon Willis has referred to these narratives as "a left-wing romantic nostalgia, and a kind of tourist reverie" (37), while Roman Gubern has warned against what he considers a tendency toward sentimentalism and a self-complacent tenderness (106). If we believe Gubern and Willis, and if we accept that a certain trend in contemporary Spanish cinema (in which I strategically frame this production directed by the Mexican Guillermo del Toro) takes part in this nostalgia for a past reset with a sentimental tone, we should ask ourselves what is questionable in this option. First, there is the problem of moral epistemology that Avishai Margalit summarizes in his canonical essay "The Ethics of Memory": "An essential element of nostalgia is sentimentality. And the trouble with sentimentality [. . .] is that it distorts reality in a particular way that has moral consequences. Nostalgia distorts the past by idealizing it. People, events, and objects from the past are presented as endowed with pure innocence" (62). This type of nostalgia puts any cultural critique about the past in an impossible situation because all criticisms directed toward a pure and innocent time necessarily turns out to be excessive, mistaken, and unjust. The happy and pure past regard the critic, as Margalit shows, as a child, dying in all of its fragility. Before such a gaze, it is logical that certain criteria of intellectual lucidity cede to indulgent empathy.

Second, this manner of presentation of the Spanish Civil War can give rise to a schematization of war or, in the words of José Luis Abellán, a "modo arquetípico [de] las características de toda guerra civil, de tal manera que la convierten [. . .] en una especie de micro-historia" (47; archetypical representation of the characteristics of *all* civil wars, in such a way that they turn it [. . .] into a type of microhistory).[9] The danger in representing the Spanish Civil War and the subsequent triumph of Francoism as a loss of youth is that of freezing the complexity of a historical process into an archetype. In this, the cultural specificity of the event itself is lost. On the other hand, if the Spanish Civil War was not "a" civil war, but instead "the" titanic clash between two abstract principles, all other military altercations seem to be reduced to simple collisions between temporary situations, mere second-class, unoriginal conflicts. This rhetoric has surrounded the Spanish Civil War from the beginning. The final result of this rhetoric is that any phenomenological, discursive, material, and ideological appearance of the Spanish Civil War becomes a superfluous wrapper behind which exists a hard nucleus: a type of *tableau vivant* that dramatizes a battle between absolute values.

CODA

In this chapter, I have pointed out some of the consequences of a certain treatment of the Spanish Civil War for the understanding of Spanish history and also for a wider geopolitical problem in which the director himself situates his project. *Pan's Labyrinth* belongs not only to a new trend of films about the Spanish Civil War but also to a family of feature-length films of very diverse provenance that deal with distinct episodes of violence from the past by way of the inevitable lens of present circumstances. From these circumstances, the temptation is to recreate scenarios (sometimes historical, sometimes futuristic) that serve to highlight the radical nature of a situation that, here and now, can seem unprecedented. Guillermo del Toro confesses, in the analysis of his work, this necessity to separate himself from his previous conceptions of violence, fear, or valor in order to observe them again in (much more negative) light of recent events. This reflection turns out to be very relevant for *Pan's Labyrinth* because its particular juxtaposition of a historical narrative with another that is fantastic (the second as a commentary on and supplement to the first) suggests the existence of an ultimate meaning of history that does not proceed from history itself, from its facts, phases, and components but instead from elsewhere, an absolute that cannot be rationalized, that only a genre such as the fairy tale can recover.

Notes

1. In these works, the war includes the Maquis's fight in the 1940s. Despite the official declaration made by the national faction, which claimed the conflict was concluded, these narratives understand the actions of the Maquis to be an attempt at prolonging the conflict at least until the end of the World War II.
2. Two of the principal criticisms of Ariès's procedures have been his almost exclusive use of French artistic and literary sources and his analysis of these sources as if they were trustworthy sociological material.
3. This perspective, which is clearly related to that of the Rousseauian "good savage," finds its complementary opposite in the consideration of childhood that, for example, William Golding suggests in *The Lord of the Flies* (1954).
4. Some memoir writers that lived through the Spanish Civil War as children agree on this association of liberty with the process of war. A paradigmatic example would be the narrative that Juan Goytisolo created in *Coto vedado* (*Forbidden Territory*). Despite the death of his mother, this author interprets his childhood during the Spanish Civil War as a time of discoveries and vital revelations of many types.
5. In both cases, this lesson could be summarized by the necessity of abiding by the rules and a structure of power instead of by certain content. In other words, in *Pan's Labyrinth*, the captain desires to cut off, even more than a certain doctrine, the very possibility of politically and emotionally imagining a reality other than that offered by the new regime.

6. Foucault affirms the following in *Madness and Civilization*: "Madness represents [. . .] a form of minority status [. . .] Madness is childhood [. . .] They [people diagnosed as mad] are regarded as children who have an overabundance of strength and make use of it" (123).
7. In *The Devil's Backbone* (2001), the fantastic plot is not imagined by any character but instead is lived by various characters, adults, and children alike as an empirical experience. In this film, for example, the ghost of a murdered child returns to the ontological sphere of the living to revenge himself against his murderer. In *Pan's Labyrinth*, the boundary between both narrative spheres is never crossed, except by Ofelia's imagination.
8. Zipes understands this type of story as a postmodern manifestation of narrative autoreflexivity by means of which the text itself "recreate[s] the rules of narrative production" (1994, 157). In del Toro's film, there are narrative strategies that explicitly inform the spectator of the intentional presence of a certain narrative genre.
9. Jo Labanyi already described this process in her study on Spanish narrative of the aftermath 1930's civil war's. Her conclusions are pertinent, and worth taking up here because Labanyi affirms that "myth is concerned with the eternal and the universal, and attempts to neutralize change; history is concerned with the temporal and the particular, and stresses the importance of change" (33). At another point, Labanyi adds that a myth can act in two ways: "By denying history, or by critically exposing the universal human tendency to mythification" (53). I would add a third form exemplified in *Pan's Labyrinth*, that consists of combining both these options: a narrative that suggests the negation of history, understood as a succession of unique and unrepeatable events, by showing the universal tendency of a character to mystify history.

Works Cited

Abellán, José Luis. "La 'Guerra Civil' como categoría cultural." *Cuadernos Hispanoamericanos* 440–41 (1987): 43–55.

Alryyes, Ala. *Original Subjects: The Child, the Novel, and the Nation*. Cambridge: Harvard UP, 2001.

Ariès, Philippe. *Centuries of Childhood: A Social History of Family Life*. Trans. Robert Baldick. New York: Vintage Books, 1962.

Corsaro, William. *The Sociology of Childhood*. Thousand Oaks: Pine Forge, 1997.

Foucault, Michel. *Madness and Civilization*. London: Tavistock, 1967.

General Assembly of the United Nations. *Declaration of the Rights of the Child*. Geneva: Office of the High Commissioner of Human Rights, 1959. Web. 6 Aug. 2007. <http://www.unhchr.ch/html/menu3/b/25.htm>.

Goytisolo, Juan. *Coto vedado*. Madrid: Alianza, 1999.

Gubern, Roman. "The Civil War: Inquest or Exorcism?" *Quarterly Review of Film and Video* 13.4 (1991): 103–12.

Harries, Elizabeth Wanning. *Twice Upon a Time: Women Writers and the History of the Fairy Tale*. Princeton: Princeton UP, 2001.

Heuscher, Julius. *A Psychiatric Study of Myths and Fairy Tales: Their Origin, Their Meaning, and Usefulness.* Springfield, IL: Thomas, 1974.

James, Allison, Chris Jenks, and Alan Prout. *Theorizing Childhood.* Cambridge: Polity, 1998.

Jordanova, Ludmilla. "Children in History: Concepts of Nature and Society." *Children, Parents and Politics.* Ed. Geoffrey Scarre. Cambridge: Cambridge UP, 1989. 3–24.

Kelleher, Joe. "Face to Face with Terror: Children in Film." *Children in Culture. Approaches to Childhood.* Ed. Karín Lesnik-Oberstein. New York: St. Martin's, 1998. 29–54.

Kuhn, Reinhard. *Corruption in Paradise: The Child in Western Literature.* Hanover: UP of New England, 1982.

Labanyi, Jo. *Myth and History in the Contemporary Spanish Novel.* New York: Cambridge UP, 1989.

Laberinto del Fauno, El. Dir. Guillermo del Toro. Perf. Ivana Baquero, Maribel Verdú, Ariadna Gil, and Sergi López. Tequila Gang, 2006. Digital videodisc.

Lesnik-Oberstein, Karín. "Childhood and Textuality: Culture, History, Literature." Introduction. *Children in Culture: Approaches to Childhood.* Ed. Lesnik-Oberstein. New York: St. Martin's, 1998. 1–28.

Margalit, Avishai. *The Ethics of Memory.* Cambridge: Harvard UP, 2002.

Reynolds, Kimberley, and Paul Yates. "Too Soon: Representations of Childhood Death in Literature for Children." *Children in Culture: Approaches to Childhood.* Ed. Karín Lesnik-Oberstein. New York: St. Martin's, 1998. 151–76.

Steedman, Carolyn. *Strange Dislocations: Childhood and the Idea of Human Interiority, 1970–1930.* Cambridge: Harvard UP, 1995.

Stephens, Sharon. "Children and the Politics of Culture in 'Late Capitalism.'" Introduction. *Children and the Politics of Culture.* Ed. Sharon Stephens. Princeton: Princeton UP, 1995. 1–48.

Stewart, Susan. *On Longing: Narratives of the Miniature, the Gigantic, the Souvenir, the Collection.* Durham: Duke UP, 1997.

Willis, Sharon. "*La guerre est finie*: The Image as Mourning and Anticipation of History." *The Spanish Civil War and the Visual Arts.* Ed. Kathleen Vernon. Ithaca: Cornell UP, 1990. 37–45.

Zipes, Jack. *Fairy Tales as Myth/Myth as Fairy Tales.* Lexington: U of Kentucky P, 1994.

———. *Happily Ever After: Fairy Tales, Children, and the Culture of Industry.* London: Routledge, 1997.

———. *When Dreams Came True: Classical Fairy Tales and Their Tradition.* London: Routledge, 1999.

CHAPTER 3

A CHILD'S VOICE, A COUNTRY'S SILENCE

ETHNICITY, CLASS, AND GENDER IN *EL SILENCIO DE NETO*

GEORGIA SEMINET

Despite the havoc being wrought on contemporary Central American societies as they struggle to integrate into the global economy (Robinson 2003; Cuevas Molina 2006), paradoxically there seems to be a glimmer of hope regarding the future of cinematic productions in the region. For example, recent publications (Alfaro Córdoba 2008; Cortés 2006) point to the increase in productions since the beginning of the millennium. Despite the extreme hardships and the numerous obstacles to producing successful films in Central America, Amanda Alfaro Córdoba claims that cinematic productions are becoming more and more viable (23).[1] For her part, María Lourdes Cortés notes that the appearance of recent Central American films in international festivals, some of which have won awards, is indicative of the growing recognition of these films by global audiences ("Más allá de" 2006). However, notwithstanding the increase in productions since 2000, Cortés affirms that Central American films are perhaps the least known, and the most invisible, of those of any other world cinema ("Centroamérica," 2006).

Within this context, the Guatemalan-US production *El silencio de Neto* (Luis Argueta 1996) stands out as "el único filme centroamericano en tener una verdadera presencia internacional" (the only Central American film [of the 1990s] to garner international attention; "Más allá de").[2] Cortés goes on to state that "y se convirtió en la película emblemática, en la prueba de que era possible hacer cine de calidad en la region con temáticas propias y talentos locales" (and it became an emblematic film symbolizing the possibility of making quality films in the region with autochthonous themes and local talent; "Más allá de"). *El silencio* is characteristic of a return to narrative films—a form that had been less cultivated in Central America during the years of social unrest and revolution (1960–1996). The return to predominance of narrative films follows an earlier proclivity, from the 1950s up to the mid-1980s, for filmmaking "conceived as a weapon for denouncing injustices and for social combat" ("Más allá de").[3] This period exemplified the idea that "una cámera se consideraba tan importante como un fusil" (a camera was considered as important as a rifle; "Más allá de"). In this respect the goals of Central American directors were in lock-step with those of other Latin American countries that by the late 1960s had coalesced around the ideological assumptions of New Latin American Cinema.[4] Given the social and political conditions in Central America prior to the mid-1980s, it is not surprising that the camera was considered a weapon of ideological warfare. However, according to Cortés (Más allá de"), subsequent to the mid-1980s, and owing to a period of relative peace and hope, Central American filmmaking was characterized by a return to storytelling. This period holds sway up to the beginning of the new millennium when a greater number of films, with a wider variety of themes, are produced.[5] As one of the earlier and most popular Guatemalan films to exemplify this return to narrative ("Más allá de"), *El silencio* employs the widely used discursive mechanism of the child focalizer.

The use of the child focalizer to embody history in film is a common strategy in Latin American cinema. Two recent examples pertinent to Central America are the Mexican-Salvadoran production *Voces inocentes* (*Innocent Voices*; Luis Mandoki 2004), which narrates the heart-wrenching story of a young boy who is kidnapped and forced to fight in his country's brutal civil war; and the French–Costa Rican film *El camino* (*The Path*; Ishtar Yasín Gutierrez 2007), which relates the journey of two young Nicaraguan children as they set out alone in search of their mother who is living and working in Costa Rica. Although *El silencio* also uses a child protagonist, its representation of history and society is not nearly as bleak. The tone of *El silencio* is distinguished from that of *El camino* and *Voces* by the young Neto's successful coming-of-age narrative, which culminates in a timidly celebratory ending. The purpose of this essay is to problematize the representation of history as it is portrayed through the eyes of Neto, the child focalizer. Furthermore, the essay proposes that *El silencio*'s nostalgic reconstruction of a Guatemalan childhood, as well as its representation of childhood as a period of innocence, reenvisions history from a perspective that is bound tightly by the social class, gender, and ethnicity of the child focalizer. Typically, Latin American cinema uses the child focalizer to denounce the civil violence that has traumatized the citizens of the region, such as in the Argentine production *Kamchatka* (Marcelo Piñeyro 2002), the Peruvian film *Paloma de papel* (*Paper Dove*; Fabrizio Aguilar 2003), or the Chilean film *Machuca* (Andrés Wood (2004). Children and adolescent focalizers are also employed to expose and critique the social conditions that lead to crime and violence such as in the Mexican film *Amores perros* (*Love's a Bitch*, Alejandro González Iñáritu 2000), the Brazilian film *Cidade de Deus* (*City of God*; Fernando Meireilles 2002), or the Colombian *María llena eres de gracia* (*Maria Full of Grace*, Joshua Marston 2004). As these examples attest, in films that stage childhood as an allegory for the nation or that critique corrupt societies that fail to protect the future of their youth, happy endings are rare. However, *El silencio* counters this trend, projecting a positive outlook for Guatemala's future even though in the film the country has just undergone a military coup whose leaders are bent on violent repression of the opposition. *El silencio* associates a tumultuous and devastating moment in Guatemalan history with a triumphant coming-of-age story that conflates the destiny of the child focalizer with that of the nation. The conflation of the two is problematic because Neto is an upper-class Ladino[6] male, and thus he does not represent a large segment of the nation or at least not the segment that had so much to lose with the exile and deposition of President Jacobo Árbenz (1913–71).

Árbenz was the democratically elected president of Guatemala from 1951 to 1954. His administration continued, and intensified, land distribution initiatives begun under his predecessor, Juan José Arévalo (1904–90). However, land distribution and a tolerant attitude toward the communist Guatemalan Labor Party brought Árbenz into direct conflict with the CIA, sectors of the Guatemalan military, the Catholic Church, conservative landowners, and the United Fruit Company. Historian Edwin Williamson ties the coup of Árbenz's government to the political environment in Guatemala and the world at the time:

> The Cold War anti-communism of the USA was reflected in Latin America by the exclusion of communists from government, and even from political life in some countries. Yet the communist threat was more a figure of political rhetoric than a reality, and tended to be invoked by the USA whenever it saw fit to practise "big-stick" diplomacy. In Guatemala the radical nationalist government of Jacobo Árbenz was accused of being a stalking-horse for the Communist Party by the US government, which had been upset by proposals for land reform affecting the immense holdings

of the United Fruit Company. Árbenz was duly overthrown in 1954 by an invasion force financed by the CIA. (353)

Williamson's description of the effects of the Cold War on Guatemala summarizes the political strife that punctuates *El silencio*. During the Cold War era, opposing political views in Latin American countries risked provoking the suspicion of the US government and the CIA, so silence was often imposed on dissident views or on anyone opposing the assumed rights and demands of Western capitalist concerns, specifically those of the United States. Therefore, though in the film's title silence is attributed to Neto, it may also refer to the silencing of the Guatemalan people who elected Árbenz to be their voice. The main conspirators of the coup supported the business interests of the United States, and the United Fruit Company, who took advantage of the indigenous population as a source of cheap and expendable labor. Thus the social reality outside the frame, so to speak, leads spectators to conclude that Neto's silence is a metaphor for the Guatemalans who were silenced following the coup, as they lost hope for fair and decent working conditions and land distribution, changes that Árbenz was promoting.

El silencio is, at its core, a compassionate and nostalgic coming-of-age story set during the 1954 coup that deposed President Árbenz. The drama is constructed around the Yepes family, and in particular young Neto's struggle to move out of the shadows of his authoritarian father, Eduardo. Neto's mother, Elena, and his father's brother, Uncle Ernesto, are sympathetic to Neto's plight, though he is constantly made to feel immature by his overly critical father. The majority of the film takes place in a prolonged flashback following the news that Neto's beloved Uncle Ernesto has just died. At the funeral, Neto enters one of the chapels of the cathedral, and while praying alone he is approached by his uncle's ghost who will be his "guide" throughout the film. Uncle Ernesto, Neto's namesake, is the polar opposite of Neto's stern father. As an outspoken and ardent supporter of the Árbenz government, Ernesto does not censor his ideological leanings, nor his distrust of the imperialist motives of the United States in Guatemala. Uncle Ernesto's ghost, who frequently appears to Neto as a benevolent counselor/uncle in a white suit, is Neto's link to Guatemala's brief experience with a democratically elected government. Coupled with his uncle's ghost, Neto's character thus represents a conduit for the dream of democracy and social justice in Guatemala. In other words, the child focalizer's coming-of-age process runs parallel to the resurgence of hope in Guatemalan society.

Three plot strands compose the drama: personal identity, political/historical contextualization, and family tension. Foremost is Neto's struggle to define his own identity, which is symbolized by two important endeavors he is compelled to undertake. First, along with his two best friends, he will climb *Volcán de Agua*. Second, he is driven by the need to construct and fly his own mini hot air balloon, a task charged to him by Uncle Ernesto. The historical narrative is represented in six scenes of the film depicting anti-Yanqui protests over US involvement in Guatemala's sovereign affairs and the bombing of Guatemala City that causes the family to flee to Uncle Ernesto's home in Antigua. Finally, the third strand is represented by the underlying tension within the Yepes family. As the revelation of national and personal histories progresses, the third plotline reveals that the Yepes family is burdened by the past, especially a triangular relationship between Eduardo, Elena, and Uncle Ernesto. It is intimated on more than one occasion that Elena and Ernesto were in love with each other prior to her marriage to Eduardo. The resulting tension in the Yepes family stemming from the rivalry between the brothers is palpable in all the scenes in which Eduardo and Ernesto appear together.

Director Argueta characterizes Neto's coming-of-age as representative of the country's attempt to define its own identity. In a quote that appears on the commemorative DVD box he states, "*El silencio de Neto* is the silence of all Guatemalans. It is a profound silence inculcated in all aspects of our culture by the events of the last 40 years of the twentieth century, and which finally we have begun to break" (*El silencio*). Taking him at his word, it becomes clear that Argueta develops Neto's coming-of-age story as a metaphor for Guatemalan history in which Neto's ultimate triumph over silence likewise symbolizes the nation's triumph over silence and repression, albeit not fully realized until the culmination of the Esquipulas Process in 1996.[7]

However, the film's representation of history is colored by the nostalgic representation of an innocent childhood that glosses over the political turmoil of Guatemala in 1954, such that Neto's personal triumph cannot seamlessly be equated to the triumph of women and the indigenous.[8] In fact, the film's narrative might lead us to the opposite conclusion. Neto's successful rite of passage could be interpreted as disenfranchising those who are silent—that is, women and the indigenous population, whose voices are subsumed by the focus on the coming-of-age of an upper-class Ladino male.

The incongruity between the intentions of the director and the implied message has not gone unnoticed. US film critics were critical of the implication that Neto's childhood could represent Guatemala's childhood. Bill Staments, writing for the *Chicago Sun Times* is highly critical of the silence the film perpetuates rather than overcomes. "*The Silence of Neto* feels more like an after-school special preaching self-esteem, than one of public television's P.O.V. inquests into U.S. intervention in a tiny, troubled country. [. . .] For his first feature, Argueta slights his homeland's rich political drama" (40). David Rooney, writing for *Variety*, is less critical of the lack of ideological rigor in the film, though he does point out that "the film's political agenda lapses in and out of focus" (50). The criticism underscores the obstacles inherent in an autobiographical approach laden with nostalgia and grounded in the presumed innocence of childhood.

Perhaps one reason for this discrepancy lies in the implicit representation of different historical periods that reflect (1) the political reality depicted in the film, and (2) the film's moment of production. The historical narrative of the film is grounded in the six months leading up to, and including, the coup against Árbenz. However, the tone of the film is also influenced by the time period in which *El silencio* was produced, an optimistic period prompted by a negotiated peace after two decades of civil war. In the early 1990s, aspirations for Guatemala's future were hopeful. From 1960 to 1996, Guatemala had endured a relentless, violent civil war; but in 1993, steps were taken to begin the peace process. The 1996 release date of the film situates the production process in this period of transformation and reorganization following almost four decades of a traumatically devastating internal conflict.[9] Writing on film productions in Central America in the 1990s, Cortés explains, "It was a time of peace and hope, but disenchantment reined over the lost, or more precisely, betrayed, revolutions. [. . .] The great social revolutions are followed by the battles for rights of the indigenous populations, as well as rights for Afro-Caribbeans and women" ("Más allá de"). Thus the restrained optimism regarding Guatemala's future projected vis-à-vis Neto's childhood is plausibly due more to the moment in which the film was produced rather than to the chaotic period that is reconstructed in the narrative.

As a product of this expectant moment in history, *El silencio* equates the cautious, albeit brief, hopefulness of the 1990s with the apprehensive but exhilarating times surrounding the presidency of Árbenz before the threat of US intervention. Though the expectations for the Árbenz government were prematurely dashed by the coup, the ending to *El silencio* returns the viewer full circle to that moment in time, instilling spectators with optimism for the future vis-à-vis Neto's triumph. In this case, would it be fair to view *El silencio* as a romanticized history of Guatemala? Possibly. But director Luis Argueta, as well as informed viewers, is well aware of the trajectory of Guatemalan history subsequent to the 1954 coup. So has this coming-of-age story of an upper-class Ladino child like Neto (based on Argueta himself), who symbolically represents the nation, been decoupled from the extradiegetic historical narrative? Argueta claims to have gone to tremendous lengths to construct the mise-en-scène with authentic objects from the period,[10] and indeed the historical context is meticulously and accurately reflected as regards Neto's privileged childhood. Argueta also readily admits that *El silencio* is a highly personal film in which he seeks to pay homage to his family and personal history (DVD). In light of this, the film is an authentic portrayal of the social class that Neto represents, but given the highly stratified and rigid social structure of Guatemala, as true in the period in which the film is set as it is today, Neto may not be an ideal candidate to represent, or embody, the voice of silenced Guatemalans.[11]

The commemorative edition of the DVD is one of the few sources available that provides documentation on the origins of the film as well as on Argueta and his cowriter of the screenplay, Justo Chang, a fellow Guatemalan. Chang, whose dedication to the screenplay is highly praised by Argueta, died in 2006, but many of his comments about the screenplay, and about their vision for the film, are included in the commemorative DVD. Chang describes it as a "nostalgic film" supported by attention to the details of the historical context. Argueta, on the other hand, is very emphatic that for him the film is an homage to his family and his country based on memories of his own childhood (DVD). As the director, Argueta's camera becomes the eyes and voice of the film, choosing what he wants the spectator to know of Neto as well as Guatemalan history and society. In this respect however, the film belies its limitations, as Neto's triumphant attainment of voice and vision are incompatible with those of the indigenous population and women of all social classes.

In her study of childhood and film, Karen Lury affirms that "the child figure acts as a vehicle for an adult agenda [. . .] in autobiographical stories: the child that is now the adult author or director who remembers and revisits his wartime experiences" (109). The representation of childhood in the film falls squarely within this description, presenting personal memory as history. Argueta affirms that in the making of the film he has remained as faithful as possible to his childhood memories (DVD), and as a result we are presented with a nostalgia-tinged reproduction of the past. Thus to understand the film's place in Central American film history, we must discern the nature of the "adult agenda" represented in the film by Neto's childhood. Given that Neto's coming-of-age story runs counter to the coming-of-age of Guatemala, the adult agenda seems to focus more on the semiautobiographical story of Argueta's childhood rather than a problematization of Guatemalan history. As Rooney writes of the film, "Argueta opts for a rather straightforward narrative approach, but his strongest suit is a breezy handle on the innocent pursuits of adolescence" (50). The metaphorical structure of the film implied by Argueta derives from the fact that both the child and the nation are captured at the moment of coming-of-age. However, the association between the two becomes problematic because just as Guatemala embarks on a fresh period of social democracy its "new life" is cut short by the coup. Neto, unlike the nation, overcomes the authoritarianism of his father who threatens to stunt his coming-of-age process. Why is it, then, that Neto succeeds in the rite of passage (symbolized by his successful ascent of the *Volcán de Agua*) but Guatemala fails? The difference, I believe, lies in the fact that Neto is from a wealthy Guatemalan family and does not typify the nation. However, before moving on to the roles of class, ethnicity, and gender in the film, I will first speak of the repercussions of the use of nostalgia and its coupling with the myth of childhood innocence and how these two elements contour the representation of history in the film.

History, Nostalgia, and Innocence

The representation of Guatemalan history through the eyes of Neto is problematic because his triumph (the successful journey to the top of the volcano) is at odds with the fate of the nation. Critic Tzvi Tal has commented that filmic narratives focusing on childhood and adolescence are often deployed as allegories of national identity that include the "production and reproduction of the past" (137). Tal also states, "La imagen del pasado en el cine contribuye a fortalecer el sentido de continuidad mientras la sociedad y su cultura viven transformaciones profundas" (140).[12] Though this may at first seem to be the case in *El silencio*, the creation of a sense of continuity is problematic because it disenfranchises a large segment of the population. While the film may be seeking to embody continuity with the past, and many spectators interpret it that way, it is problematic for spectators to assume uncritically that Neto represents Guatemala. As spectators witness Neto's ultimate triumph on screen, the moment when he is finally able to fly his balloon, it becomes suddenly apparent that the birth of a modern Guatemala will, unlike Neto, cease to emerge, never having had the opportunity to cross the threshold from childhood to maturity. Thus, on close scrutiny, the continuity between the past and the present that Tal notes in the films *Kamchatka* (Marcelo Piñeyro 2003) and *Machuca* (Andrés Wood 2004), though certainly implied in *El silencio*, is really an effect of nostalgia. For the astute viewer, Neto will ultimately be dissociated from his relationship to the nation given that his and Guatemala's parallel paths will diverge. Nostalgia is powerfully coupled with the myth of childhood innocence to reproduce the sense of historical continuity mentioned by Tal.

As the reconstruction of Argueta's own childhood, the film is characterized by the nostalgic tone of remembered experiences. According to sociologist Fred Davis, nostalgic experience functions by "encompassing some necessary inner dialogue between past *and* present" (448). In *El silencio*, the child focalizer becomes the location of this dialogue. As Davis goes on to explain, we cannot assume that "the two sides in the dialogue are of equal strength, independence or resonance or that there is any serious doubt over which way the conversation is destined to go . . . for nostalgia's mise-en-scène to fall into place, it is *always* the adoration of the past that triumphs over lamentations for the present" (448). Thus Argueta's own obvious nostalgia for his childhood meshes with an "adoration of the past" that conflates his personal childhood with that of the nation's history, and herein lies the incongruity.[13] Though the film is optimistic, Neto is implausible as a representative for the disenfranchised sectors of society that were/are seeking, indeed fighting for, a greater voice in Guatemalan politics.

Neto's silence is in part what contributes to the creation of nostalgia and innocence, and molds the character of the *infans* that he portrays in the first half of the film. Vicky Lebeau equates the small child in film to the *infans*, or the state of infancy, "literally, without language" (16). Though Neto, at age 12, is not a "small child" and can obviously talk, symbolically he has not yet fully developed his own voice. His silence can also be equated to living in a stern household that reflects the mores of the traditional, patriarchal family. Neto's silence, he is shy and reserved, allows the spectator to sympathize with his guileless point of view because he does not understand the undercurrents of discontent in his family and country until near the end of the film.

However, it is not only nostalgia that shapes the representation of history. The myth of childhood innocence is also at play in the film, evoking a conservative vision of the past that is at odds with Argueta's stated intentions. Henry Jenkins writes of "the myth of childhood innocence" that it "presumes that children exist in a space beyond, above, outside the political; we imagine them to be noncombatants whom we protect from the harsh realities of the adult world" (2). Whereas on the one hand, the older Yepes generation represents politics and history as burdensome, unresolved conflicts whose origins have been obscured, or intentionally ignored, Neto's childhood is untainted by such worries. He is the consummate innocent child who stubbornly inhabits an apolitical space. His detachment from history and politics is symbolized by his desire to fly a balloon, to let a small piece of him soar above the messy predicament of his family and country. Jenkins goes on to debunk the "myth of childhood innocence," equating it to a nostalgic, but ultimately misleading, vision of the past that smoothes over the rough edges of historical reality. This representation of childhood deprives the child of agency and "affects not only how we understand the child, its social agency, its cultural contexts, and its relations to powerful institutions but also how we understand adult politics, adult culture, and adult society, which often circle around the specter of the innocent child" (Jenkins 1998, 2). In light of Jenkins comments, it is problematic to accept the film as emblematic of Guatemalan history and society without delving further into the representations of ethnicity, class, and gender.

Ethnicity, Gender, and Class

While Neto's transition provides a happy ending, the same is not true for his country. The marginalization of the indigenous population is exemplified through their status as servants, and their wardrobe marks them as "other." An attentive viewing reveals that they are only the center of the frame if they are accompanied by one of the Ladino, Western-dressed characters, or if they are in the kitchen or performing household or childcare duties. Even in the church, where the indigenous choir sings during the funeral for Uncle Ernesto, they are set apart by their dress and confinement to the choir. A clear example is found in a scene depicting Neto's birthday. Two indigenous women and their children pass by the entrance to the patio. The camera captures them from a distance, framed by the doorway that leads into the Yepes's beautiful patio where children are playing with toys and adults, including the local priest, are enjoying the food and drinks being served by Nidia and Rosa, the cook.[14] The visually striking scene shows the clear boundary between the status of the two cultures. The indigenous women, with baskets on their heads, create a striking contrast to the dress of the Ladina women at the party, who are, incidentally, being served by Nidia and Rosa, attired in indigenous clothing. The indigenous servants, especially Nidia, are intimately woven into the everyday lives of the Yepes family. However, despite the interdependence of the two ethnic groups, there are cultural boundaries that cannot be crossed. Another instance depicting the ethnic divde is found in an earlier scene in which Eduardo chastises his wife Elena for allowing Nidia to speak to her indigenous father at the front gate of their home. Though the spectator knows that Nidia's father needs money for medicine for her mother, it is striking that Eduardo does not want the man's presence near his home, especially in an area where others can see him.

Early in the film, Neto is often paired in scenes with his indigenous nanny, Nidia. As a representative of the Mayan culture, Nidia exemplifies freedom from the conventions of Western culture, and she is a link to Guatemala's unique heritage. In one of the early scenes in the film, Nidia comforts Neto who is in the midst of an asthma attack. She takes the inhaler out of his hands, puts it aside, and pulls him to her breast, as a mother might, to comfort him. The medium close up in the bedroom of Neto and his brother makes it a tender scene, but the viewer also senses Neto's budding interest in sexuality when Nidia embraces him. He obviously enjoys having his head rest against her breast, thus her motherly overture can also be read as highly suggestive in the racist and exploitative context of postcolonial Guatemalan society.

Subsequently, while spying on Nidia, Neto sees her relenting to the passionate overtures of his cousin Rodrigo. He becomes jealous of her, and a few scenes later he insults her by calling her a "dirty Indian."[15] The slur masks his adolescent desire for the female indigenous other, and his repudiation of her when he realizes that he cannot possess her reenacts the drama of conquest and colonization, a leitmotif in the film constructed around the presence of Nidia, and her fellow servant Rosa, revealing yet another layer of silence characterizing Guatemalan society. Furthermore, not only is Neto's reaction to Nidia governed by their unequal class relationship, but gender also plays a role. As an upper-class male, Neto feels entitled to possess Nidia and misinterprets her "otherness" as something to possess, an odious but understandable position (given the sociohistorical context) that he later reconsiders.

The silence of women is another striking element in the film. In the presence of men, the Yepes women are subdued and acquiescent. In the few scenes where Elena Yepes appears with her sister-in-law, they are chatty and animated, but when Eduardo and Ernesto are present, they are quiet. Our first viewing of Elena in the film is through Neto's eyes. He walks in on his parents late at night after they have received the call informing them of Ernesto's death. They are dressing to leave, and as Neto opens the bedroom door, his mother, dressed only in a slip, is snapping the garter belt to her hose. When she looks up to see Neto, she quickly pulls her slip down over her thigh. As the camera closes in on her legs and her quick movement, through the direction of Neto's gaze we immediately understand that he is about to enter puberty.[16]

The social class of the Yepes family is also an important factor influencing the film's optimistic ending. Neto's privileged childhood has sheltered him from the reasons for political violence and family dissention. His silence is related not only to his youthful naïveté but also to the fact that it is part of the legacy of his family and country. The Yepes family, specifically Neto's parents, does not speak out about the injustices in Guatemalan society. As Neto matures, the accumulated knowledge he gains through quiet observation, naturally encompassing a broader social milieu over the course of the film, ultimately prepares him to assert his own voice and point of view, something denied to Nidia, for example, as well as Neto's mother, even though she is part of the upper class.

It is apparent from the settings, the characterization, and the composition in the film that Argueta's childhood memories are inextricable from the place in which they were formed. The choices made by Argueta regarding the mise-en-scène exemplify the relationship that Maurice Halbwachs (sociologist of memory) defines as the importance of "place" in the evocation of memory: "Place precedes not only recognition, but the evocation of memories, and it seems to determine them. Place contains the substance of memory . . . it is a reflection, in the form of ideas, enclosed in concrete events . . . In that sense, place will explain memory" (118–19). Halbwachs's theory is epitomized in the attention paid to the details of the setting that exemplify Neto's privileged heritage. For example, the family photographs on the walls of Eduardo and Elena Yepes's bedroom are from the Argueta family (DVD). The scenes in the home of Eduardo, as well as those in the home of his brother Ernesto, were shot in different homes in Antigua and another town to recreate as closely as possible the memories of Argueta's childhood home. Even some of the mischievous deeds of Neto and his friends stem from the director's personal memories (DVD).

The settings and symbols associated with Neto, his beautiful home, a private school, his uncle's sports car, his father's large sedan, all classify him as an upper-class child. Furthermore, in two scenes in the film, the family refers to the appropriation of their lands suggesting that they had at one time been large landholders in Guatemala. The level of education of the family members (Eduardo is a judge), their home, car, and other possessions all mark them as privileged among the majority of poor Guatemalans. The matriarch of the Yepes family, *abuela* Mercedes (Frida Henry) laments the loss of the family's land to the "communists," a reference to the Árbenz government and its policies of land redistribution. Her anti-Árbenz stance puts her at odds with her favorite son Ernesto, who is frustrated by his mother's lack of understanding of the abysmal inequalities in Guatemalan society. Though the Yepes family has obviously benefited from a wealthy colonial heritage, Eduardo and Elena neither zealously oppose President Árbenz nor defend the actions of the Árbenz government against the "gringos" as does the more openly political Ernesto. The film implies that they might be pro-Árbenz, but they are silent throughout the chaos of the coup, never explicitly voicing their ideological or political views, as does their anti-Árbenz mother or the pro-Árbenz Uncle Ernesto.[17]

Neto does not endure extreme violence, loss, or exile as a result of the political situation in Guatemala. He is rather the stereotypical child character who represents innocence, optimism, and hope but who must struggle to find his voice amid the violence and trauma. Young Neto and the adult Neto, Argueta himself, are a team that offers the spectator both a story about childhood and a reenvisioning of Guatemala's history based on the childhood memories of the director. In Neto's childhood, we perceive the double-voiced quality that Lury ascribes to the child figure in autobiographical films, "The child's limited and often unconventional view of the world and war is framed by the adult's knowingness and retrospective understanding" (109). Argueta's conscious decision to film and produce *El silencio* in Antigua, Guatemala, despite the numerous technical and professional challenges that this implied also reflects his concern for authenticity in the mise-en-scène. On the other hand, his personal narrative subsumes the voices of women and the indigenous in the recreation of nostalgia.

A Problematic Metaphor

The final scenes of the film bring us back to the present: the funeral of Uncle Ernesto. In the first scenes of the film, we learn of Uncle Ernesto's death, but approximately eight minutes into *El silencio* the story lapses into a flashback comprising the six months that led up to the coup. It is during the first eight minutes of the film that Neto's dependence on Nidia is established, and his asthma, a source of fear for Neto and his mother, is at its worst. Nidia is again a central figure in the final scenes of the film. Neto encounters Nidia leaving the Yepes household and returning to her home. He and his friends have left the funeral and have run up the mountain to fly a balloon in Uncle Ernesto's honor. It will be the first balloon that Neto flies without help from an adult, and it represents an important rite of passage. At this point, Nidia tells her young charge that she wants to return to her village to have her baby among "her people." Though indigenous identity is often associated with repression, this scene clearly associates her with an attempt to escape Western, colonial culture. Neto, who had once denigrated the heritage of his caretaker, now accepts her as an equal subject, and his appreciation for her is apparent when he tells her, "Nidia, let your child speak" (DVD). Neto, who has only recently felt himself liberated from the suffocating conventions of his traditional family by defying his father and climbing the volcano, is now mature enough to recognize the need in others to live their own lives, become agents of their own desire, and speak out for themselves. His Uncle Ernesto had always told him that he needed to speak out more, that all Guatemalans needed to speak out more, and at this point in the film it becomes apparent that Neto has chosen to identify himself with the worldview of his Uncle Ernesto. This is an exhilarating ending to the film that could symbolize an affirmation of the need for respect for the indigenous other. But though we may rejoice in Neto's growth and his newly acquired social consciousness, we also know that Nidia's freedom and the future of her unborn child are not as likely to break the cycle—created by colonization and ethnocentrism—of poverty and servitude that they face in Guatemala's future.[18]

Finally, one of the most important aspects of the film is its semiautobiographical reconstruction of childhood memories that focus on a violent and traumatic episode of Guatemalan history. The attention to detail in setting creates a feeling of nostalgia around Neto's childhood. Neto's experiences in the diegetic present of the film and the representation of the memories of the adult director, supplemented by his knowledge of the historical period, compose a nostalgic view of Guatemala's traumatic history. However, given the economic and social class to which Neto belongs, and Argueta's desire to create a tribute to his childhood, the film does not endeavor to undermine an idealized recreation of childhood. Neto's childhood has only been minimally traumatized by the violence and cruelty that others experienced when they tried to speak out. Rodrigo, a marginal character, but a member of the Yepes household, for example, protests against the Yanquis in the film and disappears after the coup.

Neto's increasing independence as the film progresses through frames that are very tight at first, and become looser and more open as the film progresses, attest to his successful coming-of-age. On the other hand, we only need think of the postcoup years up to the present to realize that the struggle for social justice in Guatemalan society continues for the indigenous, poor, women, and of course children who are not as fortunate as Neto. In what at first appears to be a heartwarming and uplifting metaphor, breaks down under further scrutiny when we realize that Guatemala's silent "others"—particularly women and the indigenous population—do not acquire a voice in the film, Neto's encouragement notwithstanding. Therefore it is problematic to understand Neto's childhood as representative of the nation. Whether or not it is Argueta's intention, the nostalgic representation of an innocent childhood actually smothers the voices that are ostensibly being liberated through Neto's personal emancipation from his father.

Whether referring to women or the indigenous poor, the silenced voices represented in the film do not overcome the rigid class structure and ethnic divisions within Guatemalan society that serve to perpetuate their marginalization. Neto's first steps toward autonomy have thus been awkward though personally rewarding. However, as many spectators realize, Neto's coming-of-age cannot stand as a metaphor for Guatemalan history, as the country did not achieve political autonomy at that point in history. Nevertheless, the emotionally powerful representation of nostalgia and childhood innocence serve to keep hope alive for future generations, a sentiment that may reflect the cautiously optimistic period of the film's production in which a return to democracy seemed viable. This view is reinforced in the final frames of the film, which include the ghost of Uncle Ernesto, Nidia, and Neto and his friends as they successfully launch the small, homemade hot air balloon that Neto created, symbolizing his successful rite of passage.

CONCLUSION

El silencio de Neto is a nostalgic commemoration of the lost, innocent childhood of the nation as represented through young Neto. The travesty of Guatemalan history is juxtaposed against the celebration of an almost ideal childhood in which Argueta captures the essence of life in the upper class during the 1954 coup. Neto listens and observes; he learns; he is exposed to different views and different sectors of society; ultimately, he makes a decision to speak out, following the advice of his beloved Uncle Ernesto who had always urged him not to keep silent. Neto learns to think for himself, to assess a situation and have the confidence to reach his own conclusions. It is a noble lesson that at the end of the day exposes the deficiencies of the adults whose lives are tied to an allegorical interpretation of history; and to Guatemala's heritage of patriarchy, ethnocentrism, and authoritarianism. However, in his personal triumph, Neto is decoupled from his privileged heritage, and is instead metaphorically aligned with the ghost of what *might have been* Guatemala's future, and a new-found appreciation for Guatemala's indigenous heritage through his friendship with Nidia. The realignment of the child focalizer with a legacy of social justice and egalitarianism that had been suppressed since the coup recreates the tenderness, innocence, and nostalgia for an idealized childhood, and for what could have been a foundational moment in Guatemalan history. Thus the child focalizer is utilized to reframe history and give voice to its ghosts, striking a balance between pessimism over the past and hope for the nation's future, leaving the spectator to reflect on the bittersweet reality of contemporary Guatemala.

Notes

1. On the other hand, she does call for caution given that hope for the growth of the film industry in Central America has been inspired in the past, only to be "truncated" later (16).
2. Henceforth, all translations to English are mine.
3. Cortés writes, "Este cine es, ante todo, arma de denuncia y de combate social: (Más allá).
4. Cortés remarks that Central American Cinema of the period was "En claro diálogo con las tendencias cinematográficas en boga en el resto del continente latinoamericano, los pequeños países de Centroamérica, por primera vez en su historia, produjeron textos audiovisuales de manera sistemática, considerándolos, además, expresiones genuinas de sus idiosincracias" (Clearly in dialog with the cinematographic tendencies in vogue in the rest of the Latin American continent, the small countries of Central America, for the first time in their history, systematically produced audiovisual texts, considering them to be genuine expressions of their idiosyncrasies.) ("Centroamérica").
5. Alfaro Córdoba points out very specific "semantic axes" that inform recent Central American cinema produced since the late 1990s: resistance to domination, the distinctive natural environment of Central America, and individualism vs. collectivism (19-20). Thus film as a voice raised against social injustice is still a central element of Central American filmmaking.
6. Nonindigenous, or mestizo. The ethnic breakdown in Guatemala, according to the CIA World Fact Book is: Mestizo (mixed Amerindian-Spanish - in local Spanish called Ladino) and European 59.4%, K'iche 9.1%, Kaqchikel 8.4%, Mam 7.9%, Q'eqchi 6.3%, other Mayan 8.6%, indigenous non-Mayan 0.2%, other 0.1% (2001 census).
7. Jordi Urgell García writes of the arduous road to peace in Guatemala and Central America: "In the absence of viable or relevant regional institutions in Central America, the Contadora process emerged in the early 1980s to create a less formal regional diplomatic framework for dialogue, confidence-building and inter-governmental cooperation. Contadora culminated in the Esquipulas II agreement (1987), which paved the way for elections in Nicaragua (1990), and peace accords in El Salvador (1992) and Guatemala (1996), and also established a network of regional institutions designed to enhance the pacification, democratisation and integration of the region." Unfortunately, Urgell García, in a follow-up article, laments the erosion of the Central American agreements, citing lack of implementation, social unrest and criminality, and border conflicts as some of the obstacles to success ("Lessons from Esquipulas").
8. In this respect, it is worth comparing Neto's Guatemalan childhood with those represented in other narratives such as *El norte* (Gregory Navas 1983), from the point of view of two Mayan Guatemalan teenagers who are forced to flee the country due to the genocide of their people perpetrated by the ethnocentric Guatemalan government. Other significant examples include Arturo Arias's

After the Bombs (1990), and the nonfiction *Rites: A Guatemalan Boyhood* (Victor Perera 1994).
9. The Esquipulas Peace Agreement was initiated in the mid-1980s to bring peace to Central America. Following Esquipulas, the Oslo Accord was initiated in the early 1990s specifically for the purpose of constructing a lasting peace in war-weary Guatemala. Some of the most important aspects of the accord were implemented much later. For example, the Agreement of the Rights and Identity of Indigenous People (1995), and the Agreement on Socio-economic Aspects and the Agrarian Situation (1996) are both momentous agreements in the history of Guatemala. See Conciliation Resources at http://www.c-r.org/accord/guatemala.
10. In the DVD version distributed in 2003, Argueta describes the effort put into locating authentic props for the film as well as how important it was to him to recreate his childhood as closely as possible to his Guatemalan boyhood memories.
11. The CIA *World Fact Book* reports that "the distribution of income remains highly unequal with the richest 10% of the population accounting for more than 40% of Guatemala's overall consumption. More than half of the population is below the national poverty line and 15% lives in extreme poverty. Poverty among indigenous groups, which make up 38% of the population, averages 76% and extreme poverty rises to 28%. 43% of children under five are chronically malnourished, one of the highest malnutrition rates in the world."
12. "The image of the past in film reinforces a sense of continuity as society and culture both undergo profound transformations."
13. On the commemorative DVD, Argueta—apparently addressing comments regarding Neto's ideal childhood—admits that the representation of childhood in the film is idealized. But he adds that in many respects his own childhood was ideal. Therefore, not only does nostalgia play an important role in the representation of history through the child focalizer in the film, but the myth of childhood innocence is also perpetuated in the life of an upper-class child and becomes part of the fictional reconstruction of Neto and history.
14. More could be written about the function of sound and the postcolonial interpretation of history in the film. Often the offscreen diegetic sound is traditional music with elements of indigenous instruments. Also, in the early part of the film there is a series of direct cuts accompanied by a blaring sound from an indigenous (Mayan) instrument.
15. It is also interesting that when Nidia replies to him, saying, "*Nene*, in this country we are all Indians," Neto yells back at her, "Not me!"
16. There are approximately six scenes that focus on the children's, especially the boys', growing interest in sexuality. The first is when Neto sees his mother dressing. The other scenes involve friends: Neto and his friends spy on the girls during a ballet lesson; they pay Neto's cousin Rodrigo to show them pictures of naked women in a magazine; they put rocks inside the front of their swimsuits at the pool to tease the girls; they also put mirrors on their shoes at school one day to be able to look up the girls' skirts; and finally, in a more romantic display

of sexuality, Ani kisses Neto on the cheek at school. These scenes punctuate the film and represent a sentimental performance of childhood sexuality.

17. During a scene in Neto's school, the children are teasing Neto, calling his dad a "revolucionario." Neto fights back, saying that his dad is not a revolutionary. The implication is that Eduardo Yepes is a supporter of the Árbenz government. This is consistent with Eduardo's stress over the looming coup, but he does not openly speak either positively of Árbenz or critically of the opposition.

18. The brunt of Guatemala's civil war (1960–96) was borne by the indigenous populations. Nidia walking alone to her village inspires dread in the spectator who must realize that Nidia and her child will most likely not be safe in the future. The *CIA World Factbook* reports that during the civil conflict in Guatemala, 1960–96, "more than 100,000 people [were left] dead and [the conflict] had created, by some estimates, some 1 million refugees."

Works Cited

Alfaro Córdoba, Amanda. "La producción cultural en Centroamérica: El caso del cine." *Anuario de Estudios Centroamericanos* 33–34 (2007–8): 15–28.

Central Intelligence Agency. "Guatemala." *World Factbook*. Washington, DC: Central Intelligence Agency, 2012. Web. 20 Oct. 2011.<https://www.cia.gov/library/publications/the-world-factbook/geos/gt.html>.

"Conciliation Resources." Web. 10 Oct. 2011. <http://www.c-r.org/accord/guatemala>.

Cortés, María Lourdes. "Centroamérica en el celuloide: Mirada a un cine oculto." *Istmo: Revista virtual de estudios literarios y culturales centroamericanos* 13 (July–Dec. 2006): n. pag. Web. 22 Sept. 2011. <http://istmo.denison.edu/n13/articulos/celuloide.html#titulo>.

———. "Más allá de la pantalla rota (Cine y video en Centroamérica)." *Miradas: Revista del audiovisual* n.d: n. pag. Web. 22 Sept. 2011. <http://www.eictv.co.cu/miradas/index.php?option=com_content&task=view&id=287&Itemid=48>.

Cuevas Molina, Rafael. *Identidad y cultura en Centroamérica*. San José: EUCR, 2006.

Davis, Fred. "Yearning for Yesterday: A Sociology of Nostalgia" (Excerpt in) *The Collective Memory Reader*. Ed. Jeffrey K. Olick, Vered Vinitzsky-Seroussi, Daniel Levy. Oxford: Oxford University Press, 2011. 446-496.

Halbwachs, Maurice. *Les cadres sociaux de la mémoire*. Paris: Albin Michel, 1994.

Jenkins, Henry. "Introduction." *The Children's Culture Reader*. New York: New York UP, 1998. 1–37.

Lebeau, Vicky. *Childhood and Cinema*. London: Reaktion, 2008.

Lury, Karen. *The Child in Film: Fears, Tears, and Fairy Tales*. New Brunswick: Rutgers UP, 2010.

Robinson, William. *Transnational Conflicts: Central America, Social Change, and Globalization*. New York: Verso, 2003.

Rooney, David. "The Silence of Neto." *Variety* 17 Oct. 1994: 50.

Silencio de Neto, El. Dir. Luis Argueta. Perf. Oscar Javier Almengor, Eva Tamargo Lemus, Herbert Meneses, and Julio Díaz. Maya Media Corporation, 2005. Digital videodisc.

Staments, Bill. "Guatemalan Politics 'Quieted' in Silence." *Chicago Sun Times* 7 July 1995: 40.

Tal, Tzvi. "Alegorías de memoria y olvido en películas de iniciación: *Machuca y Kamchatka.*" *Aisthesis: Revista chilena de investigaciones estéticas* 38 (2005): 136–51.

Urgell García, Jordi. "Cross-Border Peacebuilding in Central America: Contadora and Esquipulas." *Conciliation Resources*. 2011. Web. 15 March, 2012. <http://www.c-r.org/accord-article/informal-regional-diplomacy-esquipulas-process>

———. "Lessons from Esquipulas." *Conciliation Resources*. 2011. Web. 15 March, 2012. http://www.c-r.org/accord-article/informal-regional-diplomacy-esquipulas-process

Williamson, Edwin. *The Penguin History of Latin America*. London: Penguin, 2010.

CHAPTER 4

CHILDREN'S VIEWS OF STATE-SPONSORED VIOLENCE IN LATIN AMERICA

MACHUCA AND THE YEAR MY PARENTS WENT ON VACATION

CAROLINA ROCHA

Machuca (Andrés Wood 2004) and *The Year My Parents Went on Vacation* (Carlos "Cao" Imperio Hamburger 2006) are two South American films that have children as central characters and are set in the region in the early 1970s. In addition to having been well received by the public, both domestically and internationally, these films were also chosen to represent their countries as Best Foreign Language Film nominees at the Academy Awards. These films present the representation of a turbulent period as seen through the eyes of two boys: Gonzalo Infante in *Machuca* and Mauro Stein in *The Year My Parents Went on Vacation* (from now on *The Year*). These films show the young boys as focalizers and representatives of their nations whose childhoods took place during the recent dictatorships in Chile (1973–90) and Brazil (1964–84), respectively.

At first, it would seem that the success of these films was based on the truthful depiction of twentieth-century Latin American political violence, given that children figure prominently and spectators tend to rely on the authenticity of their accounts about tumultuous times.[1] As childhood has traditionally been associated with the realm of innocence, it would seem that these children's stories, set during the months immediately before and during military regimes, can be taken at face value.[2]

However, in his review of *The Year* in the *Washington Post*, John Anderson points to a cinematic formula that consists of "kids. Old people. Cuteness. Dire circumstances that don't interfere with the cuteness but imply gravity nonetheless—the old '*Life Is Beautiful*' gambit." Given this statement, two questions arise: Do these films indeed follow the same method for box-office success and critical acclaim? If so, what are the strategies of this formula and how do these techniques shape the authenticity of what these children experienced and witnessed in these films?

Before tackling these questions, it is pertinent to make some clarifications about contemporary Latin American filmmaking and its deployment of young protagonists. The existence of a formula in these films is triggered by the demand for films' profitability, as the sources financing Latin American film productions are becoming increasingly transnational. Since Latin American directors receive only a fraction of production costs from local sponsors, courting foreign investors undoubtedly affects the choice of techniques and the configuration of the plots so as to maximize a film's broad appeal and to ensure its wide appeal. For instance, *Machuca* was the result of a transnational film production, which entailed the partnership of investors from France and Great Britain. In addition it received funds from Ibermedia, a Spanish-Hispanic American common fund. Of its budget of 1.2 million dollars, only 125,000 dollars were provided by the Chilean government's funds for the arts (Jelly-Schapiro 30). For its part, *The Year* was also financed by national and international companies, including Gullane Films, Caos Produções, and Miravista (created by Walt Disney Latin America and Buena Vista Films to produce films for the Brazilian and Mexican market). *The Year* also received 9 percent of its budget from RB Cinema, Brazil's first equity investment film fund (Hopewell 2007). Hence these two films clearly sought to be commercially lucrative cinematic productions so as to attract local and international audiences and investors. As such, they could be considered part of a new transnational cinema aesthetics, which according to Lúcia Nagib addresses the interests of "the enlightened middle classes, not necessarily motivated by the imperatives of the old left, but imbued with politically correct principles, who prefer instructive and constructive films" (96).

Besides their transnational aesthetics, *Machuca* and *The Year* are also part of a cinematic trend that makes use of young protagonists to depict historical events for multiage national and international audiences. These films are not necessarily aimed at children, but rather by alluding to childhood, they reinforce the connection between the past and the future (Douglas and Vogler 9).[3] As film scholar Stinne Krogh Poulsen puts it, "the connection between the concepts of history, memory and nostalgia creates a double address which makes the childhood film an outstanding genre among several generations" (10). To be financially viable, films focusing on childhood—and these Latin American films fit into this pattern, rather than constitute an exception—need to cater to the tastes of domestic audiences.[4] Appealing to domestic audiences posits a problem, however, particularly when the representation of the past amounts to revisiting periods in which societies were deeply polarized by opposing ideological beliefs. That is to say, to what extent can plots overcome the divisiveness of the past so as to guarantee these films' acceptance?

It could be said that one such strategy is the use of children dual role of actor and witness. Their presence engages spectators, who identify with their powerlessness and limited agency. As focalizers, children, who have traditionally been associated with purity, seem to provide audiences with a neutral view of a tumultuous past. Consequently, their innocence is emphasized so as to highlight how traumatic violence irrevocably marks them as survivors and witnesses. It should be noted, then, that despite their uncontaminated view of the past, these films fully participate in the politics of memory of each society. In these films children allegorize the projects of the Latin American Left that failed to mature and were sharply interrupted by authoritarianism.[5] Furthermore, whether expanding or corroborating other representations of a traumatic past, these films undoubtedly engage with the construction of cultural and historical memory for as Miriam Hansen observes, "The predominant vehicles of public memory are the media of technical re/production and mass consumption" (5). So this brings me back to my initial question, do *Machuca* and *The Year* share the same cinematic formula by relying on young protagonists?

Even though both films present 12-year-old boys who are the directors' young alter egos—Wood (born in 1965) and Hamburger (born in 1962)—it is my contention that these films are not based on the same box-office formula. In fact, the young protagonists have slightly different roles that mirror the way in which their societies still grapple with their past dictatorships. As my analysis will demonstrate, *Machuca* offers a more unsettling representation of the past than *The Year*, for unlike Mauro, Gonzalo's role is that of bearing witness to a painful past. Because he loses his innocence and comes of age during this time, his involvement in the past is that of a young adult.[6] On the contrary, Mauro remains a child and, thus, is shielded from the more brutal aspects of political violence in Brazil.

MACHUCA: GAZING AT CONFLICT

Machuca presents a brief period in the life of two boys Gonzalo Infante (Matías Quer) and Pedro Machuca (Ariel Mateluna). As Tzvi Tal observes, *Machuca* does not intend to be an all-encompassing depiction of the turbulent early 1970s in Chile, but rather a story about characters whose lives are dominated by family conflicts, friendships, and studies (141). Pedro, along with other students from a shantytown in Santiago, is part of a program to increase the diversity of the upper-class St. Patrick's School for Boys. At the initiative of the school principal, Father McEnroe (Ernesto Malbrán), the school began integrating a handful of underprivileged students to a first-class academic experience.

Machuca's first part is structured around Gonzalo Infante's gaze, which provides a disturbing view of the period preceding and immediately after the Chilean coup d'état of 1973. At the beginning of the film, Gonzalo presents the perspective of an outsider child who curiously observes the events around him. In her study of German literature, Debbie Pinfold explains the importance of a child's point of view: "Using the child's viewpoint is a particularly effective defamiliarizing device, for a child has not had time to become jaded by the process of habitualization . . . it has not yet been weighed down by 'custom,' but instead experiences the world with the kind of intensity evoked by the phrase the 'eye among the blind'" (4).

As the "eye among the blind," Gonzalo has a defamiliarized perspective about the three institutions to which he belongs: family, school, and country. Within his family, his seemingly smooth upper-middle class life hides both his mother's (Aline Kuppenheim) disengagement from the familial routine and her relationship with a married man. Gonzalo, forced to accompany her when she visits her lover, becomes an involuntary witness of her infidelity. The fact that his father and sister may be unaware of his mother's betrayal emphasizes Gonzalo's vantage point. When he later confirms his mother's physical liaison, he grapples with the possible end of his family unit, which is as unstable as Chile's sociopolitical life in the early 1970s.

Representing an outsider's perspective, Gonzalo is also the "eye among the blind" at school. The first indication of his insightfulness is when the timid and humbly dressed Pedro is introduced to his class. As Gonzalo looks at him, he perceives his despondency and sense of isolation, which mirrors his own inadequacy in a family that is falling apart. Later, Gonzalo differentiates himself from his fellow classmates who hold Pedro down trying to convince Gonzalo to hit the new arrival. Unlike his peers, Gonzalo refuses to take part in the violence, exhibiting a more mature behavior than his friends. It is this act of courage that allows him to enter into Pedro's life. From that moment on, a silent bond of friendship develops between both boys.

When Gonzalo enters figuratively and literally into Pedro's existence, he gains access to a unique perspective about Chile's economy, social classes, and political turmoil and is thus confronted with the life of the lower classes, which Pedro represents. One day Pedro offers Gonzalo a ride home that proves to be an eye-opening adventure for Gonzalo as he is introduced to Chilean politics. Escaping from his family's strained atmosphere, he joins Pedro and his friend, Silvana (Manuela Martelli) at two events sponsored by the opposing sectors dominating Chile's politics in the early 1970s: Salvador Allende's supporters (who include Socialists, Communists, and workers) and his detractors (encompassing right-wing groups and the upper classes). The two mass mobilizations in which the boys take part are crucial events that depict not only the heightened tension during the last months of Allende's government but also Gonzalo's immersion into the social and political conflict dividing Chilean society.

Gonzalo's view is progressively enlarged thanks to Pedro's friendship. When Gonzalo is invited to his house, he has to cross a river (a metaphor for class division) and a soccer field (an area of communal recreation) to arrive at a world that he did not know existed before.[7] Hence he is introduced for the first time to a new socioeconomic reality. His impression of life in the shantytown is conveyed through the light-drenched shots that portray a peaceful community working together in a collective orchard. Gonzalo immediately perceives—and as do spectators—the degree of organization and physical labor that informs the lives of the poor. But he also notices Pedro's precarious existence once he is inside his friend's home. Dark and gloomy, the modest hut insinuates the isolation and deprivation that these characters face privately.

Back at his home, Gonzalo's status as an eye among the blind also allows him to see a side that he previously ignored when he realizes that his family is inexorably disintegrating. First, at his older sister's birthday party, he acts as an enforcer of limits and rules and is the silent witness of her adolescent transgressions, a fact that she notices and tries to stop by asking him twice, "What are you looking at?" Gonzalo also confirms his mother's extramarital liaison—glimpsing her naked body through a partially opened door—sensing the probable end of his family. Just as his private universe is slowly coming apart, so is Chile's unstable sociopolitical life. Shattered family and fractured society both spur on Gonzalo's initiation into adulthood.

Gonzalo's passage from childhood to adolescence follows a natural process of development in which his sexual awakening is portrayed in one remarkable scene, when he and Silvana share a can of condensed milk and kisses. This scene, which takes place by the riverbed, continues with a sequence of running water that signals the end of Gonzalo's childhood and his entrance into the adult world. When he loses his childlike innocence—the defamiliarized gaze as an eye among the blind—he moves into a period in which he will no longer be an observer of reality but rather a participant in his country's tense atmosphere.

Gonzalo's transformation is clearly portrayed when he returns to the shantytown as a young adult who no longer shares interests with his poor friends, showing that he has abandoned his former childhood ideals and values. First, he gazes at Silvana with desire, objectifying her through the act of looking at her. Second, he embraces the class divisions between them that he had previously ignored. When Silvana ridicules his belief in the narrative of *The Lone Ranger*, saying that the friendship between a white person and an Indian is unbelievable, Gonzalo does not contradict her. In addition, when Pedro's father challenges his son's friendship with a member of a different social class, Gonzalo again remains silent, suggesting agreement with Mr. Machuca's stance. With these gestures, he separates himself from the pure, naïve and class-blind child that he was at the beginning of the film and accepts Chilean society's ideology of class separation. His passivity and silence emphasize the insurmountable differences between members of different ethnicities and social classes in Chile in the early 1970s.

Despite Father McEnroe's integration project at school, two crucial events take place in Gonzalo's life that stress his socialization as an upper-middle class adolescent. First, his father, a supporter of the Socialist Party, accepts a position in Italy after admitting that "socialism may be good for Chile but not for us." These paternal doubts about the efficiency of socialism slowly distance Gonzalo from his previous alliance with the lower classes. Without the paternal presence, Gonzalo accommodates his views to those of the only adult remaining in his family: his mother, a staunch opponent of socialism in Chile and a self-centered woman. These changes in his family's dynamic further push Gonzalo to join in the violence. In one key scene he buys two lollipops and when Pedro's is taken by the other boys, Gonzalo abandons his role as spectator of violence and resorts to the use of force to recover the candy. Another instance of his joining in violence takes place when Pedro and Silvana temporarily hide his bike. Ignoring the fact that it is a childish prank, Gonzalo reacts by reproducing the position of the social class he represents and calls the cousins "rotos," an epithet that degrades their social class. For scholars Luis Martín-Cabrera and Daniel Noemí Voionmaa here,

"Their friendship (and the relationship with Silvana) breaks into pieces and this process parallels that of the end of Allende's socialist regime" (63). In my opinion, the bond between Gonzalo, Pedro, and Silvana is not yet broken, as the former returns one more time to the shantytown to witness the magnitude of state-sponsored violence.

Machuca's final part shows Gonzalo's double status as a witness and participant. As a witness, he perceives a latent desire on the part of adults to shield children from the pervasive social and political violence. For instance, when Silvana is cheated on by the right-wing Pablo, Gonzalo's mother tries to protect her describing her as "a little girl." However, her use of language shows the ways in which youth have become socialized by a conflict-ridden public discourse that posits one class against the other. Not even Father McEnroe—who strives to shield children from the new order imposed by the military authorities, asking, "What are you doing? They are children"—can prevent the spread of violence. The children and teenagers shown in *Machuca* are no longer innocent bystanders, as Gonzalo's behavior has shown. The political tensions have also reached them, making them reproduce adults' acts of brutality. Indeed, as a participant, Gonzalo is present in the shantytown during a military raid. He witnesses the violence directed at the poor community and Allende's supporters and sees Silvana's father as he is savagely beaten without attempting to help him. Moreover, when he is also mistreated, he denies belonging to the neighborhood, stressing his lighter skin and the quality of his clothes that mark him as someone from a higher social class. With this gesture of disloyalty, Gonzalo betrays his former friends one final time.

Despite his cowardly behavior, Gonzalo is forever defined as the witness who survives. Referring to the consequences of witnessing, scholars Ana Douglas and Thomas A. Vogler state that "for survivor witnesses, witnessing itself becomes a part of the trauma, since the pain of seeing others perish is added to the suffering of those who do not" (36). Gonzalo's sense of guilt stems from his status as a surviving witness, particularly of Silvana's sacrificial death, which symbolizes the end of the awareness and participatory progress of the lower classes under Allende. Douglas and Vogler explain that "when victims are considered innocent, like children, the violation is considered more heinous . . . ('innocents' = incapable of inflicting harm, from in = not + nocens, present participle of nocere, to harm, hurt)" (23). Despite the fact that Silvana has been shown in the first part of the film as a precocious teenager, in the raid her innocence is stressed both by her white shirt, denoting purity, and by her childish act of defending her only parent, seemingly oblivious of the ensuing risks. Gonzalo's gaze records her futile struggle and makes him a survivor and eyewitness to a crime that will probably remain unpunished. This act of witnessing imposes the duty of having to provide testimony about the violent acts of the military authorities. Nevertheless, fearing for his well-being, and as a result of the trauma he experiences, Gonzalo is a mute witness, unable to speak for his former friends. His only gesture of resistance is leaving his exam blank to illustrate his self-censorship. In this sense, I propose that the title *Machuca*, which means "to hurt," does not refer to Pedro's last name, as has been previously suggested.[8] Rather, it concerns the pain and trauma of the Chileans who, like Gonzalo, were silent witnesses or even participants of the cruelty of the military regime. As such, they are all marked by a loss of purity and collectively share the guilt of past atrocities.

As corresponds to a coming-of-age film, the final takes of *Machuca* are deeply nostalgic for they present a counterpoint between past and present. When Gonzalo observes the erasure of the shantytown formerly occupied by the poor families, he grasps the magnitude of the displacement that has taken place both literally and figuratively. The poor working classes have been removed from sight and the empty space that has replaced it is a place filled with nostalgia of a nation that could have been a family and of the friendships that were destroyed. As Marianne Hirsch and Leo Spitzer explain, nostalgia "has broadened over the years to encompass 'loss' of a more general and abstract type, including the yearning for a 'lost childhood,' for 'irretrievable youth,' for a 'vanished world of yesterday'" (82). Indeed, all those feelings influence Gonzalo as he looks at a familiar place that is irrevocably gone, just as his own innocence is also a thing of the past. The wound produced by his witnessing of the repression is still an unresolved consequence of political violence and one that affects more than the youthful protagonist of *Machuca* given that it also encompasses other Chilean survivors and witnesses.

THE YEAR MY PARENTS WENT ON VACATION: A PARTIAL VIEW

In *The Year*, viewers are introduced to the life of Mauro Stein (Michel Joelsas) during several months in 1970 when his parents take him from Belo Horizonte to São Paulo to stay with his paternal grandfather Mótel Stein (Paulo Autran). Mótel's death the same day that Mauro arrives complicates the plans laid out by his parents, who thought they were leaving him in good hands while they go "underground." The revolutionary status of Mauro's parents characterizes this film as one in which politics has a central place, according to Doris Fagundes Haussen (7–8). However, in my view, his orphanhood deflects the importance of politics and focuses on his survival in an unfamiliar space. In the absence of his grandfather, Mauro is taken in by one of his neighbors, Shlomo (Germano Haiut) who, as a bachelor, is ill-suited to deal with a young non-Jewish boy.

From the beginning, Mauro is presented as a child shielded from the political tension in which Brazil is immersed. The first scenes show him playing soccer with imaginary players, unaware of his mother's anxiously waiting for his father's arrival. Also, as the family travels to São Paulo, He is oblivious of his parents' apprehension when they encounter a military truck with armed soldiers. Sitting in the backseat, Mauro ignores the potential threat to his parents that the truck may represent. Instead, his attention is focused on the comments made by a radio talk show host about the composition of the Brazilian national soccer team. This scene is crucial as it shows Mauro's gullibility and lack of critical skills when he believes the opinions expressed by the radio host, which are quickly dismissed by his father. Viewers also briefly observe Mauro's defamiliarized gaze when the family arrives in São Paulo and he is introduced to the city's impressive architecture and strange population of Orthodox Jews in the district of Bom Retiro where Mauro is left by his parents. They only explain that "they are on vacation," thus neglecting to inform him about their whereabouts.

The Year develops in an idyllic district populated by immigrants who act as protectors of Mauro's innocence. His defamiliarized gaze or outsider status appears circumscribed to the Jewish community and its customs. His boredom at his grandfather's funeral and discomfort when using the *kippa* (yarmulke) for the first time show him as a stranger to Jewish religious rites. He curiously witnesses Shlomo's morning prayer of the siddur and notices his tallith. But when Shlomo sees him, the old man closes the door in a gesture that reinforces Mauro's status as an outsider to Jewish rites. His limited view is also reinforced because as a child he does not have access to his grandfather's apartment, a fact that leaves him distanced not only from his family's possessions but also from his own cultural genealogy. In this regard, the scene in which the ringing of the phone literally "calls" him into his grandfather's apartment signals his entrance into a different universe. When he finally manages to have the door of the apartment opened, he steps into a new world in which he finds all sorts of strange objects, such as a typewriter with Hebrew letters. Back at Shlomo's apartment, he continues to observe his caretaker's unfamiliar routine and different eating habits. As will be apparent in the last part of the film, his curiosity and careful attention to Shlomo's customs constitute steps toward his adaptation to a different way of life.

As Mauro becomes a resident of the Bom Retiro neighborhood, he is also sheltered from the more menacing aspects of the state repression under way in Brazil at that time. In this new environment, Mauro's gaze is oriented toward identifying his peers. He first sees Hannah (Daniela Piepszyk) on the day of his arrival. In their second encounter, she observes his frantic attempt to reach his grandfather's apartment. Displaying her insider's perspective and common sense, Hannah directs Mauro toward the janitor who has keys to all the apartments. Later, Mauro sees her as she leads a group of children in her mother's business: peeking at her customers while they try on clothes. While this childish prank allows Mauro to peek inside a forbidden space of privacy, he does not discover, as Gonzalo does in *Machuca*, the tensions of the period. Rather, he sees Irene, an important character in his new neighborhood. This is a key scene for two reasons. First, Hannah obstructs Mauro's gaze, an act that reinforces the idea that this young character's view is limited. Second, unlike the older boys' reaction, Mauro projects on Irene his need for maternal love and attention, not sexual desire. Contrasting with innocent Mauro, a savvy Hannah guides him in his process of familiarization in his new environment, but this is mainly confined to their building and the areas of the neighborhood. Unlike Pedro in *Machuca*, Hannah does not expand Mauro's gaze to see social conflicts; by acting as his protector and displaying a mixture of alternatingly nurturing and calculating gestures, she simply integrates him into the community.

The Year chronicles the enormity of Mauro's personal plight, downplaying the importance of politics, which appears as backdrop. By showing in detail his struggles and challenges as he seeks to survive without his parents, the film adopts Mauro's perspective. John Beifuss holds that "director Cao Hamburger strikes no false notes. He keeps the viewer's identification focused on Mauro, so the ideological struggle boiling beneath the surface remains mostly outside of our notice." Indeed, the day after Mauro's arrival in São Paulo, after having upset Shlomo, he bunks in his grandfather's apartment. From the balcony, he sees graffiti spelling "abaixo a ditadura" (down with the dictatorship) something viewers saw being painted during the night. Nonetheless, Mauro's view is more focused on his private universe, following Shlomo's movements as he leaves for work than on inquiring about the graffiti's significance. As pertaining to a child, Mauro's gaze and interests are oriented mostly toward his private universe.

Furthermore, even in a time of conflict, *The Year* primarily stresses the idea of harmony. When Shlomo expresses his resistance to being in charge of Mauro, the small Jewish community meets to discuss what to do with

the boy and starts to speculate about Mauro's parents whereabouts—
"eles estão metidos en politik" (they are mixed up in politics). The rabbi
quickly deflects any possible excuse for abandoning Mauro and makes
the point that it is God's will for the community to take care of Mauro
independently of the reason for his parents' absence. Their "vacation,"
albeit suspicious, does not constitute, in his opinion, a valid motive for
Shlomo to be released from his moral and religious duty toward Mauro.
The rabbi's mention of Moses's story is particularly significant for three
reasons. First, Shlomo calls Mauro this name. Second, Moses's story is
also narrated by one of the Jewish ladies who invites Mauro for lunch, a
gesture that illustrates that she not only feeds his body but also educates
him about a key episode of Jewish tradition. Third, and most importantly, one of the meanings of Moses is "saved from the waters," a possible
allusion to Mauro's own salvation from the political conflicts that were
affecting Brazil in the late 1960s and early 1970s. Mauro's survival is
possible thanks to the solidarity of the Jewish community, which acts as a
protective and nurturing environment.

Mauro's insertion into a close-knit ethnic community shapes his
protected view of Brazilian society in the 1970s. When he states that
"São Paulo e tão grande que cabe gente de toda forma" (São Paulo is so
big that people of all different backgrounds fit in), he is displaying the
acceptance of differences that he witnesses every day in Bom Retiro, portrayed as the home of Jewish, Italian, and Greek immigrants who coexist
side by side, united (or divided) by the very Brazilian passion for soccer.
The sense of unity, despite divisions, is evident, for instance, in the soccer match in which the Jewish team faces the Italian team. The Jewish
team, whose players and supporters are mostly Ashkenazi—that is to say,
Eastern European Jews and Jews from Germany, Austria, Hungary, and
Czechoslovakia—has a black goalkeeper, Edgar (Rodrigo dos Santos).
Upon learning about his talents, Mauro confesses "Eu queria ser negro
voador" (I wanted to be a flying black), a statement that betrays his previous color blindness. Brazilian scholar Elionora Silvéria da Costa interprets Mauro's words as an instance of his embracing the "other," stating
that "Mauro projeta uma visão infantil não contaminada pelo ranço do
preconceito contra os diferentes" (Mauro projects a child's point of view
uncontaminated by discrimination against those who are different; 5).
Mauro's wish clearly indicates his innocence by simplifying the dynamics
of a multiracial society.

Mauro's shielded gaze is spared the ugly side of Brazilian repression
in two instances. The first one deals with the state of his parents' apartment in Belo Horizonte when Shlomo visits it so as to find clues about the

whereabouts of Mauro's mother and father. The camera blurs the contours of the furniture as if to distort the fact that the apartment has been searched and ransacked, probably by the military authorities looking for them. Without experiencing the trauma of seeing his home searched, Mauro considers Shlomo's trip a success as it yields the two goalkeepers that he needed to play. These game pieces—as well as the fact that Shlomo brings a cot to make Mauro more comfortable—show that his stay in São Paulo may be longer than he anticipated. It also signals that the parts of his small universe are being arranged to re-create his home in São Paulo. The second occasion in which Mauro's view of the political anxiety of the times is obstructed when Shlomo contacts Italo (Caio Blat), a socialist sympathizer, to request his help in locating Mauro's parents. As Shlomo and Mauro meet Italo, they are monitored by a civilian who may be an informant for the military authorities. However, neither Shlomo nor Mauro is aware of his presence, and when the conversation between Shlomo and Italo takes place, Mauro is encouraged to view a soccer match as a way to distract him from what is going on. These events can be related to the title of the film, which in the opinion of Brazilian scholar Scheilla Franca de Souza refers to the process of hiding the real consequences of the Brazilian dictatorship (10).

The World Cup of 1970, in which the Brazilian team is a favorite to win, serves as a major diversion for Mauro and many adults, distracting them from the political situation. Mauro's preparation for the first game speaks of the importance that this event has in his young unproblematic life. The first match is also an opportunity for the socialist-leaning Brazilian youth to imbue the Brazil-Czechoslovakia game with a subtext in which the advantage of the Czech team should be interpreted as an indication of the superiority of socialism. When the match begins and the Czech team scores first, the Brazilian socialists cheer but it is a meager demonstration given that when Brazil scores its first goal, their celebration is much noisier and emotional. In a similar way, elder Jewish males and females are shown cheering and enjoying Brazil's soccer feats. Brazilian soccer is a passion for all ages and one in which different ethnic groups come together. Nonetheless, for Mauro, the coming together of all the neighbors to watch the soccer matches constitutes a bittersweet experience because it makes his parents' absence more pronounced, as they had promised to be reunited on that day. As a result of the exaltation of the nation's unity driven by the success of the national soccer team, Mauro is not exposed to traumatic experiences that could have prompted his transition into adolescence.

Even when the facade of normality begins to crack, Mauro is only marginally aware of the newly visible traumas all around him. When the celebration of a Bar Mitzvah that he is attending is interrupted by the noise of the horses used by the military, raiding the university campus and violently rounding up students, Mauro manages to see only a fraction of violence. His universe is later disturbed when he finds Italo wounded and helps hide him. Once again, the film depicts Mauro, replicating Shlomo's protective ways and proving that his socialization in a strict but caring environment has resulted in his compassion and nurturing gestures. Yet, in one telling scene, he asks Italo if his parents will return, doubting for the first time their reason for being away. By reaffirming the notion that Mauro's parents are on vacation, Italo keeps the young boy's dissociation from the political grip that is closing in on him. In spite of this protection, Shlomo's arrest deeply disturbs Mauro. In a reversal of roles, he, the child, now seeks help for his guardian in the same place where he found refuge: the Jewish community.

The final scenes focus on Mauro's limited interests: soccer and his family. Before the World Cup's final match, Mauro silently prays for his parents' return. He watches the first part of the game in the company of those who have become his friends, but as soon as he learns of Shlomo's release, he heads to the place that has now become his home. As he walks back to his grandfather's apartment, his step does not show either hope or optimism although he is relieved to see Shlomo back unharmed. Yet the long-awaited reunion with his mother is far from the joyous event that he had imagined. His mother's sadness and deteriorated physical condition suggest the ordeal that she has endured. In addition, his father's absence—he is probably dead—and the fact that Mauro later becomes an exile when he and his mother leave the country speak of the many losses he will have to face as he gains awareness of history. Throughout all of this, however, he continues to exhibit a childish innocence that is evident in his final positive voice-over, which refers both to the international soccer tournament and to the naïveté regarding national politics "o Brasil está ganhando" (Brazil is winning). This statement seeks to appease the spectators' conscience while deflecting any possible traumatization that Mauro may experience at losing his father by indirectly pointing out that repression is a necessary evil for the country's well-being.

It is precisely this perspective that confirms that the child Mauro, who has seen glimpses of the political repression, has not lost his naïveté. His voice-over displays the acceptance of an adult's version, which he parrots just as he does with the title of the film. Historian Bruno Groppo states that "cualquier sociedad confrontada con un pasado trágico y difícil de asumir desarrolla mecanismos de inhibición, esforzándose por olvidar los acontecimientos y las experiencias cuya evocación provoca sufrimiento y amenaza a su identidad, su autoestima o su equilibrio" (any society facing a tragic and difficult-to-overcome past develops mechanisms that inhibit memory, willfully attempting to forget the events and experiences that provoke suffering and threatens its identity, self-esteem, and stability; 31). In the same way, Mauro's account, which affirms and omits, is a product of both memory and oblivion. Hence his final words mask the true dimensions of the tragedy affecting his family and his country. His inability to express the real cause of his father's absence can be read in two ways. On one hand, it may exemplify a denial of the traumatic experiences he has just undergone, particularly because, unlike in *Machuca*, where the break up of Gonzalo's family is a metaphor for the divisions affecting Chile, in *The Year* the fracture of Mauro's family is clearly shown as an exception and contrasting with the country's exultant mood as a three-time soccer champion. On the other hand, Mauro's accepting remarks about his situation may point to his "learned" ability to mimic Brazilian adults who use euphemisms to downplay the scope of the dictatorial repression. Rita De Grandis interprets his final words as vacating "the word *exile* of its political content" (239), thus presenting an easy-to-absorb examination of a tumultuous past in line with Brazil's process of coming to terms with state-sponsored violence has been slowed by the impunity given to military leaders and by a lack of mobilization of civil society compared to that of the Southern Cone countries. Like Mauro in *The Year*, Brazilian society still resorts to the security (and delusion) of euphemisms so as to preserve the discourses of national harmony and unity.[9] *The Year* exposes the politics of memory (and oblivion) because as Sander Gilman reminds us, "The cinema, like all art forms, levels the moment of its own origin and becomes part and parcel of the viewers own time" (305). Hence both films discussed here tell us as much about the present as they do about the particular moment in the past that they reference.

***

Machuca and *The Year* make use of child narrators to represent life in Chile and Brazil in the early 1970s amid a climate of political division and internal strife. While both films have been commercially successful, both in their countries of origin and abroad, my analysis has shown that there is not a shared, common formula in these two films. In *Machuca*, Gonzalo's gaze encompasses his family's breakup as well as Chilean society's disintegration. These traumatic experiences mark his passage into adolescence. In *The Year*, Mauro is not fully exposed to the class and political conflicts dividing Brazilian society. On the contrary, he is surrounded by an immigrant community that adopts and protects him. Because his gaze is mostly obstructed from the traumatic reality of the military dictatorship, Mauro does not lose his innocence and, thus, unconditionally accepts an adult-made version of the dissolution of his family. In these two films, children are used to represent the different politics of memory that are at work in both countries. At the time of *Machuca*'s shooting, Chileans were exposed to the many criminal charges against General Augusto Pinochet for his human rights violations. This painful process was represented in Wood's film as Gonzalo's coming-of-age: revisiting the past provided an opportunity not only for nostalgia but also for national growth. Gonzalo, a representative of the Chilean upper class, is portrayed as a silent witness and a participant in state repression. Produced with the intent to reach a wide transnational audience, *The Year* timidly takes part in the revisionist cinematic effort to represent the human rights abuses of the Brazilian military regime. Mauro's depiction as an unscarred child survivor of the dictatorship highlights the protective gestures of loving immigrants to preserve his innocence during the years of repression years. *The Year* closes with a happy ending that illustrates the still prevailing discomfort to fully revisit that important and tumultuous period of contemporary Brazilian history.

NOTES

1. Lúcia Nagib mentions several post-2000 films where children or elderly people represent authenticity (98).
2. Kathy Merlock Johnson holds that "prior to World War II, the image of children in American films has been one of unqualified innocence" (1).
3. Brazilian scholar Doris Fagundes Haussen mentions the reasons that motivate the reexamination of the past in contemporary Brazilian films: "Apontam tanto para uma grande preocupação em resgatar a história da construção da sociedade e da identidade nacionais como para um entendimento mais objetivo do cinema como um negócio lucrativo para diversos segmentos" (They point as much to a big concern with rescuing the history of the development of society and of national identity as to a more objective understanding of cinema as a lucrative business for various groups; 12).
4. Ariel Dorfman's *La muerte y la doncella* (Death and the Maiden; 1991), a play that revisited the violence of the dictatorship, was not well received in Chile, but it was very successful in the United States and England (Richard 20).
5. Nelly Richard states that "the most emblematic definitions of the intellectual in Latin America had been those traditionally forged by leftist thought" (69).
6. Here I disagree with Kenneth Turan of the *Los Angeles Times* who holds that "the best thing about *Machuca*, however, is its exceptionally balanced tone. There is no sense of special pleading about Wood's direction, no giving in to

easy sentimentality. No matter where it goes, it gives you the sense that this is the way it must have been, and it is hard to ask for more than that."
7. Other critics have pointed out related metaphors. For example, Luis Martín -Cabrera and Daniel Noemí Voionmaa state that "the field separating Pedro and Gonzalo (and their impossible friendship) is a metaphor of class conflict during the time of Allende" (64).
8. Rita De Grandis perceptively notices that "by inverting the protagonism of Pedro's voice despite the deceiving title, the film reaches wide national and transnational audiences" (242).
9. In an article written by Robert Stam, João Luiz Viera, and Ismael Xavier in the mid-1990s, these scholars proposed that "any definition of Brazilian nationality, then, must be antioriginary (seeing the nation as narrated, constructed, diacritically forged by difference), must take into account, must allow for racial, gender, and sexual difference, and must be dynamic, seeing the 'nation' as an evolving, imaginary, deferred construct rather than as an originary essence" (396). More recently, Nagib, writing about *Central do Brasil*, states that this "landmark of the Brazilian film revival" presents a "reconciling ending and harmonious mingling of races and creeds, despite the violence" (96).

Works Cited

Anderson, John. Rev. of *The Year My Parents Went on Vacation*, dir. Cao Hamburger. *Washington Post* 28 Mar. 2008. Web. <http://www.washingtonpost.com/gog/movies/the-year-my-parents-went-on-vacation,1146894/critic-review.html#reviewNum1>.

Ano em que meus pais sairam de férias, O. Dir. Cao Hamburger. Perf. Michel Joelsas, Germano Haiut, Paulo Autran, Daniela Piepszyk, 2006.

Beifuss, John. "A Pair of Films Translate the Human Condition Well." *The Commercial Appeal.* Scripps Interactive Newspapers Group, 18 Apr. 2008. Web. 20 Apr. 2009. <http://www.commercialappeal.com/news/2008/apr/18/a-pair-of-films-translate-the-human-condition/>.

"Celulloid Dreams Buys Brazilian Films." Web. 7 Dec. 2008. <http://reelsuave.com/2008/08/19/celloid-dreams-buys-brazilian-films/>.

De Grandis, Rita. "The Innocent Eye: Children's Perspectives on the Utopias of the Seventies (*O ano em que meus pais sairam de férias, Machuca*, and *Kamchatka*)." *The Utopian Impulse in Latin America.* Ed. Kim Beauchesne and Alessandra Santos. New York: Palgrave Macmillan, 2011. 235–58.

De Souza, Scheilla Franca. "Imaginário, identidades, linguagens e nós, outros: Um diálogo multiculturalista através de representações cinematográficas." *Intercom —Sociedade Brasileira de Estudos Interdisciplinares da Comunicação* 2008. 1–15 Web. 20 Apr. 2010. <http://www.intercom.org.br/papers/regionais/nordeste2008/resumos/R12-0428-1.pdf>.

Douglas, Ana, and Thomas A. Vogler. *Witnesses and Memory: The Discourses of Trauma.* New York: Routledge, 2003.

Gilman, Sander. "Is Life Beautiful? Can the Shoah Be Funny? Some Thoughts on Recent and Older Films." *Critical Inquiry* 26 (2000): 279–308.

Groppo, Bruno. "Traumatismos de la memoria e imposibilidad del olvido en países del Cono Sur." *La imposibilidad del olvido: Recorridos de la memoria en Argentina, Uruguay y Chile.* Ed. Bruno Groppo and Patricia Flier. La Plata: Ediciones Al Margen, 2001. 19–42.

Hansen, Miriam. "*Schlinder's List* Is Not *Shoah*: The Second Commandment, Popular Modernism, and Public Memory." *Critical Inquiry* 2.2 (1996): 292–312.

Haussen, Doris Fagundes. "A política nos filmes brasileiros: Relações com a economia, a cultura e a identidade nacional." (2007). Web. 20 Apr. 2010. <http://www2.eptic.com.br/sgw/data/bib/artigos/f469b1ac55c468d3d2af5c8adc126cee.pdf>.

Hirsch, Marianne, and Leo Spitzer. "We Would Not Have Come Without You: Generations of Nostalgia." *Contested Pasts: The Politics of Memory.* Ed. Katharine Hodgin and Susannah Radstone. London: Routledge, 2003. 79–96.

Hopewell, John. "Film Distribution Pick Up 'Parent.'" *Variety* 10 Feb. 2007. Web. 8 Dec. 2008.

Jelly-Schapiro, Joshua. "Making Movies in Latin America." *Berkeley Review of Latin American Studies* (Winter/Spring 2006): 26–30. Web. 20 Nov. 2008. <http://www.clas.berkeley.edu/Publications/Review/Winter2006/Winter2006-Machuca.pdf>.

Machuca. Dir. Andrés Wood. Perf. Matías Quer, Ariel Mateluna, Manuela Martelli, Federico Luppi. 2004

Martín-Cabrera, Luis, and Daniel Noemí Voionmaa. "Class Conflict, State of Exception and Radical Justice in *Machuca* by Andrés Wood." *Journal of Latin America Cultural Studies* 16.1 (2007): 63–80.

Merlock Johnson, Kathy. *Images of Children in American Film: A Sociocultural Analysis.* Metuchen, NJ: Scarecrow, 1986.

Nagib, Lúcia. "Going Global: The Brazilian Scripted Film." *Trading Culture: Global Traffic and Local Cultures in Film and Television.* Ed. Sylvia Harvey. Eastleigh, UK: Libbey, 2006. 95–104.

Pinfold, Debbie. *The Child's View of the Third Reich in German Literature: The Eye among the Blind.* Oxford: Oxford UP, 2001.

Poulsen, Stinne Krogh. "History, Memory and Nostalgia in Childhood Films." *Cinemascope* 13.5 (2009). Web. 19 Apr. 2009. <http://www.cinemascope.it/Issue%2013/PDF/STINNE%20KROGH%20POULSEN.pdf>.

Ramírez, Roxana. Rev of *Machuca*, dir. Andrés Wood. *Film-Forward* 19 Jan. 2005. Web. 15 Dec. 2008. <http://www.film-forward.com/machuca.html>.

Richard, Nelly. *The Insubordination of Signs: Political Change, Cultural Transformation and the Poetics of the Crisis.* Durham: Duke UP, 2004.

Rocha, Carolina. "Jewish Cinematic Self-Representations in Contemporary Argentine and Brazilian Films." *Journal of Modern Jewish Studies* 9.1 (2010): 37–48.

Silvéria da Costa, Elionora. "Salve, salve meu rei, versus Brasil, ame-o ou deixe-o." *Baleia na Rede*. Web. 25 Apr. 2009. <http://polo1.marilia.unesp.br/Home/Revistas Eletronicas/BaleianaRede/Edicao04/salve.pdf>.

Stam, Robert, João Luiz Viera, and Ismael Xavier. "The Shape of Brazilian Cinema in the Postmodern Age." *Brazilian Cinema*. Ed. Robert Stam and Randall Johnson. New York: Columbia UP, 1995. 387–472.

Tal, Tzvi. "Alegorías de memoria y olvido en películas de iniciación: *Machuca* y *Kamchatka*." *Aisthesis: Revista chilena de investigaciones estéticas* 38 (2005): 136–51.

Traverso, Antonio. "Contemporary Chilean Cinema and Traumatic Memory: Andrés Wood's *Machuca* and Raúl Ruiz's *Le Domaine Perdu*." *Interactive Media* 1.4 (2008): 1–26. Web. 19 Apr. 2009. <http://nass.murdoch.edu.au/issue4/pdf/IM4_traverso.pdf>.

Turan, Kenneth. "Review of Machuca, dir. Andrés Wood." *Los Angeles Times*. Los Angeles Times Media Group, 29 Apr. 2005. Web. 12 Dec. 2008.

CHAPTER 5

ENABLING, ENACTING, AND ENVISIONING SOCIETAL COMPLICITY

DANIEL BUSTAMANTE'S *ANDRÉS NO QUIERE DORMIR LA SIESTA*

JANIS BRECKENRIDGE

El cine es un campo de conflicto entre las diversas memorias.[1]
—Tzvi Tal

Black screen. Cut. A fenced-off, seemingly abandoned building. Cut. Running. Heavy breathing. Cut. A boy, crying and begging to go, says he doesn't want to play anymore. Sounds of shattering glass. Cut. Shouts of "You're nothing!" and "You're going to die!" punctuate childlike drawings of actors as credits begin to appear. The viewer, from the perspective of someone hiding, at first catches only fragmented glimpses of neighborhood children playing *poliladrón*, an eerie blend of hide-and-seek and cops and robbers. As the disturbing opening sequence continues, the ruthless game becomes increasingly sinister: a gun points to a boy's head; a sniffling girl pleads to be released because the handcuffs hurt. It is with these haunting images of an otherwise familiar childhood game that Daniel Bustamante evocatively replicates the violence and terror of 1977 Argentina and introduces his first feature-length film, *Andrés no quiere dormir la siesta* (2009).

Appropriately described as a family drama that functions as a societal mirror (Martínez 2010), *Andrés* offers an unflinching critique of the impact of collective indifference and complicity on a generation coming-of-age during the last military dictatorship.² Thus Bustamante directly addresses what has seemingly become a taboo subject in postdictatorship filmic production in Argentina for, as Susana Kaiser notes, the polemical topic of society's role during the dictatorship has been largely ignored in national cinema (105). The film chronicles a pivotal year in the life of the young protagonist, the curious and headstrong Andrés (played by Conrado Valenzuela), who would rather watch *Kung Fu* than sleep the siesta and who prefers to organize back-lot marble competitions with his friends than compete in the club-sponsored sports that please his estranged father.³ Following the (accidental?) death of his liberal and leftist-sympathizing mother (Nora, played by Celina Font), the child finds himself abruptly relocated to his rather austere grandmother's home (Doña Olga, played by Norma Aleandro) and once again under the disciplinary control of his angrily aggressive father (Raúl, played by Fabio Aste). This sudden dislocation—one not entirely unlike the nation's transition from democratic rule to dictatorship—signifies a new set of regulations and expectations, requiring the boy's immediate adaptation and significant changes in his behavior. Throughout the course of the film, Andrés at first resists the seemingly arbitrary rules he does not understand (at times suffering unjust and harsh punishments for his transgressions) until he gradually comes to incorporate the attitudes and behaviors demanded in this conservative, middle-class household.

Uniquely focalized through the young Andrés, Bustamante's film presents childhood as a microcosm of a bewildering world in which most of the adult characters tenaciously cling to traditional social values in the face of extreme political repression. As a result, these formative years, in turn, become an intense training ground for learning how to navigate a complex, and often hostile, social landscape. Nevertheless, *Andrés* is neither an intimate portrayal of an innocent boy in an unjust world nor a typical Bildungsroman whereby the process of maturation and self-realization lead to the creation of a sympathetic hero; instead, Andrés's identity formation—his psychological and moral development—challenges the adult viewer to an uneasy if not outright discomfiting identification with the conflicted and at times heartless child protagonist. In short, *Andrés* problematizes facile reception with the young protagonist while questioning "los grados de la responsabilidad individual y social" (degrees of individual and societal responsibility; Bellon 2010).

CHILDREN: BEST SEEN, NOT HEARD?

The fact that film can serve as a battleground for diverse and often competing memory constructions, as Tzvi Tal suggests, becomes apparent with a brief survey of the better-known representations of Argentina's so-called dirty war (*guerra sucia*) in national cinema. These productions display distinct thematic and stylistic approaches ranging from melodrama to suspense and horror.[4] Significantly, with the exception of *Andrés*, no fictional filmic representation to date has set out to depict the generational effects of societal complicity and indifference. To be sure, Argentina's postdictatorship cinema has not yet directed its critical lens at the seemingly less dramatic but equally traumatic impact of extreme repression on quotidian reality, particularly everyday life in middle-class households and neighborhoods. The topic demands critical revision, and the use of a child narrator offers a particularly apt vehicle for questioning the ongoing effects of enforcing traditional values and conservative ideals on a generation growing up under military rule.

Andrés is not the first Argentine film to approach the dirty war from a child's perspective. Darío Stegmeyer's short, *El balancín de Iván* (*Ivan's See-Saw*, 2002), and Marcelo Piñeyro's feature-length film *Kamchatka* (2002, based on Marcelo Figuera's book of the same title) also depict political repression from the young protagonists' point of view.[5] Not surprisingly, all three of these films emphasize the family, particularly the impact of parental involvement in revolutionary politics, and point to the traumatic repercussions of losing one or both of these loving figures. Despite overwhelming political oppression and societal fear, each of these productions avoids overt violence and instead features heartening domestic settings. Particularly significant are childhood games and pastimes that take on highly charged, metaphoric import.

In addition to similarities in narrative content, the films share remarkably parallel narrative constructions: both *Iván* and *Kamchatka* offer a nostalgic retelling of the distant past filtered through an adult consciousness. Karen Lury, in her recent study *The Child in Film*, explains the possible ramifications of this common strategy. In her estimation, employing a "double-voiced" form of representation where "the child's limited and often unconventional view of the world and war is framed by the adult's knowingness and retrospective understanding" (109) runs the risk that the child protagonist—rather than representing the interests, experiences, anxieties, dislocations and traumas of childhood—can easily become erased and merely serve the purposes of an adult agenda. In other words, although these films show children's experiences, their voices remain superseded or supplanted by mature ruminations. Children may be seen, but they are not, strictly speaking, heard *as children*. Additionally, as seen in both *Kamchatka* and *Iván*, the requisite temporal remove distances viewers (who already more readily identify with the adult narrative voice situated in the present) even further from the child protagonists. The result is a sentimental account that idealizes childhood and romanticizes long-lost parents who are cast in the stereotyped roles of selfless protectors valiantly sacrificing their lives for their ideals, both personal and political.

El balancín de Iván utilizes the technique of a prolonged flashback to recall the overwhelming anxiety and tensions of a family living in hiding while the father actively participates in leftist militancy. The protagonist Ana, now an adult, returns to her childhood home and relives the traumatic events that culminated in her mother's abduction. Perhaps as a result of limited time constraints or, more likely, a consequence of its focalization, *Iván* falls victim to the simplistic dichotomy of "good" victims persecuted by "bad" men along with predictable typecasting: loving, protective parents who stand in direct opposition to a brutal political regime ultimately personified as ruthless paramilitary thugs. *Kamchatka* also offers an intimate portrayal of a family in hiding. Similarly focalized from a child's point of view, it likewise remains framed by mature philosophical reflections on the past and its aftermath. The child comes to understand (and directly communicates to the audience) that the game referred to in the title (Risk or TEG) symbolizes determination, solidarity, and resistance. The adult narrator of *Kamchatka*, who like Ana reconstructs the past in a conscious act of self-reflection and introspection, stands in sharp contrast to *Andrés*. Set entirely in 1977, Bustamante's film eschews the use of flashback and depicts the child protagonist's daily life as it unfolds under military rule; in this way, the child's perceptions remain unmediated by future adult contemplation and judgment.

What sets *Andrés* apart, then, is a highly nuanced exposition of social reality made possible, in part, by maintaining the child's naïve perspective for the duration of the film. In sharp contrast to idealized recollections filtered through the comprehension and security that comes with hindsight, *Andrés* projects with immediacy the uncertainties faced by the young protagonist as he struggles to make sense of what seem to be capricious rules, harsh punishments, and deceptive behavior. Moreover, by withholding the adult protagonist's mature reflection and relying solely on the child's incomplete understanding of social norms and political contexts—not to mention an individual code of ethics still in the early stages of formation—it remains impossible to incorporate intellectual or moralistic judgment from the narrator's position.

The adult viewer comes to supplant the embedded adult double of the protagonist and finds that, as Tal suggests, Andrés does not always recognize (let alone conform to) standard social practices: "The perspicacity of the young character . . . makes it possible to represent at times critically and other times pedagogically, aspects of social life that hegemonic ideology has 'naturalized' and transformed into 'quotidian logic'" (142).[6] In other words, a child's ingenuousness and fresh insight can be employed to question what others simply take for granted. Nor does Andrés always live up to accepted notions of right and wrong. In addition to a radical disparity in comprehending and accepting the status quo, this ethical gap augments tension for the viewer caught in a position that calls for identification with an unflinching child narrator. In this way, the film goes beyond the veneration of familial efforts to protect innocent sensitivity in a cruel world and instead depicts the incomprehensible and often traumatic challenges of learning to negotiate a hostile environment.

COMPLEX REALITIES, LIMITED PERSPECTIVES

A pivotal question underlying *Andrés*, one that directly echoes the central line of investigation in Vicky Lebeau's *Childhood and Cinema*, becomes, "What does a child see and know? What of a child's world can be represented to and for adults as well as other children?" (44). Significantly, although a child assumes the narrative position in *Andrés*, he does so without narrative authority. The impact of now-iconic imagery such as the ominous green Ford Falcon and, even more notably, the sinister presence of a clandestine torture center in the heart of the middle-class neighborhood, while tacitly understood by adult characters, remain entirely lost on the naïve protagonist.[7] Refusing to provide overt and didactic commentary within the narration, Bustamante instead relies on the viewer's knowledge of Argentina's recent history. Those sharing Andrés's "innocence" must learn to read the signs that, while at times subtle, more frequently simply go unrecognized. However, as Susana Kaiser reminds us, survivor testimony—not to mention investigations and documentation conducted by human rights agencies and the court system—provides a detailed understanding of how the dictatorship operated and "nos permite decodificar los mensajes que las imágenes transmiten" (allows us to decode the messages that [filmic] images transmit; 103). For informed viewers already in a position to "see"—the film's target audience—such allusions impart dread together with a profound sense of culpability.

Thrust into the same position as the child, the spectator's desire to see, hear, and know remains frustrated. Numerous point-of-view shots literally force Andrés's limited perspective on the viewer. The camera often remains at his height, providing only half-shots: a filmic technique that inhibits visual identification of and with adult characters while simultaneously denying an omniscient narrative perspective. The viewer's access to the cinematic world is further constrained spatially, limited to the specific areas that the young protagonist inhabits. The camera never strays outside of his middle-class residential neighborhood, with most scenes taking place within the strictly regimented and narrow confines of home and school. And while the streets seemingly provide an unbounded space for play, a place free from adult supervision, even here the children remain confined by less-apparent but no less stringent rules. The young Andrés (and by extension, the camera and viewer) remains absolutely prohibited from exploring certain restricted areas of the neighborhood.

In this way, Bustamante's skilful camerawork makes apparent the child's point of view while subtly demarcating the children's territory from the adult realm. In the same vein, representations of Andrés's interpersonal relationships make it clear that the adults keep children peripheral to important events and major decisions. Lury has pointed out a paradox frequently underlying films that feature young protagonists: "While the children are undoubtedly the centre of attention for the viewing audience, they are marginal presences for most of the adults in the film" (44–45). Indeed throughout *Andrés*, family members and teachers enforce innumerable rules, often with no more explanation than "because I said so." Important conversations frequently take place off camera, intentionally away from dismissed children. As a result, the spectator also remains excluded from crucial exchanges of information. But even when the young protagonist is present for such conversations, it becomes apparent that "kids have no say in adult matters," as Doña Olga uncompromisingly declares when Andrés voices an idea contrary to her own. This perceived insignificance of the child's views creates another level of narrative tension that further hinders the identification process: the adults' attitude of inherent superiority deprives Andrés, and by extension the viewer, of agency.

There remains yet another layer of complexity to complicate the use of Andrés as the point of narrative focalization. Not only do doubts arise regarding his ability to see and understand the events taking place around him, but the viewer also begins to question the child's reliability in reframing what he does experience. Significantly, the spectator witnesses Andrés's storytelling expertise as he relates his participation in the game of cops and robbers depicted in the opening sequence. Despite his tender age, the child readily tailors his depictions to his various audiences. To the charismatic and commanding Sebastián (played by Marcelo Melingo), a swaggering, self-assured figure whom Andrés admires and befriends but whom the audience uneasily associates with a secret detention center, Andrés confidently asserts that only *this* time has his prisoner escaped. Afterward he proudly boasts to his grandmother that as a cop he successfully captured more robbers than anyone else. In sharp contrast, when his mother voices sympathy for "poor Clara," the girl whose handcuffs hurt, Andrés immediately highlights his own compassion and insists that he personally allowed her to escape. Even more significantly, over the course of the film the child becomes, like the adults that surround him, adept at lying.[8] Again, the viewer's discomfort with Andrés arises not solely in response to the boy's incomprehension (for which the apt viewer often compensates) but from being obliged to identify with a duplicitous and at times cruel character whose behavior one would rather not claim as his or her own.[9]

Significantly, Andrés remains carefully shielded from much of the danger and violence that surround him. Yet, ironically, the very rules, restrictions, and prohibitions meant to protect him naturally pique his curiosity and, as the film's title suggests, Andrés often rebels against tradition and authority. Inquisitive and industrious, he surreptitiously turns to spying. In her study of representations of children in modern fiction, Susan Honeyman cites spying (together with lying) as a common tactic of childhood subversion and disruption. However, voyeurism and eavesdropping, especially by someone unable to fully process the information obtained, produce only partial knowledge, vague notions, and incomplete understandings. Accordingly, subtle inferences and narrative ambiguity (what is intentionally obscured from him, what remains unseen, and what he simply fails to grasp) become central characteristics of Bustamante's film.

The boy's unsophisticated perceptions, in part, allow Bustamante to present characters that eschew stereotyped representation. Not only does the director avoid casting Andrés in the typical role of the innocent child-victim, but he also further rejects conventional, one-dimensional depictions of repressors. In Andrés's eyes, Sebastián is not a formidable member of a military task force but rather a cool guy who expresses genuine concern when Andrés gets hurt, plays soccer with him, and generously rewards him with gifts and money. Moreover, and again partly a result of Andrés's lack of insight, many unresolved, if not altogether irresolvable, plot points leave the viewer with ever-increasing tension and doubt. Many questions hauntingly linger: Was Nora's death an accident or a politically motivated homicide? What specific factors lead to Alfredo's disappearance and who is ultimately responsible? And finally, can Andrés be held partly accountable for the death of his grandmother?

As a result, the film's subtlety and frequent lack of resolution require active rather than passive spectatorship. At the same time, the child's evolving ethical standards allow for inconsistent and at times unexplainable moral comportment. Adult viewers, believing themselves superior to the child narrator both intellectually and morally, cannot always easily resolve these conflicts; they find themselves trapped in a challenging narrative position. I would suggest, therefore, that Bustamante's film not only questions what a child can know but also simultaneously asks what, in fact, a viewer, when limited to a child's naïve perceptions, can know with authority.

TURNING A BLIND EYE: PLOTTING *PERCEPTICIDE* AND SOCIETAL INDIFFERENCE

Perhaps the most persistent and troubling question underpinning *Andrés* is what a *society* can be held responsible for seeing and knowing. In her insightful study of public spectacle, spectatorship and performance surrounding Argentina's "dirty war," Diana Taylor coined the term *percepticide* to describe a willed self-blinding adopted by a fearful and quiescent population in response to state terrorism. Taylor argues that, terrified by the fact that citizens were detained and disappeared in full public view and threatened by the presence of clandestine torture centers on busy downtown streets and in residential neighborhoods, "people had to deny what they saw and, by turning away, collude with the violence around them" (123). Bustamante likewise takes a close look at societal acquiescence, indifference and complicity in this film.[10] By utilizing the child's gaze, he is able to project radically contrasting perspectives whereby commonly accepted norms and attitudes are held up to scrutiny, observation, and questioning without imposing moralizing or didactic overtones. Not insignificantly, as many of the adults appear to lose sight of social reality, Andrés, in turn, becomes an increasingly active witness. This in turn leads him to attempt greater involvement in family and community affairs, acts that result in even more aggressive marginalization.

As might be expected, in exploring the dismissive adult's apathy and blind adherence commonly expressed as "*en esto no me meto*" (I don't get involved), "*por algo será*" (there must be a reason) and "*algo habrán hecho*" (they must have done something), *Andrés* is replete with references to seeing: from the opening sequence where children playing "cops" call out "I see you" as a powerful form of intimidation to the closing sequence featuring close-ups of Andrés's aggressively impassive eyes as he pretends to take no notice of his grandmother's fatal heart attack. Such references likewise insinuate adult characters' relative power and ideological positioning. For instance, Sebastián's privileged capacity for observation and knowledge create a sense of omnipotence as he boasts to Andrés, "I know many things. I am like God, I am all-knowing, all-seeing." In contrast, Alfredo's rhetorical question, "We're not going to look the other way are we?," implies that people have a moral obligation not only to see but also to take action. With respect to the dangers of seeing and the populace's ingrained behavior of looking the other way, three scenes remain particularly salient and merit more in-depth attention.

Andrés's conservative but seemingly apolitical family displays the fear that Taylor describes of the Argentine citizenry: "People dared not be caught seeing, be seen pretending not to see" (122). Like Doña Olga, Raúl remains intent on protecting the family. Outraged by evidence of the mother's personal involvement with Alfredo (a relationship he prefers to ignore), and intolerably anxious on finding compromising pamphlets in Nora's home, Raúl accusingly raises the question, who knows what the kids saw?[11] Recognizing the danger of seeing, he frantically burns not only the leaflets but also all traces of her existence while adamantly insisting on a pact of silence. Not coincidentally, only the child looks on in horror as his adult relatives remain complacent if not openly participatory in this grotesque *auto de fé*. The traumatic effects that the erasure of the mother's existence has on the child become apparent in his thwarted efforts to intervene and impede his father's enraged denial of Nora's personal and political involvements. Despite the boy's frantic pleas and distressed sobs, physical obstruction and verbal abuse literally force Andrés's compliance.

A parallel act of repression occurs when Andrés attempts to report, with great excitement, something that he has discovered when venturing into a forbidden zone in the neighborhood. "You won't believe what I saw!" he exclaims, only to find that the adults refuse to listen. His father and grandmother respond to his disobedience by mercilessly burning his favorite toys and with this harsh punishment he is effectively silenced. To again cite Honeyman, "Though disallowed engagement by lack of necessary language skills or willing (able?) adult listeners, literary children are frequently idealized as sites of resistance to the inflexible, systemizing logic of adult discourse" (116). As with the callous burning of his mother's possessions, the boy's indignant anger and emotional shock once more seem to cast him in the complex role of innocent yet defiant victim; as a young character, he is neither resigned nor indoctrinated and thus deemed likely to rebel in the face of injustice.

Bustamante's representation of middle-class *percepticide* reaches an alarming climax when Andrés witnesses a forced disappearance in the movie's only overtly violent scene. Peering curiously through semiclosed blinds, he looks on as members of a task force discover compromising leaflets (reminiscent of the scene described earlier), viciously assault prisoners, and scream "you're already dead" and "you're nothing," shouts that eerily echo the children's game depicted in the opening sequence. Significantly, after the teary female makes direct eye contact with Andrés (and consequently the viewer), she is brusquely hooded (with a *capuche* meant to blind, disorient, and erase personal identity) and dragged away. At that very moment, Doña Olga suddenly covers Andrés's mouth as she forcefully pulls him away from the window so that he sees no more. Her abrupt actions unwittingly mirror those of the repressors.

A sharp discrepancy arises between Andrés's desire to comprehend the brutality he has witnessed—made apparent as he attempts to ask questions—and the grandmother's adamant refusal to acknowledge or discuss the event.[12] It is in fact her calm denial of this distressing scene the following morning that remains truly horrifying. "You dreamed it" she insists, no fewer than three times, much to the boy's (and the viewer's) shock and dismay. Nevertheless, and as if in confirmation of the appropriateness and necessity of her outlook, Andrés observes a neighbor nonchalantly hosing down the blood on the street thus casually eliminating the few existing traces of the dictatorship's "atrocities given-to-be-invisible" (Taylor 1997, 119).

In each of these scenes, then, Andrés displays actions and attitudes that openly conflict with adult conduct and expectations. His boundless curiosity leads to the gradual discovery of the intricate lies, elaborate subterfuges, fear, and propensity for violence that constitute the grown-up world. Bustamante's complex and highly nuanced depiction of this child protagonist complicates Honeyman's theory that "unsuspected and overlooked, literary children demonstrate the ability to upset adult authority through honest observation and thinking from outside of established language and logic" (125). With his unclear understanding of the societal forces at play combined with intentions and motives that remain obscured, it becomes difficult for the spectator to judge Andrés's (deliberate?) participation in the dramatic events that result in Alfredo's disappearance.

By the film's conclusion, however, the audience witnesses the profoundly negative impact the family's self-imposed "blindness" has had on the impressionable Andrés. The film culminates with the sudden death of Doña Olga. Despite her repeated demands that he look at her when she speaks, the child not only defiantly ignores her admonitions but remains utterly impassive as she dies from a heart attack. Even more appalling than this deliberate aloofness is his subsequent deliberate and nonchalant refusal to acknowledge her death, an act of silence that reflects and perpetuates her previous denial of the brutal abduction. The viewer is left with no doubt that Andrés, in turn, has mastered the art of percepticide.

This pivotal scene refuses to resolve the issue of whether Andrés engages in a "disrupting discourse" in which the child character consciously and deliberately turns the adults' power and indifference back on them in a powerful display of resistance and agency (Honeyman 2005, 128) or whether the child instead unconsciously enacts the role of apt pupil, coming to exemplify the very ideology the film sets out to critique. Either way, the oppressive family atmosphere reproduces the nation's hierarchal power structure. Much as Andrés struggles to meet the demands of a newly adopted conservative household, so too must an oppressed citizenry learn to conform to the expectations of a repressive military regime. Andrés, in his gradual transition from innocent, naïve victim to unfeeling perpetrator embodies the dangerous repercussions of a society's willed percepticide.

Growing Pains: Breaking the Silence by Means of Child Subjectivity

Throughout *Andrés no quiere dormir la siesta*, Daniel Bustamante attempts to see beyond the "perceptual blind spot" regarding the representation of child protagonists and avoids stereotypical characterization whereby "children are helpless; children should be protected; and if children do wrong, it is because they do not know any better" (Honeyman 2005, 2) even as he explores the politics of authority—parental authority, dictatorial authority, and narrative authority. The film, an exposition of social interactions as seen through the eyes of a child, depicts myriad ways in which a repressive sociopolitical reality is personally experienced in one's home and neighborhood rather than as an invisible force that transcends quotidian existence.

The film initially projects a seemingly insurmountable power differential between the child protagonist, Andrés, and the adults who control his environs; decide how much information to impart and what to withhold; and determine (as well as carry out) punishments they deem appropriate. While at times aloofness remains a voluntary choice—the boys opt not to view their mother's body at her funeral for example—more often than not Andrés's ignorance, distance, and disassociation are forcefully imposed. At first the spectator empathizes with the charming protagonist, a boy whose mother dies and who resists familial efforts to erase all traces of her existence for their own protection. However, as the film progresses he moves from this position of blameless victimization to one of unlikable complicity as he gradually begins to display monstrous behaviors he has learned by example. *Andrés no quiere dormir la siesta* exposes the dangers and vulnerabilities inherent in feigning blind ignorance. The film envisions the monstrous effects of utter indifference and unspeakable acts of quiet compliance by directly engaging the theme of societal collusion, a topic essentially unrepresented in postdictatorial Argentine cinema (Kaiser 2010, 107). Daniel Bustamante deliberately disrupts this culture of silence and contributes to an ever-growing body of memory discourses with this uniquely uncompromising indictment of middle-class complicity.

Notes

1. "Film is a field of conflict between diverse memories." This and all subsequent translations from Spanish are mine.
2. "Relato familiar que también es espejo social."
3. *Kung Fu*, an American television series starring David Carradine that aired from 1972 to 1975, featured a socially committed protagonist roaming the western frontier in search of his half brother. The show highlighted frequent flashbacks to a time when, as an orphaned boy, he was sent to a Chinese monastery; spiritual lessons learned in childhood continue to guide him as an adult. Though not explicit in the film, Andrés's favored program—with its emphasis on childhood training, social injustices, and ethical behavior—clearly resonates with themes presented in Bustamante's film. *Kung Fu* offers the young protagonist a heroic role model, one that serves as a counterpoint to many of the adult figures he encounters.
4. *La historia oficial* (1985) dramatizes in melodramatic fashion the nation's turbulent transition to democracy. With an emphasis on coming to terms with recent national tragedy on both a personal and collective level, the landmark production provided Argentine filmgoers with a cathartic experience. As film historians Eduardo Jakubowicz and Laura Radetich note, "La trama permite, a partir de la victimización de Alicia, la expiación de las culpas de la clase media argentina" (The plot allows, given Alicia's victimization, an expiation of guilt for the Argentine middle class; 168). In contrast, *Garage Olimpo* (1999), with its focus on the relationship between a prisoner and her captor, graphically depicts the horrors of clandestine imprisonment. An accompanying publicity campaign, an urban intervention whereby Argentina's capital was inundated with stark images of the blindfolded protagonist, offered a startling intrusion into the collective amnesia endorsed by Menemist politics. As Valeria Manzano explains in her insightful study, "La intervención reinscribía el pasado dictatorial en el entramado de la Buenos Aires de los noventa" (The intervention reinscribed the dictatorial past onto the framework of a 1990s Buenos Aires; 156). *Crónica de una fuga* (2006), in turn, capitalizes on the techniques of suspense and horror to recreate the extraordinary and harrowing escape of four *desaparecidos* from Mansión Seré.
5. *Cordero de Dios* (2008) remains focalized through an adult who reflects on her traumatic childhood during the dictatorship; *La noche de los lápices* (1986) and *La cautiva* (2004), take on the subject from an adolescent perspective. Other fictional films that directly represent Argentina's last dictatorship include *Sur* (1988), *Imagining Argentina* (2003), and *Hermanas* (2005).
6. "La visión del personaje infantil . . . posibilita representar a veces en modo crítico y otras pedagógico, aspectos de la vida social que la hegemonía ideológica ha 'naturalizado' y transformado en la 'lógica cotidiana.'"
7. For more on the iconic status of the Ford Falcon in Argentina's postdictatorial cultural production, see Fernando Reati's study "El Ford Falcon: Un ícono de terror en el imaginario argentino de la posdictadura."

8. Lies subtly reveal characters' personalities. That Andrés's father says Nora is sick rather than dead shows the depth to which he can deny reality. Doña Olga takes calculated risks, such as inviting Alfredo to enter the very room where Raúl sits, having claimed he was not at home. Andrés lies in an effort to join the expensive swimming club and pretends to mourn his mother in order to skip class. As the film progresses, the lies become increasingly sinister—for example, Andrés's grandmother insists she has not been in Andrés's house and subsequently refuses to acknowledge having witnessed an abduction; Andrés maintains absolute silence regarding his grandmother's death.
9. Identification with Andrés may be problematic; however, a select generation of viewers—Argentines, especially male, who were of elementary school age in the late 1970s—will readily relate to his sociocultural milieu. Familiar cultural references abound, from television programming to toys, from music to clothing and hairstyles.
10. I discuss Bustamante's depiction of middle-class complicity in a forthcoming article coauthored with Bécquer Medak-Seguín: "Norma Aleandro Fashions Herself as Argentina's (Post) Dictatorial Middle Class," in *Latin American/ Latino Icons*, ed. Patrick O'Connor and Dianna Niebylski.
11. The presence of a detention center is not the neighborhood's only *secreto a voces*, or public secret. When Doña Olga condemns Nora's choice in men and expounds the neighbors' insidious gossip and repeated warnings regarding Alfredo's continued influence on the children, Raúl accusingly asks his mother, "You knew and you didn't say anything to me?" Her irritated response of, "What was I supposed to say to you, Raúl? You're a man; you're not a child," draws attention to what *adults* should see and know. Moreover, the fact that Alfredo disappears not long after this conversation chillingly conveys the power of neighborhood vigilance, insinuation, and *complicity*.
12. Honeyman states that in asking questions children can engage in powerfully subversive resistance while safely avoiding suspicion: "The most effective way to disrupt adult discourse and yet be sheltered by the imposed guise of innocence is in the form of a question" (133). Emilio A. Bellon, in his review of *Andrés*, affirms that the film "nos lleva a reconocer la mirada de un niño, Andrés, quien desde sus nueve años, nos hará llegar su mundo de interrogantes" (leads us to acknowledge the gaze of a child, Andrés, who, as a nine-year-old, brings his world of questions to us; 2011).

Works Cited

Andrés no quiere dormir la siesta. Dir. Daniel Bustamante. Perf. Norma Aleandro and Conrado Valenzuela. Ansia Producciones, 2009. Film.

Bellon, Emilio A. "La monstruosidad de lo siniestro." *Página/12.com*. Página/12. 4 Feb. 2010. Web. 20 Dec. 2011. <http://www.pagina12.com.ar/diario/suplementos/rosario/12-22535-2010-03-01.html>.

Honeyman, Susan. *Elusive Childhood: Impossible Representations in Modern Fiction*. Columbus: Ohio State UP, 2005. Print.

Jakubowicz, Eduardo, and Laura Radetich. *La historia argentina a través del cine: Las "visiones del pasado" (1933–2003)*. Buenos Aires: Crujía Ediciones, 2006. Print.

Kaiser, Susana. "Escribiendo memorias de la dictadura: Las asignaturas pendientes del cine argentino." *Revista Crítica de Ciencias Sociais* 88 (2010): 101–25. Print.

Lebeau, Vicky. *Childhood and Cinema*. London: Reaktion, 2008. Print.

Lury, Karen. *The Child in Film: Tears, Fears and Fairy Tales*. New Brunswick: Rutgers UP, 2010. Print.

Manzano, Valeria. "*Garage Olimpo* o cómo proyectar el pasado sobre el presente (y viceversa)." *El pasado que miramos: Memoria e imagen ante la historia reciente*. Ed. Claudia Feld and Jessica Stites Mor. Buenos Aires: Editorial Paidós, 2009. 155–80. Print.

Martínez, Adolfo C. "Retrato familiar que también es espejo social." *La Nación .com*, 4 Feb. 2010. Web. 20 Dec. 2011. <http://www.lanacion.com.ar/1229145-relato-familiar-que-tambien-es-espejo-social>.

Reati, Fernando. "El Ford Falcon: Un ícono de terror en el imaginario argentino de la posdictadura." *Revista de Estudios Hispánicos* 43.2 (May 2009): 385–407. Print.

Tal, Tzvi. "Alegorías de memoria y olvido en películas de iniciación: *Machuca y Kamchatka*." *Aisthesis: Revista chilena de investigaciones estéticas* 38 (2005): 136–51. Print.

Taylor, Diana. *Disappearing Acts: Spectacles of Gender and Nationalism in Argentina's "Dirty War."* Durham: Duke UP, 1997. Print.

Part II

Childhood and Paths to Citizenship

CHAPTER 6

INNOCENCE INTERRUPTED

NEOLIBERALISM AND THE END OF CHILDHOOD IN RECENT MEXICAN CINEMA

IGNACIO M. SÁNCHEZ PRADO

The emergence of a major cinema trope within a national tradition is, at times, traceable to a memorable scene. The end of childhood through sexual initiation acquired a front-and-center position in contemporary Mexican cinema in one of those cinematic moments: the kiss and the suggested sexual encounter between Julio (Gael García Bernal) and Tenoch (Diego Luna) at the end of Alfonso Cuarón's *Y tu mamá también* (2001). The film's success in redefining the terms of Mexican national cinema (Baer and Long; Saldaña Portillo), along with the failed attempts at censoring the film via a C rating (the Mexican equivalent of an NC-17), had an important outcome: the development of narratives representing the end of childhood, teenage sexuality, and the perils and pressures faced by young Mexicans on the verge of their integration into society. In what follows, I will explore one of the themes central to these narratives: the use of sexuality as a threshold between the innocence of childhood and adults as citizens.

In the very last scene of the film, Tenoch and Julio meet for the last time in a restaurant, where we find out that Tenoch is studying economics. One of the implications of this fact is obvious to most viewers: that he has given up his aspirations to be a writer and, more crucially, that he has ended up on a professional path more appropriate to his class position, one surely encouraged by his father, a politician of the ruling party. Most analyses of *Y tu mamá también* have focused on topics such as the film's sly subversion of gender expectations, masculine selfhood, national identity and even class narrative (Acevedo Muñoz 2004; Finnegan 2007; De la Mora 2006, 163–80; Lewis 2009) or on the film's role in establishing coproduction schemes between Mexico and Spain (Smith 2003; Linhard 2008). Nonetheless, Cuarón's key decision is to use the final sexual encounter between his characters to deplete their joyfully subversive masculinity, one that resisted, up to this point, Tenoch's family's social status and his class difference vis-á-vis Julio. The film's conclusion inscribes them into the normalized life paths that they declaredly pursue at the end of the film. In my view, this is perhaps the most striking aspect of the film. In spite of its subtle critique of nationalist, gender, and class expectations, *Y tu mamá también* is ultimately a film about the inescapable fate of middle-class adulthood in neoliberal times, where the Dionysian rituals of young male bonding are nothing but a carnivalesque stop along the irrevocable route toward citizenship.

The proliferation of narratives about childhood, youth, and the path to (middle-class) citizenship in the wake of *Y tu mamá también* provides clear evidence of two intertwining phenomena. First, it is one of the first successful attempts to capture the teenage audience as a potential market for the emerging Mexican market, which became commercially viable in the wake of box-office hits of the late 1990s. Also, it becomes a key vehicle in the construction of the ideological trope of the meanings and perils of growing up in a society where the traditional values of the family and the nation are in crisis. Youth, the prolonged threshold between childhood and maturity, is represented by many films as a crucial and dangerous territory of transition in which success means becoming part of the bourgeois mainstream and failure results in being an outcast. The effects of neoliberalism have undermined and altered the traditional quadrants of nation and family and have exacerbated an already unequal economic system. Under these circumstances, youth has emerged as a critical space for the articulation of citizenship. The vast number of films about growing up produced in Mexico in the 2000s (including those I will discuss in what follows: *Amar te duele*, *Temporada de patos*, *Niñas mal*, *Año uña*, *Soba*, and *Drama/Mex*) is an indicator of an emerging concern regarding adulthood and citizenship in what Roger Bartra has famously called the "post-Mexican condition."[1] To be sure, this concern is not exclusive to Mexico, and scholars of different film traditions have posited the importance of the trope in various national contexts.[2] However, the marked increase in the theme's centrality in the past ten years in Mexico, compared to a lower incidence of youth-related topics and younger characters in the cinema of the 1990s, indicates the persistence of the question regarding the new paths toward citizenship in the new post–Partido Revolucionario

Institucional, post–North American Free Trade Agreement Mexican reality.³ By shooting films about the passage from childhood to maturity, Mexican filmmakers highlight the question of new societal configurations through the moment of articulation. In these terms, my analysis will be concerned with the ways in which the interruption of innocence marks a stepping-stone toward citizenship faced by young Mexicans. I will also show, throughout different examples, that youth is not a category that should be read in isolation but, rather, that its class articulations are crucial to understanding the way in which individual representations of childhood and youth operate as ideological configurations. Finally, I will spend the latter part of the paper discussing the way in which gender problematizes the question of citizenship given that narratives of formation, like the one presented by *Y tu mamá también*, traditionally privilege masculine subjects.

Laura Podalsky has already identified the centrality of youth in contemporary Mexican cinema. In her article, Podalsky recognizes a wide array of films focused on youth, from Televisa star vehicles and early New Cinema works of the 1980s to the blockbusters of post-NAFTA cinema ("The Young and the Damned"). Her analysis encompasses two issues: the conservative portrayal of youth as a collective of "ungovernable bodies" resulting, according to her, from the emergence of the *chavo banda*⁴ subculture; and the music video aesthetics that, in her view, introduce a major formal change in Mexican cinema.⁵ In identifying macro trends such as family dysfunction in a wide corpus, Podalsky overlooks some important subtleties in the very concept of youth deployed in each individual film. My aim here thus is to supplement arguments such as the one set forward by Podalsky by showing how the growing-up narrative is marked by gender and class in order to create significantly distinct scenarios of the threshold between childhood and citizenship.

An interesting first example is offered by Jonás Cuarón—Alfonso Cuarón's son—in his *Año uña* (*Year of the Nail*; 2009). The film presents Diego (Diego Cataño), a 14-year-old boy, as he falls in love with Molly (Eireann Harper), a 21-year-old exchange student from the United States. The film is constructed through a very interesting formal conceit: the entire film is a slideshow of still photographs, accompanied by dialogue and the character's inner thoughts in voice-over. Thus while the film is not a flashback, the action happens as if it were a remembrance, in which the still images register those moments to be recorded in the memory of their protagonists. The film is very effective in representing the inner lives of both Diego and Molly. Diego's hormone-ridden mind functions in the tension between his emerging and intense sexual desire and the new emotions that gradually become the focus of his affective life. Molly's thoughts represent a Sofia Coppolaesque young woman disconcerted by the strangeness of a foreign country and by the uncertainties of the adult life she is about to face. The intimate tone of the film is undoubtedly assisted by the fact that the film is a family affair: Harper is Cuarón's real-life girlfriend, Cataño his half-brother, Diego's mother is played by their actual mother, and father Alfonso is the producer of the film. These formal and extradiegetic factors frame Diego's story as a tender memory of childhood, a time he is not quite ready to let go. Despite his best efforts, which include an impromptu trip to New York to see Molly, Diego never actually consummates his desire for her, allegorizing his unreadiness to integrate into society as an adult.

The plot is marked by two significant elements that show the ideological conceits underscoring Diego's bittersweet experience. First, it is precisely Diego's imperiled middle-class status that makes the romance possible in the first place. The reason why Molly ends up in his house is that Diego's grandfather is diagnosed with cancer and his mother puts a room in the house up for rent to help with the expenses. This side plot signals the middle class's loss of the networks of social protections—given that the reason why cancer would be an economical issue is related to the vanishing structures of public health in Mexico.[6] Nonetheless, Diego's interest in Molly brackets this concern and places him into a space of unconsciousness. His inability to actually have sex with Molly—something that would have resulted, through allegory, in some form of maturing or self-consciousness—allows him to remain in the safe space of childhood, where he remains immune to the social pressures of neoliberalism. Second, Diego's attraction to Molly comes at the expense of his early infatuation toward his cousin Emilia, who, up to the arrival of the American student, was Diego's primary object of desire. This displacement is meaningful because his interest in an older girl certainly indicates a growth process, but it is even more relevant to point out that he substitutes a Mexican object of desire with an American one. This, along with the fact that the final scene of reckoning takes place during a stroll in Coney Island, is symptomatic of the class location of Diego's affective experience, insofar as growing up into the new neoliberal society implies a contact with the codes of Americanization established by post-NAFTA modernity.

While the film could indeed be a good example of Podalsky's point of an avant-garde narrative device in representing what may be deemed as a socially conservative story, Diego's inability to become a "deviant" kid through sexual intercourse is indicative of the close relationship between class and the right to protect childhood innocence. Another telling example of this occurs in Fernando Eimbcke's *Temporada de patos* (*Duck Season*; 2004), where an even younger Cataño plays Moko, a kid stuck with his best friend Flama (Daniel Miranda) during a power outage in the lower middle-class neighborhood of Tlatelolco. The story shares important similarities with *Año uña*. It has a similar tone of remembrance—this time through the use of black and white throughout the film—and a slightly older girl, Rita (Danny Perea), playing the role as the protagonist's object of desire. The creation of a self-enclosed world of childhood immune to the outside pressures of neoliberalism is constructed through devices such as the use of the kid's nicknames throughout the film, which has a similar effect to Cuarón's use of inner dialogue. Kate Richardson has pointed out the importance of the film being set in Tlatelolco, site of the 1968 massacre, a history about which Moko and Flama seem to be completely unaware (7). Furthermore, they have no qualms in keeping Ulises (Enrique Arreola), a pizza-delivery man, in the house when he refuses to leave because they will not pay for a pizza, which they justify by alleging that Ulises was 11 seconds late. As we learn that Ulises works at the pizza place due to his need to take care of his sick aunt, the striking feature is the indifference (a characteristic usually associated with adolescence) shown by Flama and Moko to his fate. Flama and Moko's self-centered world shows the extent to which the film uses the space of childhood as a refuge against the pressures of a modernity that lurks around the everyday experience of young Mexicans, both in the conflictive history of the country taking place in their apartment complex and in the economic uncertainty that they will most likely face when they grow up. Like *Año uña*, *Temporada de patos* is a film about not crossing the threshold to adulthood, a prerogative made possible by the privileged social status of both Diego and Moko, whose middle-class position allows them to postpone the encounter with the uncertainties of neoliberal adulthood. Cuarón and Eimbcke construct these self-enclosed childhood spaces through highly aestheticized conceits (the still photographs and the black-and-white cinematography) that aptly transmit the nostalgic and somewhat unreal world of youth to the eyes of an adult audience.[7] Childhood, thus, is an aesthetic locus that preserves the subject from becoming citizen, a postponement of adulthood marked by the impossibility of fulfilling one's first erotic desire.

At this point, it becomes clear that all these narratives are gender determined due to their focus on male protagonists and female objects of desire. Here, it is pertinent to note that the young masculine subject has been the focus of narratives of formation since the outset of modernity itself. In *The Way of the World*, his landmark study on Bildungsroman, Franco

Moretti argues that narratives of formation tracing back to novels such as Johann Wolfgang van Goethe's *Wilhelm Meister* became central to modernity due to the ability of the trope of youth to "accentuate modernity's dynamism and instability" (5). Following this idea, one could argue that Mexican cinema turns youth into a forceful matrix of narratives and allegories to express the instability underlying the path to citizenship. Insofar as neoliberalism constitutes a narrative of modernization that breaks away from the quadrants of identity formation designed under postrevolutionary narratives, Mexican cinema in the 2000s follows a trend analogous to that established by the Bildungsroman at the outset of modernity, a focus on youth as the site of a changed notion of citizenship. In these terms, the nostalgic, slow-tempo narrative of *Año uña* and *Temporada de patos*, located on the verge of adulthood, represents childhood as a holdout to the dynamic development of a youth exposed to vertiginous modernity, as is the case in *Y tu mamá también* and even in Octavio's (Gael García Bernal) story in Alejandro González Iñárritu's *Amores perros* (2000).[8] In of all these cases, youth is embodied in a masculine figure that either remains in the safety of the family home shielded from the outside pressures of neoliberalism (like Moko and Flama) or faces a sudden integration to modernity via either sexual fulfillment or personal trauma (like Julio, Tenoch, and even Octavio).

Fernando Sariñana's *Amar te duele* (*Love Hurts*; 2002), one of Mexico's most successful films of the past decade, provides a very meaningful example of the tensions introduced into growing-up narratives when class and gender are explicitly factored into the plot. The film is a Romeo-and-Juliet story centered on the relationship between Renata (Martha Higareda), an upper-class prep school girl, and Ulises (Luis Fernando Peña), a working-class young man who works in his parents' market stand. The story is strategically set in Santa Fe, Mexico City, a neighborhood notorious for the radical economic inequality of its inhabitants, which range from the poor people that have historically lived on the city's edge to the elite that took over parts of Santa Fe when it became a hub of corporate business. The film is constructed on the contrast between the sweet love story and the violent reluctance of their friends and families to their bridging the boundaries of class. Thus the film builds a crescendo of interclass violence that includes Renata's former boyfriend Francisco's (Alfonso Herrera) attack on Ulises and the retaliating attack on the male students of the prep school by the working-class teens. The conclusion takes place in a bus terminal, where Renata and Ulises's attempt to run away is foiled when Francisco attempts to kill Ulises but shoots and kills Renata by mistake. Ana León Távora and Itzá Zavala-Garrett have suggestively read this plot as a foiled "foundational romance,"[9] since Ulises' and Renata's relationship would have meant a potential symbolic reconciliation between Mexico City's upper and lower classes into a unified identity. Renata's tragic death thus "reaffirms the immobility of the social structure and the persistence of *clasismo*" (83). One should add here that a gendered double standard is also present in this ending. For Ulises, the experience, bitter as it is, is ultimately his entrance to neoliberal society, where he will go ahead with his life as a young man unable to achieve his dreams of upward mobility, since we know his dream of attending art school is not an option for him. Conversely, Renata's class transgression makes her unable to become a full-fledged woman within the upper class. Since her rejection of Francisco indicates her inability to conform to the relationship standards of the elite, therefore, she has to die. To be sure, this gendered conclusion appears in other films, most notably Gerardo Naranjo's *Voy a explotar* (*I'm Gonna Explode*; 2008), where Maru (María Deschamps) dies as a result of her illicit relationship with Román (Juan Pablo de Santiago), the son of a powerful politician, who also enters adulthood through the mourning of his young love interest. The fact that male characters ultimately enter society, even if it is in a traumatic way, while young female characters die within the same plot is telling. It speaks, in a way, of the inadequacy of Mexican cinema to deal with the idea of young women transcending social norms, since their transgressions lead, unlike their male counterparts, to their ultimate inability to enter the social.

 The eruption of reality at the end of *Amar te duele* results from the inability of childhood to remain as a shelter against neoliberalism for a young working-class boy like Ulises. At the beginning of the film, Ulises lives in a form of preserved childhood, spending most of his time with his friend Genaro (Armando Hernández) in a world of arcade videogames, skateboarding, and comic books—not unlike Moko and Flama. This space is preserved in one of his moments with Renata, where he tells her the story of a comic book mythology he has been devising—one unsurprisingly set in a world where social difference does not matter—as we see his drawings emerge on the screen. Even in the early love forays of these characters, childhood remains a space of aesthetic safety. However, Ulises's encounter with Renata is from the beginning a reckoning with society, given their unbridgeable social differences. Tellingly, Renata and Ulises do fulfill their sexual desire near the end of the film, unfolding in part the tragic resolution. Therefore, as the film progresses, the iconology of Ulises's childhood progressively fades away, giving way to the violence unleashed by their transgression of class boundaries.

It is also relevant to note here, in a more contextual sense, that *Amar te duele* provides a significant departure from Sariñana's early career, which, in turn, shows some of the underlying reasons behind the rise of growing-up narratives in 2000s Mexican cinema. Sariñana is one of Mexico's most successful and influential directors, and he made his name in the late 1990s with a combination of critically acclaimed films of social vocation (like his debut film *Hasta morir* [*'Til Death*; 1994]) and commercially successful films on the life and times of Mexico City's professional middle class (most notably his comedy *Todo el poder* [Gimme the Power; 2000]). Given his insight on the audiences of Mexican commercial cinema, his turn toward youth and away from his 1990s interest in young urban professionals as subjects of representation is representative of a turning point also signaled in sociological studies. Lucila Hinojosa Córdova, for instance, shows that, in 2001, young people emerge as an audience due to the introduction of promotional pricing on Wednesday and the uses of cinema as a dating practice by young people (103). I would argue that, in the wake of *Y tu mamá también*, *Amar te duele*'s success represented an apt reading of this phenomenon in a moment when teenage and young adult audiences became visible in market analyses of cinema. Given the tight control on the television airwaves held by the Televisa/Televisión Azteca duopoly, in which prime-time slots are usually taken over by *telenovelas*,[10] cinema became a viable venue for media aimed at youth, particularly as the private exhibition chains opened new complexes in shopping malls.[11] In this context, *Amar te duele* became hugely successful—raising 6.6 million dollars in the domestic box office—by tapping into that market. It is also important to note here that the very success of *Amar te duele* is as class determined as its plot. Higareda and Ximena (Sariñana's daughter, who also plays Renata's sister in the film) became two of the most iconic film stars in the country, gracing the covers of magazines like *Rolling Stone* and *FHM*, while Luis Fernando Peña, perhaps due to his working-class looks and his dark skin, was confined to a more low-profile career. In any case, this last point indicates the same issue discovered by Sariñana in this film: the importance of middle- and upper-class youth in the construction of Mexican cinema. Not surprisingly, the film confirmed its success when it beat Carlos Carrera's *El crimen del Padre Amaro* (*The Crime of Father Amaro*; 2002), Mexico's biggest box-office success to date in the 2003 MTV Movie Awards Mexico, where it won favorite movie, favorite song, favorite actress and favorite villain awards. *El crimen del Padre Amaro* raised over 16 million dollars, mostly banking on a controversy around its religious subject, which attracted a very wide demographic. Nonetheless, it is important to note that young viewers were important to this number due to the presence of

Gael García Bernal (fresh out of his double success in *Amores perros* and *Y tu mamá también*) and Ana Claudia Talancón, who became, along with Higareda, one of Mexico's most popular young actresses of the 2000s. It is also important to note that the awards are named "favorite" rather than "best" because they are based on audience votes. The fact that *Amar te duele* prevailed in the MTV demographic is a good indicator of the point about the youth audience tapped by Sariñana. It is significant, though, that while Higareda was selected as favorite actress over Talancón, the voters chose Gael García over Peña, in part due to the former's bigger name, but surely also due to the ethnic undertones mentioned before. Finally, the "favorite song" award, won by Natalia Lafourcade's title song, shows the importance of music videos and Mexican pop stars in recruiting young audiences to films such as this.

Sariñana's next film featuring Higareda, *Niñas mal* (*Charm School*; 2007) shows the way in which his cinema adjusts the growing-up narrative to tailor it specifically to his middle-class audience. Higareda plays Adela, the rebellious daughter of a major conservative politician, Senator Martín León (Rafael Sánchez Navarro), who sends her off to a femininity course at charm school to stop her from undermining his aspirations to run for office. In the charm school, Adela finds a group of young women seeking integration into society: Valentina (Ximena Sariñana) is a young lesbian sent there to reconsider her sexual orientation; Pía (Camila Sodi) is a brilliant economics student who agrees to attend the course to address her mother's worry that she cannot meet a man; Maribel (María Aura) is a clueless young woman who wants to no longer be clumsy; and Heidi (Alejandra Adame) is sent there by her future in-laws so she can be the perfect wife for her upper-class future husband. The film's title is a play on the notion of "niñas bien," which implies well-behaved, upper-class women. While the characters are not strictly children (they are all supposed to be in their late teens and early twenties), they are subject to infantilization by Maca (Blanca Guerra), their etiquette instructor, who calls them "*niñas*" all along.

A few striking features emerge in the context of the present discussion. First, Sariñana completely eliminates the issue of class conflict from this film. All five girls clearly belong to the upper class, to the point that they are somewhat connected to each other through political and economic relations: Heidi's future father-in-law is one of Senator León's donors, Pía's love interest is Senator León's economic advisor and personal assistant, while Valentina is the niece of a prominent bishop with political ties to both Heidi's and Adela's families. The only reference to someone outside the plutocracy comes from Fina, Maca's maid, whose son Emiliano,

Adela's love interest, is completing an MA in aerodynamics with Maca's support. Unlike Renata, who gets punished for crossing class lines, Adela is able to become a respectable person because her transgressions are not irreversible: after derailing Heidi's wedding and her father's candidacy due to a misunderstanding, she ultimately puts together a new ceremony that redeems her in the eyes of everyone. Still, for Emiliano to be an acceptable suitor, he has to be on his way to becoming part of the elite, which he can only do thanks to Maca, who provides an exception to Mexico's lack of social mobility. Furthermore, it is important to note here that, with the exception of Valentina, who becomes a pop singer, all other four girls achieve feminine realization when they meet a man: Pía and her economist boyfriend move to Harvard so she can study her PhD in economics (as many members of the elite aspire to do), Heidi gets married after Adela has no choice but to validate her decision to be the perfect wife, and Maribel meets someone to lose her virginity. While the girls' integration to society is not determined by a traumatic event, the happy ending of the film is clearly class determined: the five girls are allowed to enter society after they are able to "fix" the rough edges that kept them from doing so. These changes undoubtedly improved the film's standing among the MTV audience to the point of creating a spin-off television series, also titled *Niñas mal* and produced in Colombia, which currently plays on MTV Tr3s in the United States and MTV Latin America across the continent.

Niñas mal is the pinnacle of a series of films that addressed middle- and upper-class girlhood within a similar discourse of integration into adulthood through (class-appropriate demonstrations of) sexuality and the acceptance of social norms of womanhood. This is the case, for instance, of Alejandro Gamboa's trilogy *La primera noche* (*The First Night*; 1998), *La segunda noche* (*The Second Night*; 2001), and *La última noche* (*The Last Night*; 2005). The films are not directly connected to one another; their only link is the actress Mariana Ávila, who plays an altogether different character in each film. All three are stories of the sexual awakening that marks the end of girlhood and is necessary to integrate into society. Ávila, whose red hair and facial features are strongly reminiscent of Molly Ringwald, embodies an earlier stage of the film persona that would be perfected by Higareda: a girl whose growing-up process exists on the line between awkward sexuality, a rebellious nature, and a need for social acceptance and integration. A similar character may be found in Gabriela Tagliavini's *Ladies' Night* (2003) in which Alicia (Ana Claudia Talancón), a highly infantilized young woman named after *Alice in Wonderland* who dreams of living a fairy tale romance, endangers her impending marriage by falling in love with a male stripper during her bachelorette party. Like Ávila and Higareda's characters, Alicia's affective formation is also a matter of class position: her transgression is forgiven because her fiancé and her friend Ana (Ana de la Reguera) are in love with each other anyway. The difference is that Alicia does perform a class transgression and a moral one. I would contend that the substantial distinction here is that the director and scriptwriter is a woman, while in all other cases, male directorial gazes narrate the young women's stories. Still, the film's ending is not such a big departure, as Alicia's ultimate realization and her becoming woman are tied to her relationship to a man, which, as implied by the very last line of dialogue, means to renounce "knowing Wonderland"—that is, by marking the end of the protective space of childhood.

The point that must not be missed here is that success narratives are the prerogative of cinematic subjects of privileged economic positions whose youthful transgressions are not so grave as to preempt successful integration to society. Narratives focused on young women become the most symptomatic exploration of this point precisely because they introduce a gendered element that allows us to see the gap in traditionally masculine narratives of formation. A case in point is Gerardo Naranjo's first film, *Drama/Mex* (2006). The film follows the parallel story of two young women, Fernanda (Diana García) and Tigrillo (Mariana Moro), in the pivotal moment of sexual discovery on the threshold of adulthood. Fernanda is an upper-class girl whose former boyfriend, Chano (Emilio Valdés), a strong masculine character, reappears after leaving her behind to escape from Acapulco with her, at the expense of her current boyfriend Gonzalo (Juan Pablo Castañeda). Fernanda's relationship to Chano is highly dysfunctional, as attested by their first encounter: he rapes her, which shockingly makes her realize how much she misses him. Gonzalo's friends inform him of Chano's return and he tries to get Fernanda back. In the end, Fernanda opts to go back to Gonzalo, reintegrating herself to the social tissue of Acapulco, a coastal city with a less dramatic but still significant class gap. As we can see, the upper-class girl has familiar undertones: a young woman who meets a transgressive man but ultimately recognizes her mistake and is allowed a return to normalcy. This conventional story acquires more interest as a counterpoint to that of Tigrillo, a working-class girl. We meet her on her first day as a "*yajaira*," part of a girl's gang that makes money hustling foreign and older tourists. During the day, she meets Jaime (Fernando Becerril), an older man who leaves his home and his work to run away from an incestuous relationship with his teenage daughter. Tigrillo takes a liking to Jaime, to the point that the audience almost feels she is falling in love with him, and she does ultimately prevent him from committing suicide. Unlike Fernanda, who ultimately reintegrates into society, Tigrillo's traumatic experience result in a will to leave Acapulco for good, since staying would mean to continue a life as a potential prostitute.

The fact that the working-class girl is subjected to a far more traumatic story than the upper-class female character, with undertones of incest and pedophilia, clearly shows that Mexican cinema's ideology of working-class girlhood goes beyond sordidness. One has to remember a film with an even more drastic storyline: Alan Coton's *Soba* (*Beating*; 2004). In this film, Claudia Soberón plays Justina, a 15-year-old girl on the verge of her sexual awakening. Making good on her name, which is reminiscent of one of Marquis de Sade's most memorable characters, she seduces her stepfather, who is ultimately murdered by her mother. In a scene that challenges verisimilitude, Justina is cast away by her mother in a revealing night robe, which leads her to be arrested for prostitution. In the police station, she is subject to gang rape by a whole police unit, until one of the officers (Dagoberto Gama), notorious for torturing his suspects, rescues her. She has no choice but to accuse him of the rape and send him to prison, where we see her, at the end of the film, visiting him in jail. The truly distasteful nature of the film, which ends up being ridiculous in its excessive plot twists and its ethically questionable portrayal of Justina (who was in fact played by a 27-year-old actress), shows an extreme example of the way in which girlhood can be represented in oversexualized, overdetermined, and punishing ways in Mexican cinema. The film is entirely shot in black-and-white, adding a perverse twist to the flashback connotations of this cinematic resource in films like *Temporada de patos*. Justina's sudden adulthood is one of destruction and madness, where her closure lies in being tied to one of her rapists. In a way, *Drama/Mex* and *Soba*,[12] in their violent appeal to sexual taboo, show the inability of Mexican cinema (and perhaps of Mexican culture) to grant a narrative of formation to young women outside of the upper classes that is equivalent to that of their male counterparts.

In conclusion, I want to point out that all the films discussed here show that the emergence of youth as a cinematic topic is as much a matter of emerging audiences as it is a vehicle for expressing the ideologies of citizenship and formation in a transitional society. In neoliberal Mexico, this trend has been translated into an idea of social formation that reproduces class privilege and access to a symbolic economy that only recognizes valid affective experiences in classes. Renata's death in *Amar te duele*, and Justina's and Tigrillo's sordid experiences in *Soba* and

Drama/Mex, respectively, are only possible in a film culture that is unable to imagine cultural and affective citizenship for women who transcend and transgress the social mores of a cultural and economic regime defined by inequality. I would thus contend that, adding to the work done by authors like Timothy Shary and Podalsky, childhood and youth narratives in contexts like that of contemporary Mexican cinema give us a vantage point to understand the way in which social ideals problematically interweave youth and citizenship formation with gender, class, and race hierarchies. If, as José Manuel Valenzuela Arce forcefully argues, "youth identities are sociohistorically located and signified constructions [and y]outh is not a crystallized social sector, but a polysemic and variable one" (35; my translation), cinematic representations of youth must respond to current cultural configurations of the transition from childhood to adulthood, particularly if they seek to appeal to that very demographic. Thus films of particular commercial success (like Cuarón's or Sariñana's) and those who explore the forbidden limits of youthful experience (like Naranjo's or Coton's) offer important insights on both the agendas and blind spots of the ideologies of youth in societies where formation is an allegory of citizenship and social integration. Also, the ability of young stars like Higareda or García Bernal to occupy iconic places in the cultural imaginary, and the plasticity that actors like Ávila or Cataño deploy in representing distinct narratives of youth provide literal embodiments of social ideals of race, gender, class, beauty, and affect. In all cases, as I have shown, the interruption of innocence through a traumatic or formative event shows important differences in the right to childhood and to adulthood determined by class and gender lines. In conclusion, the ultimate aim of the brief readings I have presented so far is to underscore a crucial analytical point regarding childhood and youth within cinema: it is not a single trope but rather a set of clearly differentiated discourses that together interweave a network of symbolic imaginaries, which underlie the social ideology of identity formation. It is thus in the differentiated analysis of discourses of youth in their specificity, rather than in the assertion of a trope of youth at large, that we find the true insights that cinema of formation has to give. In the gap that separates Tenoch and Adela from Ulises and Tigrillo, we have an iconic space of signification for the abyss that separates upper and lower classes in the intrinsic inequalities of neoliberal life.

Notes

1. By this, Bartra means a way of articulating subjectivity in Mexico beyond the ideologies of *Mexicanidad* that were part of the hegemonic project of the now fallen postrevolutionary regime. See Roger Bartra's *Blood, Ink, and Culture*.
2. See particularly the essays collected in Shary and Seibel, *Youth Culture in Global Cinema* and Hardcastle, Morosini, and Tarte, *Coming of Age on Film*.
3. The issue of citizenship in neoliberal times has been famously addressed by Néstor García Canclini in *Consumers and Citizens*. Here, I will use a more flexible notion where citizenship means, more generically, "integration to society" given that consumption, García Canclini's main trope, is not of particular relevance to my analysis.
4. The term *chavo banda* implies a young working-class male, usually bound to gang-like social communities.
5. I fully agree with Podalsky's assessment of the tension between ideologies of social conservatism and avant-garde formal work in contemporary Mexican cinema, which I identified in my article on *Amores perros*. See Sánchez Prado, "Exotic Violence and Neoliberal Fear."
6. For a study detailing this process, see Laurell.
7. This technique acquires further meaning when compared with Eimbcke's second film, *¿Te acuerdas de Lake Tahoe?* (2008) in which an older Diego Cataño plays Juan, an alienated youth trying to escape the uncertainty caused by the death of a loved one. This film, which focuses on an already failed subjectivity instead of the not-yet-subject child, takes places in the ruinous edges of a provincial town, away from neoliberal modernity. The contrast between the beautiful black-and-white world of the childhood apartment and the desolate landscapes of youthful escape exemplify Eimbcke's use of ambiance and visual palette in the contrasting worlds of Moko and Juan.
8. Octavio's story follows a similar pathway: he is in the safety of a family home but, lacking the protections of middle-class childhood, he acquires an object of desire—Susana—whose fulfillment requires him to enter capitalism through the darker side of informal economy. Thus, rather than a slow-paced film with nostalgic undertones, González Iñarritu gives us a fast-paced story with a violent palette. This is, in a way, a different take on the point made by Podalsky when she speaks of "music video aesthetics," in that speed is a factor not only of visual language but of the very experience of neoliberal modernization.
9. León Távora and Zavala-Garrett extract this notion from Doris Sommer's well-known study *Foundational Fictions*, which argues that nineteenth-century romance novels may be read as allegories of national foundation.
10. Certainly, Televisa was not blind to the youth audience, which had been tapped by Alejandro Gamboa's film trilogy on young girls growing up (which I mention in another part of this chapter). By the time *Amar te duele* was released, Televisa had reserved the 7 p.m. time slot for soap operas aimed at teenagers, which was occupied in 2002 and 2003 by the hugely successful *Clase 406*. Still,

despite the even bigger success of *Rebelde* a few years later, this type of production remains rare in Mexican television; *telenovelas* aimed at older women remain the norm in primetime slots.

11. The effect of cineplexes and shopping malls on the US film audience of the 1980s has been aptly studied by Shary in *Generation Multiplex*. I would contend that by the early 2000s a similar phenomenon was taking place in Mexico, and the opening of Cinemex, Cinemark, and Cinépolis venues in malls like Plaza Universidad, frequented by youth from the many adjacent private schools, meant an exponential growth of this demographic within Mexico's film audience. Ana Rosas Mantecón shows that, in 1998, only 5 percent of Mexico City's inhabitants chose going to the films as a weekend activity, compared to 14 percent of respondents who preferred malls (276). Presumably, as multiplexes opened in malls in the late 1990s and early 2000s, film attendance was enhanced by absorbing the already existing customer base of the shopping malls.

12. It may be interesting to point out that both films were financed by director-owned independent companies—La Chancla producciones and Revolcadero films—outside of the commercial circuits of Miravista, Canana, Televicine, and Altavista, which bankrolled the more commercial films discussed in other parts of this chapter.

Works Cited

Acevedo Muñoz, Ernesto R. "Sex, Class and Mexico in Alfonso Cuarón's *Y tu mamá también*." *Film and History* 34. 1 (2004): 39–48.

Amar te duele. Dir. Fernando Sariñana. Perf. Martha Higareda, Luis Fernando Peña, and Ximena Sariñana. Distrimax, 2002. Digital videodisc.

Año uña. Dir. Jonás Cuarón. Perf. Diego Cataño and Eireann Harper. Canana, 2010. Digital videodisc.

Baer, Hester, and Ryan F. Long. "Transnational Cinema and the Mexican State in Alfonso Cuarón's *Y tu mamá también*." *South Central Review* 21.3 (2004): 150–68.

Bartra, Roger. *Blood, Ink, and Culture: Miseries and Splendors of the Post-Mexican Condition*. Trans. Mark Alan Healey. Durham: Duke UP, 2002.

El crimen del Padre Amaro. Dir. Carlos Carrera. Perf. Gael García Bernal and Ana Claudia Talancón. Columbia Tri-Star, 2003. Digital videodisc.

De la Mora, Sergio. *Cinemachismo: Masculinities and Sexuality in Mexican Film*. Austin: U of Texas P, 2006.

Drama/Mex. Dir. Gerardo Naranjo. Perf. Diana García and Mariana Moro. IFC Films, 2007. Digital videodisc.

Finnegan, Nuala. "'So What's Mexico Really Like?' Framing the Local, Negotiating the Global in Alfonso Cuarón's *Y tu mamá también*." *Contemporary Latin American Cinema: Breaking into the Global Market*. Ed. Deborah Shaw. Lanham: Rowman and Littlefield, 2007. 29–50.

García Canclini, Néstor. *Consumers and Citizens: Globalization and Multicultural Conflicts*. Trans. George Yudice. Minneapolis: U of Minnesota P, 2001.

Hardcastle, Anne, Roberta Morosini, and Kendall B. Tarte, eds. *Coming of Age on Film: Stories of Transformation in World Cinema.* Newcastle upon Tyne: Cambridge Scholars, 2009.

Hasta morir. Dir. Fernando Sariñana. Perf. Demian Bichir and Vanessa Bauche. Venevisión, 2002. Digital videodisc.

Hinojosa Córdova, Lucila. *El cine mexicano: De lo global a lo local.* Mexico City: Trillas, 2003.

Ladies Night. Dir. Gabriela Tagliavini. Perf. Ana Claudia Talancón and Ana de la Reguera. Buenavista, 2005. Digital videodisc.

Laurell, Asa Cristina. "Health Reform in Mexico: The Promotion of Inequality." *International Journal of Health Services* 31.2 (2001): 291–321.

León Távora, Ana, and Itzá Zavala-Garrett. "Romeo the Mexican and Juliet the Gypsy: Shakespeare's Hispanic Flavor in *Amar te duele* and *Montoyas y tarantos.*" *Coming of Age on Film: Stories of Transformation in World Cinema.* Ed. Anne Hardcastle, Roberta Morosini, and Kendall Tarte. Newcastle upon Tyne: Cambridge Scholars, 2009. 80–92.

Lewis, Vek. "When 'Macho' Bodies Fail: Spectacles of Corporeality and the Limits of the Homosocial/Sexual in Mexican Cinema." *Mysterious Skin: Male Bodies in Contemporary Cinema.* Ed. Santiago Fouz-Hernández. London: Tauris, 2009. 177–92.

Linhard, Tabea. "Unheard Confessions and Transatlantic Connections: *Y tu mamá también* and *Nadie hablará de nosotras cuando hayamos muerto.*" *Studies in Hispanic Cinemas* 5.1–2 (2008): 43–56.

Moretti, Franco. *The Way of the World: The* Bildungsroman *in European Culture.* London: Verso, 2000.

Niñas mal. Dir. Fernando Sariñana. Perf. Martha Higareda, Camila Sodi, and Ximena Sariñana. Columbia Pictures, 2008. Digital videodisc.

Podalsky, Laura. "The Young, the Damned and the Restless: Youth in Contemporary Mexican Cinema." *Framework* 49.1 (2008): 144–60.

La primera noche. Dir. Alejandro Gamboa. Perf. Mariana Ávila and Osvaldo Benavides. Quality Films, 2004. Digital videodisc.

Richardson, Kate. "Renegotiating Patriarchal Power: The Tlaltelolco Massacre and Mexican Cinema." *Film Matters* 1.2 (2010): 2–8.

Rosas Mantecón, Ana. "Las batallas por la diversidad: Exhibición y públicos de cine en México." *Situación actual y perspectivas de la industria cinematográfica en México y en el extranjero.* Ed. Néstor García Canclini, Ana Rosas Mantecón, and Enrique Sánchez Ruiz. Guadalajara: Universidad de Guadalajara 2006. 263–92.

Saldaña Portillo, María Josefina. "In the Shadow of NAFTA: *Y tu mamá también* Revisits the National Allegory of Mexican Sovereignty." *American Quarterly* 57.3 (2005): 751–77.

Sánchez Prado, Ignacio M. "*Amores perros*: Exotic Violence and Neoliberal Fear." *Journal of Latin American Cultural Studies* 15.1 (2006): 39–57.

La segunda noche. Dir. Alejandro Gamboa. Perf. Mariana Ávila, Sherlyn, and Irán Castillo. Warner Brothers, 2004. Digital videodisc.

Shary, Timothy. *Generation Multiplex: The Image of Youth in Contemporary American Cinema*. Austin: U of Texas P, 2002

Shary, Timothy, and Alexandra Seibel, eds. *Youth Culture in Global Cinema*. Austin: U of Texas P, 2007.

Smith, Paul Julian. "Transatlantic Traffic in Recent Mexican Films." *Journal of Latin American Cultural Studies* 12.3 (2003): 389–400.

Soba. Dir. Alan Coton. Perf. Claudia Soberón and Dagoberto Gama. Zafra, 2005. Digital videodisc.

Sommer, Doris. *Foundational Fictions: The National Romances of Latin America*. Berkeley: U of California P, 1991.

¿Te acuerdas de Lake Tahoe? Dir. Fernando Eimbcke. Perf. Diego Cataño, Héctor Herrera, and Daniela Valentine. Film Movement, 2009. Digital videodisc.

Temporada de patos. Dir. Fernando Eimbcke. Perf. Diego Cataño, Daniel Miranda, and Danny Perea. Warner Brothers, 2006. Digital videodisc.

Todo el poder. Dir. Fernando Sariñana. Perf. Demián Bichir, Cecilia Suárez, and Luis Felipe Tovar. 20th Century Fox, 2003. Digital videodisc.

La última noche. Dir Alejandro Gamboa. Perf. Mariana Ávila, Cecilia Gabriela, and Andrés García. Warner Brothers, 2006. Digital videodisc.

Valenzuela Arce, José Manuel. *El futuro ya fue: Socioantropología de l@s jóvenes en la modernidad*. Mexico City: Juan Pablos, 2009.

Voy a explotar. Dir. Gerardo Naranjo. Perf. Juan Pablo de Santiago and María Deschamps. IFC Films, 2010. Digital videodisc.

Y tu mamá también. Dir. Alfonso Cuarón. Perf. Gael García Bernal, Diego Luna, and Maribel Verdú. IFC Films, 2002. Digital videodisc.

CHAPTER 7

FROM BUÑUEL TO EIMBCKE

ORPHANHOOD IN RECENT MEXICAN CINEMA

DAN RUSSEK

The orphan is a recurring figure in a number of Mexican films. While *Los olvidados* (*The Young and the Damned*; Luis Buñuel 1950) has generally been interpreted from the point of view of juvenile delinquency and urban poverty, the dramatic role played by orphanhood in Buñuel's film has not always been fully identified. In this essay, I use *Los olvidados* as a point of departure for examining the metaphorical function of orphanhood in *Temporada de patos* (*Duck Season*; 2004) and *Lake Tahoe* (2008) by Fernando Eimbcke (born 1970). Contrary to the often melodramatic take on human relations portrayed in Mexican cinema, my analysis will showcase the understated approach that Eimbcke—part of a talented crop of emerging Mexican filmmakers, which includes Carlos Reygadas and younger directors like Amat Escalante, Rodrigo Plá, Gerardo Naranjo, and Nicolas Pereda—applies to the subject of the orphan.[1]

According to the conventional definition, an orphan is "a person, especially a child, both of whose parents are dead (or, rarely, one of whose parents have died). In extended use: an abandoned or neglected child."[2] This definition underpins more specialized perspectives on the issue. According to sociologist Judith Ennew, "Although the most usual global definition of 'orphan' used in international work is a child with two deceased biological parents, this is by no means universal; orphans may have one or both parents alive, absent, or continuing to care for them. It is common, especially in cultures in which women do not have full economic and political independence, to refer to a child whose father is dead and mother alive as an 'orphan'" (129).

The category of the orphan can be expanded to encompass "children of widows, bi-parental orphans, abandoned children, children whose fathers have abandoned their mothers and many illegitimate children" (129). For Ennew, orphanhood is traditionally linked to dependency, noting the pairing between "widows and orphans" in the Bible. The orphan is also closely associated with the image of the unhappy child. Ennew points out that orphans have become, since the mid-nineteenth century, "the focus of charitable pity" (132) or, in the words of Patricia Holland, "the most deserving of all of our sympathy and aid" (qtd. in Ennew 132).

Beyond the potential ambiguities of these definitions, my purpose is to analyze the figure of the orphan understood literally but also as a metaphor and even as a sort of cultural rubric or pattern. In this sense, the orphan evokes situations or emotions of abandonment and helplessness that a child experiences with regard to his parents even if they have not died. To be an orphan is a metaphor for an existential void, a state in which one suffers the painful effects of the absence of an authority figure (be it familial, cultural, national, etc.). In this regard, orphanhood is functional: one parent, or even both of them, may be alive, but it is as if they did not exist for the child.

Buñuel's film offers panoply of cases in which the child lacks a father, a mother, or both.[3] All major characters, as well as secondary ones, suffer this fate. The main protagonist, Jaibo, leader of the neighborhood gang, never knew his parents; Pedrito, Jaibo's younger friend and later victim, is rejected by his mother, and his father never appears or even mentioned, because it is implied that Pedrito is the product of a rape; Ojitos, the poor peasant boy, was abandoned by his father when they arrived in the big city (no mention of his mother is made); and Meche, the young girl, lives with her sick mother, siblings, and grandfather but again no father is in sight.[4]

If the definition of the orphan applies mainly to children, Buñuel suggests that adults may also feel the neglect and helplessness that characterizes orphanhood. That is the case with the blind Don Carmelo, who pines for the paternal figure of a mythical Don Porfirio (in reference to the late nineteenth-century Mexican dictator Porfirio Díaz), who would restore social order with a firm hand. It is also the case of the father of Julián, the young worker killed by Jaibo when he thinks Julián had betrayed him. After this killing, we see the father shouting and wandering, drunk, in utter despair. In this case, the roles are reversed: the father, who relied on his son for guidance and support, becomes an orphan.

As critics of Buñuel have noted, the Spanish-Mexican director upsets the generic conventions of his time by creating a work that both adopts and subverts the conventions of melodrama (Fuentes, *Buñuel* 42–47; Fuentes, *Mundos* 75–78; Berthier 153, 162; Millán Agudo 17). In his case, there are no sentimental concessions to the audience when it comes to facing reality at its grimmest and most painful (Edwards 108; Fuentes, *Buñuel* 58–60). *Los olvidados* shows the viewer the unseen back of the social fabric in the modern metropolis. The film is a matrix of fractured family relations portrayed against the grain of the patriarchal model of the Mexican family precisely when Mexican economic modernization was taking hold in the mid-twentieth century, a period known as the "Mexican miracle" (Aguilar Camín and Meyer 159).

As a counterpart to *Los olvidados*, *Temporada de patos*, and *Lake Tahoe* are focalized on young teenagers, whom I will consider functional orphans. Not entirely vulnerable but still economically and psychologically dependent on adults, they occupy an ambivalent threshold between the largely carefree existence of the child and the future trials of the adult. Eimbcke's films deftly show the growing pains of his characters as specific to their age, family position, and social status. These films, having orphanhood as a central subject, reject the well-known tropes around poverty and marginality in order to examine the effects of abandonment and hopelessness in the context of the Mexican urban middle class. They do not follow in the footsteps of *Los olvidados* in any mechanical or obvious way. Eimbcke displaces or reinterprets the Buñuelesque tropes of urban violence and orphanhood that portray the disenchanted social reality in Mexico at the dawn of the twenty-first century.

In the case of Eimbcke, the causes of this disenchantment continue to be political and economic. The middle classes have been caught in an "incomplete 'second revolution,'" to use the phrase of the authors of the volume *Mexico since 1980* (Haber et al. 3). Positioned between an emerging democratic system that still carries the heavy burden of authoritarian and inefficient political institutions, the middle classes are caught as well between the small privileged elites and the masses of the poor. The title of the last two chapters of Aguilar Camín and Meyer's study on contemporary Mexican history captures accurately the malaise that pervades Mexican society since the end of the twentieth century: the fading of the miracle and the beginning of a painful transition. These Mexican historians stress the emergence in the last fifty years of the middle classes as a new social majority that does not conform to "proud Mexican traditions or to [. . .] folkloric clichés" (260). Mexico has experienced

> a new era of younger customs and social expressions. The manifestation of this fact is quite visible on the walls of the cities painted by gangs, in the demographic statistics, in the entertainment industry that has successfully created child and adolescent musical groups on the television screens, the theaters, the radio, and the bedroom walls of millions of Mexican youth. [. . .] a new majority integrated with the perspective of modernization and approximation to the "American Way of Life," a new majority without traditions, lay, urban, and massive, without whose social and mental history it will be impossible to comprehend the Mexico we live in, or imagine, even approximately, the Mexico that will come. (260)

Temporada de patos pointedly explores this new youth reality. Selected for the Semaine de la Critique at the Cannes Festival in 2004, it is, in the words of critic Karen Backstein, "a coming-of-age tale that explores family relationships, friendships, and budding erotic desire" (61). It features a couple of 14-year-olds: Flama; Moko; Rita, a young neighbor; and Ulises, a pizza delivery guy. The action takes place on a Sunday, from 11 in the morning to 8 at night, in an apartment in the traditional neighborhood of Tlatelolco in Mexico City. The film, shot in black and white, opens with a number of scenes that depict a charmless city: gray buildings, broad avenues, and empty spaces that set the tone for the events that follow.

As a point of comparison, Buñuel opens *Los olvidados* with a voice-over that warns the viewer about the social problems of juvenile delinquency in the world's biggest cities.[5] The viewer is then taken to the poor neighborhood where a group of boys are playing by reenacting the quintessentially sacrificial bullfight. As does Buñuel, Eimbcke also begins his film with a reference to violence but in an elliptical and indirect way, a strategy that defines his cinematographic style. These introductory shots connote minimal but also inescapable signs of urban violence and decay: a medium shot of a bicycle, without the rear wheel and chained to a pole, and a basketball hoop with a torn net. It is no coincidence that this barren, unwelcome territory will soon lead the viewer to the private space of an apartment where the events take place. If Buñuel's kids belong to the street (with all the excitement, risk, and abuse associated with it), Eimbcke chooses to explore orphanhood from the alleged safety offered by a middle-class home. This move could also be read as a symbolic entrenchment: the home affords a modicum of stability in the face of the seemingly endless economic and political crisis that has marked Mexican society since the early 1980s. However, before the director lets us in, it is worth mentioning one of the last establishing shots at the beginning of the film. In a low-angle shot of the facade of a building, we read up high the name of the apartment complex "niños héroes" (literally, child heroes). The name refers to the group of six cadets who died defending their school, the Heroic Military Academy, during the American Invasion of Mexico in 1847. The brief shot is more than a historical or urbanistic reference: it is a key, both premonitory and ironic, to the events that follow.

In *Los olvidados*, the young characters, to say it with a colloquial Mexican expression, "se la juegan" (they put their life on the line). Their survival instinct is tested at every turn in the hostile environment in which they survive. In this sense, they would have the right to be seen as heroes (even Jaibo, the darkly charismatic figure of Lucifer-like traits).[6] Pedrito, struggling against fate, is a hero in a tragic sense (Edwards 92). It is worth noting that his body, thrown into the garbage dump at the end of the film, bitterly mocks, in both gruesome and trivial terms, the legendary version of the "niño héroe" par excellence, Juan Escutia, who according to popular lore threw himself down the slope of the Chapultepec Castle, site of the military academy, with the Mexican flag wrapped around him to avoid capture by the invaders. In stark contrast to the individual trials of the children and adolescents in Buñuel's film, *Temporada de patos*, full of irony and postmodern apathy, offers no hint of heroism.[7] As Mexican critic Leonardo García Tsao points out, the film is, at least at first, "una exploración del aburrimiento" (an exploration of boredom; 126; see also Ayala Blanco "La patoaventura" 126–27). Little by little, however, with an understated narrative style, anger and violence emerge.

Flama, in whose apartment the action takes places, exemplifies what I have called functional orphanhood: his parents are still alive, but on a deeper level they are absent. The story begins with Flama's mother leaving the apartment after giving her son some money to buy pizza and soda. As the plot advances, we learn that Flama's parents are in the midst of divorce proceedings. If family strife in the lower classes means on many occasions that the father abandons the home without further procedure (enacting one of the most entrenched myths about the Mexican family structure), in the case of the middle classes, family conflict most often leads to a separation through legal means that seeks the distribution of family assets. This emphasis on goods and properties, this fetishism of material belongings so common in the petty bourgeoisie, explodes toward the end of *Temporada de patos*. Flama will give free rein to his frustration and anger when he talks about his parents' behavior. Fighting over the home decorations and gadgets, they seem to care more about things than Flama's emotional well-being or the family's unity. His revenge comes when he grabs a pellet gun and begins shooting all those dear and breakable objects in the living room. Before embarking on this shooting spree with Moko, he ironically tells his friend, in reference to his own parents, "Vamos a ayudarlos a decidir quien se queda con el pinche jarroncito chino" (We are going to help them decide who keeps the damned Chinese vase). What follows is the home's destruction, literally and figuratively. Eimbcke transposes to the domestic sphere what happened in the public space in Buñuel's *Los olvidados*. At the beginning of *Temporada de patos*, the kids seem mainly preoccupied with filling their glasses to the top with soda, eating junk food until the pizza they ordered arrives, and glued to the TV while shooting at the virtual targets of a video game. By the end, the violence has become real, devastating the ornaments on the shelves and scattering pieces of pottery and glass on the floor of the apartment as if the outburst was triggered by the realization of the family's dysfunctions.

The lack of an authority figure brings to the surface a hidden violence, one that nonetheless was there from the start.

The pizza delivery guy, Ulises, perhaps in his late twenties, may have qualified as an authority figure if he himself were not so insecure and hapless. After unsuccessfully pleading with the kids to be paid for the pizza he allegedly delivered a few seconds late, he stays in the apartment and joins them in conversation. He behaves like a child when he accepts a dare by Moko: they will play a video game and if he loses, they will not pay for the pizza. We later learn about his ill-conceived plans to get money, as well as his descent into the hole of dead-end jobs that lead him to his current delivery position. His knowledge about animal behavior provides a clue about the missing link in his life (as well as in Flama's and Rita's). While everybody, seated on the couch, is looking attentively at a painting of a lake and mountains with a few ducks in the foreground, Ulises explains why ducks fly in V formation. It turns out that this shape helps them support each other by better managing the air currents. It is this "beautiful design, a remarkably cooperative one" (Backstein 62) that speaks of a marvelous, natural solidarity that is precisely what is missing in the group's social interactions. The bucolic painting, which gives the title to the film, serves as an allegorical representation (at least in Ulises's version) since it renders a moral ideal visible. For Ulises, the painting has a utopian quality, literally an escape door to greener pastures (Robey 48). The end of the film shows him riding his motorcycle with the painting on the back, in a gesture of both literal and symbolic appropriation.

Temporada de patos explores orphanhood in a variety of ways. There are clues that point to Flama's anxiety about his origins, especially in the scene where the characters—who have just eaten (unaware) some marijuana brownies that the neighbor Rita has baked—leaf through a family album. Flama, perhaps because of the drug, cannot quite recognize himself in the photographs and does not see any resemblance between himself and his parents. The rest of the characters, instead of reassuring him, suggest that maybe he is adopted. In this case, if Flama is not the son of the couple he thinks are his parents, then he is an orphan with respect to his "real," unknown parents. Eimbcke's indirect and elliptical style brings to the fore, without grand melodramatic gestures, the specter of orphanhood in Flama's life.

There are other moments like this. Just after Flama and Moko have comfortably settled in front of the TV with their snacks and sodas, the power goes off leaving them in a sort of premodern limbo.[8] Moments before, Rita rang the bell asking to use the kitchen. She spends most of the day cooking, as well as flirting with Moko. By the end, after eating the marijuana brownies that she has baked, she reveals that today was her birthday. She adds, almost crying, that "en casa se les olvidó" (they forgot about it at home). On the face of it, it is certainly odd that a family member could forget such a day. The same elliptical strategy employed by the director in the film is now assimilated by Rita, who does not reveal the situation at home, letting us only imagine what may be going on (we know that she has a mother that smokes pot "only" on weekends). If what she says, taken literally, might not seem too plausible, what transpires is again a state of helplessness and neglect. Even if we do not know who exactly is living in Rita's apartment, and who exactly forgot about her birthday, what remains is the poignancy of her feelings.

If in *Temporada de patos* orphanhood is mostly virtual, in *Lake Tahoe* (Eimbcke's second feature) orphanhood becomes literal and located at the center of the action. The film presents a day in the life of Juan, a youngster who crashes the family car in the morning and spends the rest of the day trying to fix it. The action happens in the port of Progreso, north of Mérida, in Yucatán. Juan spends the day looking for someone who could replace a broken part and along the way befriends an old and cranky mechanic, Don Heber; Lucía, a teenage mother in charge of an auto repair store (whose baby's father, yet again, is missing); and finally,

David, a young mechanic who ends up fixing Juan's car while trying to introduce him to the fascinating world of martial arts. The car as a symbol of autonomy and agency is fairly transparent: by managing to fix the broken car, Juan proves that he is now a young responsible adult.[9] His pilgrimage through the mostly desolate city streets (very much a reflection of his own state of mind) seems like a chapter of a coming-of-age story, a tale of growth and maturity that goes well beyond his immediate problem: as the plot advances, we learn that his father has recently died and his mother remains at home, depressed and bedridden. It is Juan who has to leave behind whatever is left of his childhood, overcome his daze, and face his problems in the best possible way.

The first encounter with a fatherly figure is not auspicious. Juan enters the gates of Taller Don Heber (Mr. Heber's auto repair shop) politely shouting "¡Buenos días!" (Good morning!), but the next shot shows him seated still on a chair while a sturdy dog, his back facing the camera, keeps a close eye on him. The first thing Juan tells Don Heber, who quickly enters the field of vision, is "no entré a robar" (I didn't come in to steal), to which Don Heber, who looks like an overweight and slovenly patriarch, replies, "eso se lo vas a explicar a la policía" (that you will have to explain to the police). To add to Juan's sense of helplessness, a bit later Don Heber serves himself some cereal with milk, and then pours some in a second bowl. Juan, silently seated at the table, thanks him but points out that he already had breakfast. Don Heber barely looks at him, and then calls his dog, Sica. It turns out that the bowl of cereal was not intended for Juan, but for the dog. Don Heber will not follow through on his threats and eventually Juan leaves. He later returns to Don Heber's with the car part. Before going to fix the car, Don Heber asks Juan a favor: to take the dog for a walk. Juan accepts, despite his hurry to get back to his car. Next, we see him walking the dog or, rather, being dragged by it. Interestingly, on a shot precisely outside the cemetery, we see Sica running by, unleashed, and Juan desperately shouting her name, chasing after her. He does not manage to retrieve the dog and goes back to Lucía's store. Later in the day, once the car has been fixed, Juan finds Don Heber by chance in the street. He is looking for his dog, and Juan explains to him what happened. They both get in the car and try to find the dog. Finally they see her, but when Heber realizes that the dog is happily playing with some kids in a patio, he asks Juan to drive and leave the place. The dog has found a new home, and Don Heber, now deprived of his companion, has become himself a sort of orphan.

Lake Tahoe offers fewer parallels with *Los olvidados* than *Temporada de patos*, but the contrasts between them are nonetheless revealing. In *Lake Tahoe* Juan roams the mostly deserted city streets engaged in a personal quest: no urban poverty or gang violence is in sight. In contrast to Buñuel's host of young characters, Juan shows a solid moral compass, as it is on full display with his apologies to Don Heber upon entering his house. It is the way violence is featured that sets *Lake Tahoe* apart from Buñuel's film. The daily fight for survival, central to *Los olvidados*, is lacking in the lives of Juan and David, middle-class characters who enjoy a low-key, but largely secure, existence in a sleepy provincial town. *Lake Tahoe* offers a picture of a world where violence is largely under control. In this sense, David's devotion to martial arts represents the triumph of will over blind force and raw emotion. In spite of his mellow disposition, it is Juan who performs the only explicit act of violence in the film: one directed against the car, the source of his troubles. It happens at the end of the day, after David playfully challenges Juan to fight with him. Instead, Juan, his frustrations bubbling up to the surface, smashes the hood of the family vehicle with a baseball bat. While in *Los olvidados* aggression is directed against the other, as if the city were above all a stage for collective strife, *Lake Tahoe* makes use of violence as an exceptional moment of emotional release.

If Juan is now becoming the man in the family, this role is made more prominent by the relationship he maintains with his younger sibling, Joaquín. While the film centers on Juan, his brother is no less a portrait of the orphan, and perhaps even more so. I have mentioned Eimbcke's indirect style of approaching human drama, and this is particularly true in the case of Joaquín.[10] While the camera follows Juan walking on the streets and coming in and out of houses and stores, the brother remains at home, and mostly out of sight, for the length of the film. Interestingly enough, he has become homeless in his own home: we find him spending the day in a tent he has set up in the sandy patio of the house, a child's game that is also an emblem of a precarious shelter. If Juan's mourning is cushioned by his automotive adventures, the younger brother has to suffer in silence, with some toys around him and with his depressed mother never too far away. According to Maria Delgado, Eimbcke observes his characters "from afar, respecting their privacy and secrets" (74); but in the case of Joaquín, this respect may be felt as indifference and may even border on abandonment. Not only does the father "abandon" Joaquín with his death; the mother, confined to her bedroom, largely ignores her younger son, and Juan spends most of the day in the streets. Eimbcke himself, by mostly focusing on the problems of the older brother, and hardly addressing the younger brother's pain, leaves Joaquín to his own fate.

Juan's own loneliness is apparent throughout the film, but some scenes are particularly poignant. After David verifies what part is needed to fix the car, they go back to his house, and before heading to the store to get the part, they have breakfast. There, David's mother, a devout protestant, prays and preaches the word of God to Juan. She reads a biblical passage about the corruption of the flesh and the resurrection of the dead, certainly not the most appropriate topics for a youngster grieving the recent loss of his father (and yet again, no father is present, or even mentioned, at David's house). After respectfully listening to the mother, Juan leaves the table saying that he is going to the bathroom, but decides instead to sneak out of the house. He then returns to his home to check on his brother Joaquín and his mother, who is taking a bath. She has been smoking too much and, ostensibly, crying. Interestingly, on the edge of the bathtub there are, somewhat implausibly but tellingly, two or three open family albums and some pictures, as if to emphasize the need to recreate the lost familiar presence.

Those family albums prefigure Joaquín's own scrapbook. While Juan is in charge of the family's car, the younger brother is in possession of other tangible signs of the lost father: first, he has a baseball uniform that the father used to wear; and second, an album where he keeps family pictures and other memorabilia. The scrapbook is important in a number of ways. Only there do we see, in effigy, the father. He appears in three cut-out pictures (in one of them, a close-up shows his two sons kissing him on each cheek). By the end of the film, while Juan is browsing through the album, Joaquín arrives and snatches it from his hands saying "¡Qué te pasa, es mío!" (What's the matter with you, it's mine!). Joaquín has spent the day assembling the album, a symbolic site of a possessive love whose object is hopelessly lost. Moreover, it is the scrapbook that will hold the secret of the movie's title: Lake Tahoe refers to a decal brought by an aunt and glued to the back of the car that Juan crashed. Juan rips off the decal and gives it to Joaquín who sticks it in the album. Joaquín believes that the family once traveled to Lake Tahoe, but Juan clarifies that they themselves never went there. Juan even tells him that their father never liked the decal. Thus Juan points out the disjunction between the material sign treasured by Joaquín, and the father's own dismissive opinion of the same visual token. The film ends shortly after, compounding its melancholic tone with this last reference to separation or divergence.[11]

In conclusion, if Buñuel set the stage with *Los olvidados* for an exploration of poor youths on the margins of the sprawling contemporary city, Eimbcke contributes to this filmic tradition with a study of helpless young adults from the middle class. Although Flama, Juan, and Joaquín seem to represent specific domestic situations, they could be seen nonetheless as representing the sizable population of the Latin American middle classes today.[12] In the case of Buñuel's film, the focus on the popular classes was linked to the failure of modernity in a time when national identity was being consolidated. Eimbcke's films deal with a very different social reality: one that reflects the cultural dislocations that globalization and neoliberalism have produced in Mexican society since the early 1980s.

The focalization on teenagers allows the director to explore the problems of today's middle-class youth without an explicit reference to urban decay, political crisis, or lack of economic opportunities. Too young to really care but old enough to be affected by the social circumstances around them, Flama, Moko, Juan, and David live their lives in a sort of suspension that inevitably will not last long. Eimbcke explores the ways these adolescents negotiate, from a position of both resilience and inexperience, the challenges that reality has thrown their way. They are not portrayed merely as victims of their environment, as are their counterparts in many other films about social violence. Eimbcke's films are less about social critique than about personal drama, and by avoiding sentimental, melodramatic or falsely tragic gestures, the director allows the viewer to engage with the troubles of the protagonists in an empathetic way.

Eimbcke's work has already made a contribution with his original portrayal of kids looking for direction during their tumultuous teenage years. The volatility often associated with adolescence parallels the current social, political, and economic insecurity in Mexico and the subsequent precarious situation of the middle class. Eimbcke presciently and subtly distills the metaphorical construction of orphanhood, accommodating Buñuel's portrayal of orphans to complement our evolving understanding of the repercussions of postmodern society and globalization. Though he gives prominence to the effects of personal tragedy on the middle-class family, we are also reminded of the vulnerability of youth in a country whose population under the age of 15 is close to 30 percent (United Nations 2003). *Temporada de patos* and *Lake Tahoe* are both told with sobriety and humor and achieve one of the most engaging commentaries on orphanhood in recent Mexican cinema.

Notes

1. The cinematic treatment of orphanhood in Mexican cinema can be traced to one of its foundational films, *La mujer del puerto* (*The Woman of the Port*; 1934) by Arcady Boytler. The protagonist, Rosario, cheated by her boyfriend, begins her descent into a life of wretchedness and prostitution when her father dies. While she cannot be considered a child, the helplessness in which she finds herself is as poignant as if she were a minor. Orphanhood also makes a prominent appearance in yet another iconic film, *Nosotros los pobres* (1948) by Ismael Rodríguez. This classic includes one of the highest (or, depending on the viewer's point of view, lowest) melodramatic moments in the history of Mexican cinema. The drama of interwoven lives in a poor neighborhood reaches its climax when Chachita, an orphan girl, having grown with the idea that her mother is dead, discovers that her mother was none other than the despised neighborhood's prostitute. In a wrenching scene, the poor girl finds out about this secret life on her mother's deathbed. A number of recent Mexican films feature fatherless protagonists. In *El callejón de los milagros* (*Midaq Alley*; 1994) by Jorge Fons, the tragic fate of Alma, who went from being the prettiest girl in her neighborhood to high-flying prostitute, could plausibly be traced to the lack of a paternal figure at home. In the first story of González Iñárritu's interlaced drama *Amores perros* (2000), the brothers Octavio and Ramiro live in a home without a father. A particularly interesting exploration of abuse of young women and the lack of protecting family figures in contemporary Mexican society is found in the films of Marise Systach's *Nadie te oye: Perfume de violetas* (*Violet Perfume: No One Is Listening*; 2001) and *La niña en la piedra* (*The Girl on the Stone*; 2006). In films such as *Lolo* (1992) by Francisco Athié, *Angel de fuego* (1992) by Dana Rotberg, and *De la calle* (*Streeters*; 2001) by Gerardo Tort, the absence of the father is at the center of the dramatic fate suffered by the young protagonists. The descent into urban hell featured in these last films has made critics point out their clear Buñuelesque features (Aviña, "Los Hijos" 301–4; Ayala Blanco, "El neobreviario" 76–77; Foster 85–86).
2. From the outset, it is interesting to note a different emphasis is found in the standard English definition than in the Spanish one. According to the *Diccionario de la Real Academia Española*, an orphan is "una persona de menor edad a quien se le han muerto el padre y la madre o uno de los dos" (a minor whose father and mother, or one of them, has died). The Spanish definition lacks the qualifier "rarely" that the English definition applies to the case when only one of the parents has died or disappeared. This may point perhaps to a sociocultural conception of the family in the Hispanic world that considers the absence of one of the parents more prevalent than in developed English-speaking countries.
3. Before shooting the film, Buñuel began writing with Spanish poet Juan Larrea the screenplay titled "¡Mi huerfanito, jefe!" about a child lottery vendor; it was never produced. "Huerfanito" here refers to the last lottery ticket that vendors sell (de la Colina 55). For a review of Mexican films featuring children, see Aviña, "El cine infantil y los niños en el cine."

4. Orphanhood is not merely an individual condition, but a social structure that shapes in multiple ways the characters' profiles, behaviors, and interactions. In this regard, Evans points out that "like the significantly named Ojitos, who constantly seeks his absent father and submits himself to the law of the stern patriarch Don Carmelo, Pedro also looks for the approval of surrogate fathers, constantly gravitating towards figures of male authority, such as the owner of the forge or the warden at the reformatory" (86). Evans, further commenting on the role of animals in *Los olvidados*, refers to the donkey as "a figure of surrogate motherhood—her teats sucked dry by the famished Ojitos—for Peter-Pan like boys looking for absent mothers and mother substitutes" (82). Nancy Berthier quotes a study by Julie Amiot that compares *Los olvidados* to a melodrama by Juan Orol from 1935 centered on the figure of the mother, *Madre querida* (153). In his account of *Los olvidados*, Buñuel tells the story of a hairdresser on the set who had suddenly quit during the shooting in protest of the scene in which Pedrito's mother rejects her son. By claiming that "no Mexican mother would ever do such a thing," the hairdresser gives credence to the mythic image of the self-sacrificing mother (Luis Buñuel 1983, 200). For a feminist debunking of the myth of the selfless Mexican mother, see Lamas, "¿Madrecita santa?"

5. The voice-over states, "Las grandes ciudades modernas, Nueva York, París, Londres, esconden tras sus magníficos edificios hogares de miseria que albergan niños malnutridos, sin higiene, sin escuela, semillero de futuros delincuentes. La sociedad trata de corregir este mal, pero el éxito de sus esfuerzos es muy limitado. Sólo en un futuro próximo podrán ser reivindicados los derechos del niño y del adolescente para que sean útiles a la sociedad. México, la gran ciudad moderna, no es excepción a esta regla universal, por eso esta película basada en hechos de la vida real no es optimista, y deja la solución del problema a las fuerzas progresivas de la sociedad" (Behind their magnificent buildings, all great modern cities, like New York, Paris, or London, hide humble houses full of malnourished and unclean children with no schooling. They are nesting grounds of future criminals. Society tries to correct this disease, but the results of its efforts are very limited. Only in the near future will children's and teen's rights be vindicated for them to be useful in society. Mexico, the great modern city, is no exception to this universal rule. That's why this film, based on true facts, is not optimistic. It leaves the solution up to society's progressive forces; my translation) Donna Guy, who gives a general overview of attitudes about street children in Latin America during the nineteenth and first half of the twentieth century, writes that "by the 1950s, many governments had enacted legislation to deal with abandoned infants and youths as well as with the thorny problem of juvenile delinquency" (160). The scene in the reformatory in *Los olvidados* refers to this beneficial intervention of the state. However, the film foregrounds the anxiety over modernity and underdevelopment by focusing on one of the obstacles to progress: the orphans in the street, which is a "semillero de futuros delincuentes" (nesting grounds of future criminals; my translation).

6. Julio Cortázar, in his review of *Los olvidados*, calls Jaibo "un ángel," implying that he is a fallen one.
7. In this regard, Podalsky points out that "it is now commonplace to characterize contemporary young adults as apathetic, indifferent to the horrors of the recent past, and lacking a sense of social solidarity as well as any totalizing view of society. It should be noted that many scholars do not 'blame' young adults for their apathy and lack of sociopolitical commitment, but rather see the 'apolitical sensibility' of contemporary youth as a result of the failures of social institutions (schools, family) and the larger political apparatus as well as of the seductive powers of 'postmodern culture,' often defined as the unfettered power of the marketplace" (115).
8. Perhaps we, urban dwellers, also become helpless "orphans" of modernity when the electrical power is interrupted in our daily lives.
9. A sense of continuity and development is established with *Temporada de patos*, since Juan is played by the same actor who played Moko, Diego Cataño.
10. In this case, the approach may also apply to the director himself. Eimbcke has mentioned that *Lake Tahoe* has an autobiographical origin: "Meses después de la muerte de mi padre, choqué el único automóvil de la familia, y no creo que haya sido un simple accidente. *Lake Tahoe* nació como un intento de entender las razones que me empujaron a cometer ese acto tan absurdo y tan profundamente humano" (Months after my father's death, I crashed the family's only car, and I don't think it was just an accident. *Lake Tahoe* was born from my attempt to understand what compelled me to commit such an absurd, yet very human act; Cineteca Nacional 216–17).
11. As with the painting in *Temporada de patos*, Eimbcke employs an indirect approach to point toward the unattainable desire for fulfillment. The absence of the father, of the "good" old times, and in general, of the object of longing, can never be fully grasped but only alluded to through the always precarious means of material signs, be they cheap paintings, photographs in albums, or decals in scrapbooks. Visual signs are not merely fetishes; they seem to have a life of their own, endlessly migrating with their human owners and aiding their imaginations to spin peculiar, impossible stories, as Ulises experiences in front of the painting in Flama's apartment.
12. Franco, Hopenhayn, and León point out that "in the period from 1990 to before the 2008 crisis, the number of middle-class households and their average incomes both grew" and "the number increased by 14 million households" in Mexico (23). Among the reasons they give for this phenomenon are the incorporation of women into the labor market, new consumption patterns and lifestyles, the emergence of industries that make affordable otherwise expensive consumer goods to a wide number of the population, available credit, and the increase in international trade. Their essay provides an updated bibliography on the subject of the middle classes in Latin America. See also the website of the Latin American Economic Outlook, which devoted its 2011 report to the question, "How middle class is in Latin America?"

Works Cited

Aguilar Camín, Héctor, and Lorenzo Meyer. *In the Shadow of the Mexican Revolution: Contemporary Mexican History, 1910–1989.* Trans. Luis Alberto Fierro. Austin: U of Texas P, 2001.
Aviña, Rafael. "Los hijos de *Los olvidados*." *Los olvidados: Una película de Luis Buñuel.* Ed. Agustín Sánchez Vidal México: Fundación Televisa, 2004. 285–309.
———. "El cine infantil y los niños en el cine." *Una mirada insólita: Temas y géneros del cine mexicano.* México: Oceáno, 2004. 109–17.
Ayala Blanco, Jorge. "El neobreviario de podredumbre." *La grandeza del cine mexicano.* México: Océano, 2004. 73–77.
———. "La patoaventura pasiva." *La herética del cine mexicano.* México: Océano, 2006. 123–31.
Backstein, Karen. "Duck Season." *Cineaste* 31.3 (2006): 60–62.
Berthier, Nancy. "La trasnacionalidad en el cine de Luis Buñuel." *Abismos de pasión: Una historia de las relaciones cinematográficas hispano-mexicanas.* Ed. Eduardo de la Vega Alfaro and Alberto Elena. Madrid: Filmoteca Española, 2009. 147–71.
Buñuel, Luis. *My Last Sigh.* Trans. Abigail Israel. New York: Knopf, 1983.
Cineteca Nacional. "Fernando Eimbcke." *50 Cineastas de Iberoamérica: Generaciones en Tránsito 1980–2008. 1er. Congreso de la Cultura Iberoamericana.* México: Cineteca Nacional e Instituto Mexicano de Cinematografía, 2008. 215–17.
Cortázar, Julio. "Luis Buñuel: *Los olvidados*." *Obra Crítica.* Vol. 2. Madrid: Alfaguara, 1994. 251–56.
De la Colina, José, and Tomás Perez Turrent. *Luis Buñuel: Prohibido asomarse al interior.* México: Planeta, 1996.
Delgado, Maria. "Lake Tahoe." *Sight and Sound* 19.9 (2009): 74.
Edwards, Gwynne. *The Discrete Art of Luis Buñuel.* London: Boyars, 1982.
Eimbcke, Fernando, dir. *Lake Tahoe.* Distrimax, 2008. Digital videodisc.
———. *Temporada de patos* [*Duck Season*]. Distrimax, 2004. Digital videodisc.
Ennew, Judith. "Prisoners of Childhood: Orphans and Economic Dependency." *Studies in Modern Childhood: Society, Agency, Culture.* Ed. Jens Qvortrup. New York: Palgrave Macmillan, 2005. 128–46.
Evans, Peter William. *The Films of Luis Buñuel: Subjectivity and Desire.* Oxford: Clarendon, 1995.
Foster, David William. *Mexico City in Contemporary Mexican Cinema.* Austin: U of Texas P, 2002.
Franco, Rolando, Martin Hopenhayn, and Arturo León. "The Growing and Changing Middle Class in Latin America: an Update." *CEPAL Review* 103. April 2001. 7–25. 25. Web. Mar 2012. <http://www.cepal.org/publicaciones/xml/7/44057/RVI103Hopenhaynetal.pdf>.
Fuentes, Victor. *Buñuel en México: Iluminaciones sobre una pantalla pobre.* Teruel: Instituto de Estudios Turolenses, 1993.
———. *Los mundos de Buñuel.* Madrid: Ediciones Akal, 2000.
García Tsao, Leonardo. "Patologías de hoy." *El ojo y la navaja.* México: Punto de Lectura, 2008. 125–27.

Guy, Donna. "The State, the Family, and Marginal Children in Latin America." *Minor Omissions: Children in Latin American History and Society*. Ed. Tobias Hecht. Madison: U of Wisconsin P, 2002. 139–65.

Haber, Stephen, Herbert S. Klein, Noel Maurer, and Kevin J. Middlebrook. *Mexico since 1980*. Cambridge: Cambridge UP, 2008.

"Huérfano." *Diccionario de la Lengua Española*. 2001. Real Academia Española. 25 Mar. 2012. <http://www.rae.es/rae.html>

Lake Tahoe. Dir. Fernando Eimbcke. Perf. Diego Cataño, Diego Herrera, Daniela Valentine, and Juan Carlos Lara II. [0]Distrimax, 2008. Digital videodisc.

Lamas, Marta. "¿Madrecita santa?" *Mitos mexicanos*. México: Taurus, 2001. 223–29.

"Latin American Economic Outlook 2011: How Middle-Class is Latin America?" *Latameconomy.com*. Web. 25 Mar. 2012. <http://www.latameconomy.org/en/in-depth/2011/>.

Millán Agudo, Francisco J. *Las huellas de Buñuel*. Teruel: Instituto de Estudios Turolenses, 2004.

Olvidados, Los [The Young and the Damned]. Dir. Luis Buñuel. Perf. Roberto Cobo, Estela Inda, Alfonso Mejía, and Miguel Inclán. Televisa, 1950. Digital videodisc.

Podalsky, Laura. "Out of Depth: The Politics of Disaffected Youth and Contemporary Latin American Cinema." *Youth Culture in Global Cinema*. Ed. Timothy Shary and Alexander Seibel. Austin: U of Texas P, 2007. 109–30.

Robey, Tim. "Duck Season." *Sight and Sound* 15.3 (2005): 47–48.

Temporada de patos [Duck Season]. Dir. Fernando Eimbcke. Perf. Daniel Miranda, Diego Cataño, Danny Perea, and Eduardo Arreola. [0]Distrimax, 2004. Digital videodisc.

United Nations. "América latina: Población por años calendario y edades simples 1995–2005. Latin America: Population by Calendar Years and Single Ages" *Demographic Bulletin* 36.71 (Jan. 2003): 5–26. <http://www.eclac.cl/publicaciones/xml/2/11942/LCG2197_inicio-i.pdf>.

CHAPTER 8

THROUGH "THEIR" EYES

INTERNAL AND EXTERNAL FOCALIZING AGENTS IN THE REPRESENTATION OF CHILDREN AND VIOLENCE IN IBERIAN AND LATIN AMERICAN FILM

EDUARDO LEDESMA

APPROACHES TO THE REPRESENTATION(ING) AND FOCALIZATION(ING) OF CHILDHOOD VIOLENCE

Socially motivated filmmaking involving issues of children and violence often oscillates uneasily between two opposing tendencies: the committed and the exploitative film. As Owain Jones claims, the depiction of violence by and against children is in itself a powerful and significant theme "because of the way society considers children as natural and vulnerable, the violence that they, and all, are exposed to is more visible" (201–2). One way in which films about children and youth violence might engage viewers politically and avoid the exploitative element is by bringing the adult spectator's perception closer to the child's subjective experience and worldview through the use of inner focalization. The focus of this essay shall be on the children, the violence directed against them or committed by them, and how the degree of voice and focalization they are allowed by the filmic style might either activate the audience's deepest fears or elicit sympathy and understanding, perhaps even empathy.[1] To explore these concerns I will examine two very different films that depict the lives of marginalized urban children and youth: *Rodrigo D: No futuro*[2] (Víctor Gaviria 1990) from Colombia and *El Bola* (Achero Mañas 2000) from Spain.[3]

Producing a socially committed film that depicts children faithfully, while allowing them a space of their own, is a daunting task. The tenuous boundary separating the exploitative misery porn from the committed social film might hinge on the connection that the spectator forges with the characters through a conflation of looks (of the camera, of the character, of the spectator). The success or failure of this *conflation* of looks is itself dependent on the spectator's bridging of a complex multilayered otherness that constitutes the characters, an otherness founded on cultural, linguistic, and more importantly for this essay, age-based differences.

By depicting children who are often trapped in spaces of abjection,[4] and confined by the claustrophobic poverty of the urban or sub-urban slums that surround them, these films attempt a social critique of the status quo. Children are specially poised to represent issues of marginality, on account of their special condition of alterity. According to Naomi Sokoloff, children are "the objects on whom adults foist their highest hopes and deepest fears and insecurities"; and, by virtue of their constant growth and change, they challenge adults' fixed attitudes, and therefore "children figures in narrative may serve to put into relief with special acuity the limited understandings, feelings, and perceptions of those who attempt to describe them" (239). How might the child's perspective be articulated or "focalized," to use Gérard Genette's (and Mieke Bal's) term, in the narratives of violence? Is the articulation of a child's perspective desirable, or possible, from an adult subject position?

Answering these questions might prove quite challenging. The degree to which the narrative might, at least in theory, adopt (focalize) the perspective of the child might go from one extreme (complete detachment of the spectator from the child) to its opposite, an idealized merging with the child's perspective (complete identification of the spectator with the child). Clearly, the position and use of the camera has much to do with this, as it serves the function of situating the spectator within a particular perspective. In a case of minimal focalization, the *detached* camera position is not aligned with any of the actors' point of view (POV); in an external focalization approach the perspective of one character is established through occasional POV shots and by following the character around; and in an internal focalization (the third case and closest to a complete identification), this approach is achieved by aligning the camera with the characters' exact POV, looking through his or her eyes. Naturally, this articulates the child's physical perspective, while his psychological or mental subjectivity is much more difficult to render, possibly outside of the adult filmmaker's capabilities, unless the child or youth actors are given a great deal of participation/voice in the process of the film's creation. It is altogether a different question to consider whether this type of narrative exercise is desirable or whether it amounts to a colonizing practice that imposes adult perspectives and forms of age-based oppression on the young actors/characters. Considered from this angle the adult narrative might be construed as *forcing* an adult identification on the child character, collapsing adult and child perspectives in a way that effaces the child's subjectivity and the profound differences between children and adults. Furthermore these representations of children, well intentioned or not, might result in "regimes and spaces of control, care and provision and assumptions about what individual children are and what they need. For example the vulnerable, incompetent notions of childhood can lead to children's lives being highly restricted in terms of autonomous engagement with the environment" (Jones 201). The counter argument that promotes the importance of attempting to make films from a child's or youth's perspective claims that it is desirable to do so, to the extent that the film might construct a model or worldview in which "viewing knowledge as position-dependent enhances one's ability to imagine standpoint's different from one's own," to empathize with an "other" (Margolin 41).

The issues I have outlined thus far are best explored in the context of specific films about children. From the slums of Medellín called "cinturones de miseria" (misery belts) to the working-class neighborhoods in Madrid (such as Carabanchel or Lavapiés), children who are ignored, abused, or abandoned by their families, the state, and society at large, find a voice in the films I will examine. In the case of *Rodrigo D*, the family plays virtually no role in the lives of the teen characters, while in *El Bola* the family unit is dysfunctional and plays a negative role in the child's life. These children inhabit large geographical peripheries or nomadic spaces of abjection where those displaced by poverty, drugs, and armed conflict (Colombia) or by urban growth and immigration patterns (Spain) attempt to organize their lives amid chaos and violence. *Rodrigo D* deals with the impact of street violence, drugs, and urban decay on a group of young adolescents in the slums of Medellín's *comunas* (poor neighborhoods). In *El Bola*, we are presented with a story of domestic violence, the case of a child whose father physically and psychologically abuses him.

Both films have generated debates about what type of genre they belong to, and whether they are motivated by political and social intent. Both films strive toward a *realist* portrayal of children's lives, and both projects are potentially frustrated by issues of spectator interpretation. Their filmmaking approaches differ greatly: *El Bola* uses a mostly professional cast (with the exception of the child actors), continuity editing, and a crisp scripted style, which arguably conforms to classical Hollywood films. *Rodrigo D* uses a gritty style (and no binding script), at times neorealist and at times bordering on amateur or experimental cinema, freely combining long static shots with handheld camera takes, and using a cast of nonprofessional adolescent actors.

Beyond these genre considerations, both films, I would argue, purport to offer the child's perspective, to *focalize* the child. Focalization, according to Mieke Bal, is "the relation between the vision and that which is 'seen,' perceived" ("Focalization" 116). *Rodrigo D* uses internal focalization, while *El Bola* resorts to external focalization. As Bal defines these categories, "when focalization lies within one character which participates in the *fabula* [story] as an actor, we can refer to *internal* focalization. We can then indicate by means of the term *external* focalization that an anonymous agent, situated outside the fabula, is functioning as focalizer" ("Focalization" 119). Expanding on the definition and clarifying the role of the focalizer, Bal states that in internal focalization, "the 'focalized' character sees," while in external focalization "s/he does not see, s/he is seen" (*Narrative Theory* 270). The use of several of the adolescents as internal focalizers (as we both see *them* and see *through their eyes*) in *Rodrigo D* serves the purpose of approaching the adult spectator to the youth's subjectivity, while the preponderance of an external focalizer in *El Bola* (where mainly we see Pablo from an external POV) results in a less direct identification with its child protagonist, as the spectator adopts the position of the sympathetic and protective (but distanced) adult. In the first instance, we are made to *feel* what the Colombian youths feel; in the second, we only *observe* what the Madrid children experience. In *Rodrigo D* this focal position is further complicated since the intimate filming style (i.e., gritty neorealist aesthetic, point-of-view shots) serves to meld the external and internal focalizers, achieving a conflating effect described by Bal: "The identification between the external focalizer in visual images and an internal focalizer represented in the image can [. . .] give rise to such a conflation, which would then strengthen the appeal to identification" (*Narratology* 164). The (simplified) assumption is that *Rodrigo D* renders the adolescents as free subjects with a degree of agency, while *El Bola* renders the child protagonist as an innocent victim deserving of our sympathy and protection, but/because he is unable to fend for himself. Next we will examine in what specific ways Víctor Gaviria's film *Rodrigo D* activates focalization to render a narrative of youth violence and hopelessness in Medellín, Colombia.

Internal Focalizer(s) in *Rodrigo D: No Futuro* and the Exploitation of the Image

Rodrigo D puts on display the daily life of a group of adolescent friends (*parcheros*) in the mean streets of the Comuna Nororiental (Medellín) as they seek entertainment and street credit through crime in a city that offers them no future. These nonprofessional actors *acted* real-life scenarios following a loose script, which was altered as circumstances developed, influenced by Italian neorealism as well as the tradition of *testimonio*. The looseness of the script and familiar setting facilitated a blending of reality and fiction, further enhanced through the reality of violence in the adolescent actors' lives. In *Rodrigo D*, art and life were so intertwined that several of the film's young protagonists involved in the criminal life of the *sicarios* (hitmen) or *pistolocos* (hired guns) met violent death even before the film's completion. The film serves to document the intersection between youth culture and drug violence in Medellín.[5]

After its release the film was attacked by some Colombian critics, both because of the tragic outcomes of the lives of its actors and because of the perception that it glorified the life of the cartels' pistolocos. Admittedly the premature, violent deaths of several adolescent participant *nonactors* pose ethical questions, as does the questionable dedication eulogizing them in the end credits.[6] This is why, on this account, *Rodrigo D* might be said to traffic in images, drawing on our fascination (at once attraction and repulsion) with poverty and violence, to produce a sterile and disconcerting film presenting an aestheticized violence that permeates the narrative and resides on all sides of society: the *legal* violence of the state (as represented by the torture and death of Johncito at the hands of paramilitaries) and the *delinquent* violence the teens engage in (as represented by the thefts, carjackings, mock knife fights, and the murder in the final scene). Rodrigo—the only character that might have some future for himself—commits suicide, ending his life through a desperate act of self-violence.

The shocking last sequence attempts (perhaps hopelessly) to merge the subjectivities of child character/actor and adult spectator through its cinematic technique and affective force. The senseless killing of one of the boys, Ramón, situates the spectator within the uncomfortable POV of the teenage victim, a stylistic move that warrants further discussion. Ramón's death scene(s) frames (or bookends) Rodrigo's suicide, creating a balanced triptych of despair. After considerable drinking and belligerent chatting with his fellow pistolocos, Adolfo (the ringleader) and his friends run into the hapless Ramón, who is wanted by the police and threatens to attract them to the neighborhood. Having already been warned to leave town, Ramón's presence enrages Adolfo. Words are exchanged and the boys act increasingly menacing toward Ramón, telling him again to leave Medellín. As Ramón begins to leave, Adolfo calls him back (as if on an arbitrary whim) and shoots him. The next sequence shows Rodrigo committing suicide by jumping from a downtown high-rise. Then the spectator views a *replay* of Ramón's death, from another perspective, and staged differently. The double death leads to a high degree of interpretative ambiguity: either Ramón has returned to life in order to be killed a second time (doubly disposable) in an eerie preenactment of the future of several of the adolescents, who are condemned to die twice—once figuratively as image and once literally as body; or we are seeing his execution from a different perspective, *Rashomon* style, in order to gain a fuller understanding of his experience. Gaviria has indicated that the first death is a more *objective* take (we see it from an establishing type shot) while the second is *subjective* through its use of point of view (i.e., taken from the adolescent focalizer's perspective). The *second* death scene begins with several close-ups of the aggressors as they confront Ramón. A particularly ominous, slightly low-angled, and key-lit extreme close-up of Adolfo is reinforced by his menacing words, as he remarks on the fact that since Ramón has not left to hide (*encaletarse*), perhaps they will help him hide by providing him with a "mask," presumably a death mask. The reverse shot is of Ramón's fearful face, immediately followed by more menacing close-ups of the other boys, providing a sense of encirclement, and of the impossibility of escape. The scene is carefully constructed so that the tension felt by Ramón is transferred to the adult spectator,[7] as the center of observation goes from a neutral establishing shot (externally focalized) to a perspective focalized by Ramón. The boys' cat-and-mouse game ends as Ramón tries to leave when we are presented with a shot from his perspective: Adolfo shooting three times toward the camera, followed by a close-up of Ramón's anguished look, and then another POV shot as the camera rotates and falls to the ground, fusing the physical perspective of spectator, camera, and character. The camera remains at a skew, ground-height angle, looking through Ramón's dying eyes, even as the last words of the film are spoken, "Este *man* está agotado" (This guy is spent), words that reconnect the boy's death with the concept of disposability and abjection, with the notion of something *used up* and consumed through a process that changes matter into image.

Nevertheless, the aesthetics of this carefully crafted death sequence and the attendant POV shot are problematic. In the context of a filmic structure where spectacle blends with reality the double death of a character becomes a self-fulfilling prophesy in *real* life. Ramón's death could be read as the absolute commoditization[8] of human life, as the disposable body becomes an image. The excess of the twice-represented death stages a replay not of his live image but of the moment of death. Capturing Ramón's image, Gaviria preenacts the boy's death: as the film records their images the boys leave their wasted and spent bodies in the slums of Medellín. Gaviria always already considers them as *lost*, as unreclaimable.[9]

We need not view the film through this dark lens. I wish to counter this pessimistic reading by noting that it is precisely the type of POV shots and the operation of merging the roles of the youth as focalizers and focalized—those we *see* and whose eyes we *see through*—that the film breaks through spectator reactions such as indifference, moralizing disapproval, or facile condemnation of the teenagers, opening up a space for understanding their otherness.[10] What Gaviria's film attempts, even at the risk of slipping into spectacle, is to place the viewer directly in front of—indeed, in the shoes of—this radical otherness (a double otherness, inasmuch as the categories of adolescent and "criminal" are both operative), so that he might come as close as possible to an experiential understanding, even if it is not grounded on *empathy*. The success or failure of this redemptive effort lies, in part, within the ambiguous purvey of the spectators' reaction. The spectator might choose to discard any notion of responsibility and fixate on the spectacle of obscenity and abjection, or probe the film for causes and possible solutions. The adult spectator might even try to assimilate the experience of the adolescent through his ocular witnessing, thereby bridging the gap of *otherness* and overcoming the distancing effect of the violence committed by and against the adolescents. Granted that the task of understanding such a radical otherness might be nearly impossible, as Mary Kellett suggests regarding the *gap* between the subjectivities of children and adults: "Adults simply cannot become children again because they cannot discard the adult baggage they have acquired in the interim and will always operate through adult filters, even if these are subconscious filters" (qtd. in Jones, 198). Despite these difficulties, there must be something in the filming process and in the filmic object that might predispose a spectator to approach the film in a way that does not entail aestheticized detachment or indifference ("there is nothing I can do," "I don't care") to the plight of the Colombian urban youth. What Gaviria pretends with his experimental filmic approach is precisely to eliminate the distance that separates the filmmaker (and the spectators) from his subjects.

Perhaps an overlooked point that is central to the social realist dimension of Gaviria's use of the teens as focalized/focalizers can be found in his close ties to the young subjects he has filmed, connections he has established through years of visiting and interacting with the adolescents in the comunas. As Jorge Ruffinelli has observed, without completely effacing the divide between his middle-class adult background and their marginal poverty and youth, Gaviria nevertheless has learned to listen to the adolescents. He insists on the importance of giving voice to the children, scripting (or improvising) the films in their own street language. Gaviria wants to rehumanize the youth of the comunas who are otherwise portrayed, especially by the middle-class Colombian news media, as subhuman and pathological killers engaged in an endless cycle of violence. He does not deny the existence of violence (it permeates the film), but by establishing personal ties with the adolescents until they are at ease and able to express themselves, Gaviria provides a perspective on their life that goes beyond its mere brutality. Gaviria does not speak for the adolescents but rather allows them to speak for themselves, even participate in the creation of the script, which is then *acted* using their natural language and mannerisms.[11]

As I pointed out, whether *Rodrigo D* works to witness (as a delinquent narrative variant of testimonio) or to exploit commercially the images of violence, hinges not only on its production methodology (natural actors, realist aesthetic, flexible script, etc.) but also on the spectator's reception of the film. Key to this reception is how the relationship between center and periphery is conceptualized by the film and understood by the spectator. By foregrounding the daily violence in the comunas, the film arguably tries to raise the spectator's awareness of another kind of violence exerted by the center on the periphery. By placing the camera's point of view in the eyes of different adolescent actors (as exemplified by Ramón's death scene), Gaviria focalizes the narrative and limits the spectator's perception to that of the teens, to their closed-in world, their angst, and their extreme poverty. This use of internal focalization challenges the omniscient perspective and its attendant aloof and supposedly *objective* POV (a hegemonic zero-degree focalization where the spectator can easily slip into the totalizing vision that criminalizes the youth). The shift from one young focalizer to another allows the viewer to approximate the subjectivities and emotional experiences of multiple characters. As Bal indicates, "We are shown how differently the various characters view the same facts" ("Focalization" 119). For the spectator who, aided by the film's focalizing technique, is able to empathize (and not merely sympathize) with its young subjects—acquiring an understanding that urban youth violence is generated by structural violence founded on sociohistorical factors such as class inequality, poverty, and social injustice—the film functions as politically committed filmmaking. For the spectator who, despite the built-in device of internal focalization, maintains a distance from the adolescent nonactors; the film, against Gaviria's best intentions, functions merely as entertainment, spectacle, and the exploitation of misery.

Notwithstanding important questions regarding his use of images and legitimate concerns about what happens to the young bodies those images represent, Gaviria's filmmaking signifies a level of self-awareness absent in previous Colombian productions. Through his use of natural child actors, through their active participation in the scripting and filmmaking process, and the degree of self-reflexivity in his work, it seems that Gaviria is at least keeping ethics in the foreground of his practice. Ultimately, however, he cannot fully own or determine the meaning of his images, since they are formed through a complex interplay of spectatorial mechanisms beyond the filmmaker's control *with* the production methods and style of the film. Perhaps the film unavoidably slips into what Jones qualifies as an instance of the "colonization of childhood space by an adult agenda" (202). But perhaps, by allowing the teens to present and play themselves in the narrative, Gaviria forestalls what has been called the "adultist trap," which "reduce[s] the becomings of children to adult representation" in order to "allow them to become themselves" (Jones 203–4). In that sense, his lack of control over the outcome of the film's reception paradoxically enhances its political commitment by rendering it an open text, which gives both the nonactor characters and the spectators a space for exploring *otherness*.

External Focalization in *El Bola*: Behind Closed Doors

A shift from Medellín's *colonias* (comunas) to Madrid's marginal periphery (the *extraradio* or urban outskirts) presents us with surprising similarities and stark differences. Carabanchel, where the action takes place, is a working-class neighborhood with its share of drugs and violence, but at its worse, it is not comparable to Medellín's periphery. The violence that concerns Achero Mañas's *El Bola* is of an altogether different kind, it is the domestic violence of a father who physically abuses his son within the confines of a dysfunctional family. In *El Bola* the streets represent safety, not fear, while the home environment, virtually absent in *Rodrigo D*, is transformed into a living hell. As in Gaviria's case, this is Mañas's first feature length film, and like Gaviria he chose a first-time actor for the central role of Pablo (a.k.a. el Bola [played by Juan José Ballesta]).[12] *El Bola* is filmed with classical Hollywood editing, a far cry from Gaviria's experimental style.[13] *El Bola* is also a film that does not, on the surface, pose any serious ethical dilemmas for the adult spectator: Pablo is a good kid and his father clearly abusive, which leaves little for the spectator to disagree with, or be challenged by, at least on these accounts.

El Bola is narratively constructed around the basic opposition between two families: Pablo's and Alfredo's. Pablo's father (Mariano), owner of a hardware store, is domineering and brutal and his mother is a broken, submissive woman. The dysfunctional family is completed by a senile grandmother, by Pablo himself, and by the haunting memory of Pablo's dead older brother. Alfredo's family is a bit more difficult to define. His father, José, is a tattoo artist, who lives with Alfredo's mother perhaps only part of the time (the nature of the relationship is left ambiguous) and might be bisexual; Alfredo also has a little brother. In contrast with Pablo's family, Alfredo's is loving and protective. Pablo's desire to escape his oppressive home life is actualized through his friendship with Alfredo and through the positive model provided by his new friend's family. The narrative is neatly closed when Pablo reports the abuse to the police in a dramatic final scene.

Albeit its seamless style and tidy narrative closure, *El Bola* uneasily walks a fine line between depicting and exploiting the images of children, between the melodramatic tearjerker and the socially committed exposé. Comparisons between *El Bola* and *Rodrigo D* will help establish how both deal with violence and focalization. *El Bola* purports to make something visible that has gone unnoticed: the (unexpected) abuse in the traditional family home. Mañas, like Gaviria, is committed to work with children nonactors, although with a very different methodology. In *El Bola* the children are not portraying *themselves* or their own lifestyle, they are acting a tightly scripted role. In contrast with *Rodrigo D*, *El Bola*'s meticulous and polished framing might be too controlling and "ethnographic" to accurately provide a sense of the children's inner world, imposing instead an adult projection designed to elicit sympathy and not necessarily an (empathetic) understanding of their subjectivity, their otherness.

In addition to the intradiegetic violence connected to *El Bola*'s portrayal of the dysfunctional family, there is an additional level of extradiegetic violence performed by the filmic operation against the child focalizer, indeed against the very function of focalizing. The film in several scenes *forces* the adult perspective on the children's subjectivity. The position of the adult spectator vis-à-vis the violence against and around Pablo will be mediated by the child's function as an external (and not internal, as in *Rodrigo D*) focalizer. Pablo remains within the adult spectator's purview but always as the clichéd small, frail, and powerless other who demands our protection, our sympathy. As such, Pablo's agency is limited to a few outbursts (brutally repressed by his father) and he relies on the help received from other adults. This lack of agency is symptomatic of the limited adult view of the child's world, which, as Karen Lury observes, fails to account for the fact that children "want and they act, and they should therefore be understood as agents as well as subjects" ("The Child" 308). The sympathy elicited by Pablo, however, might also suggest a possible *recognition* by the adult spectator of the child's suffering. This recognition, for Jones, means "to first acknowledge the otherness of children and the great asymmetries of body, knowledge, emotion, imagination which exist between adulthood and childhood, before we can begin to do children justice" (206).

This recognition takes place as the violence is exposed. The film's gradual unveiling of violence occurs first through the harsh words spoken by Mariano to his son Pablo and then through the physical marks left on Pablo's body, or through an ominous pair of shoes glimpsed before a beating. The violence becomes more visible as the film progresses, initially taking place behind concealing doors but later culminating in an explosion of anger out in the open for the spectator to see all the graphic details, followed by its aftermath in the emergency room. Mañas wants to make visible what occurs behind the closed doors of abusive households, forcing the reluctant adult spectator to look. Everyone in the film seems to know that el Bola is abused at home (his friends, possibly his teachers), but no one recognizes a responsibility to interfere in that abuse (until Alfredo's family does); Mañas seems to be confronting the spectator with the same issue of responsibility.

Becoming gradually aware of his father's lack of legitimacy (in view of the loving family model provided by Alfredo's family), Pablo incrementally resists the harsh rules and abuse. The violence increases proportionately, as a force of repression exerted on the body both literally and symbolically. It functions as a marker in el Bola's struggle for liberation. But how is violence represented in *El Bola*, and does the method of representation allow an intersubjectivity between adult spectator and child focalizer (as it did in *Rodrigo D*)? Through a highly controlled and carefully framed and edited narrative, Mañas directs (or forces) the spectator's gaze through a cause-and-effect-driven narrative that has little to do with the abused child's actual life experience of chaos and confusion. This dichotomy of form and content profoundly separates what is seen (i.e., the child) from what is felt—by the child character, or even less, by an abused child—negating a type of *seeing* described by Lury: "Seeing implies certain qualities and a particular response: it is an unregulated gaze, timeless and ahistorical, it also implies fascination and a sense in which effects (what is seen) are closer to affect (what is felt)" ("The Child" 308).[14]

This disjunction between the child character's subjectivity and the spectator's visual experience, between the abused child's state of confusion and the film's crisp style, distances the viewer from the child's experience, making identification with the focalizer difficult. If the spectator's and the child's perspective do not converge, empathy is unlikely to arise.

There are two key scenes in the representation of Mariano's violence against Pablo that attempt to mobilize spectatorial affect. The first occurs entirely offscreen, the second is in plain view. In the first scene, Pablo has returned from the field trip to the sierra, where he spent an idyllic day with his surrogate family. Arriving home he is greeted by his father's harsh words, telling him to never see "esa gente" (those people) again. Pablo, thinking his father was out of earshot and visibly upset by the return to the oppressive household after a day of freedom, mutters under his breath "hijo de puta, ojalá te mueras" (I wish you were dead, you son of a bitch!). An ominous eyeline match shot (from Pablo's physical perspective) toward a pair of shoes lets Pablo know that Mariano has heard, then, a reverse shot of Pablo's anguished, expectant look, in a nail-biting moment for the spectator. The screen slowly fades, leaving the violence that ensues offscreen, unrepresented, but easily imagined. The following sequence takes place in the school where Alfredo sees Pablo's empty chair, a metonymic and metaphoric marker that confirms what transpired. Further confirmation as to the severity of the beating is provided when we find out that Pablo has been absent from school for an entire week. The steady build up of the evidence of Pablo's abuse follows a logical cause-and-effect pattern that nevertheless stays away from the internal focalization we saw in *Rodrigo D*. This allows for our intellectual engagement but not a significant affective approximation into the child's subject position (we did not *feel* the blows with him), we instead have a constructed subjectivity, essentially an adult's projection of the victimized child. The narrative is building a case relying on the trope of the abused child, but nothing experientially new is revealed to the adult spectator. This seems to disregard one of the advantages of using a child as focalizer/focalized agent—namely, "their offering the adult spectator a challenging position which defamiliarizes 'what we know'" (Lury, "The Child" 310). When Alfredo attempts to see his friend, he is confronted by a closed door; and when the spectator is finally allowed to see Pablo's slightly hunched over frame, it is from behind, leaving the details of the violence as *unknown* and *invisible*. This presentation seems to deny violence as spectacle, rejecting the possibility of any perverse viewing pleasure of the violent act and the exploitation of Pablo's (fictive) pain. We are not privy to the beating, but we are shown its social ramifications and consequences. Mañas is obviously trying to negotiate the boundary between revealing the invisibility of the brutal domestic abuse, which occurs in the private sphere, and avoiding making a *public* spectacle out of human suffering. Unfortunately, by not engaging cinematically with the possibilities of the child as internal focalizer, we are not able to *feel* with Pablo, since we are merely shown—or not shown—what has happened to him. Pablo remains a passive agent and Mañas does not facilitate the adult spectator's connection with the child character on anything beyond superficial sympathy.

The second violent scene occurs after the police detain Pablo for playing on the railroad tracks. Arriving home late for dinner, he is confronted by his father, who demands to know where he has been. When he catches Pablo lying (the boy tells his father he was at school), Mariano becomes increasingly enraged. The scene is filmed in a progression of shot-reverse shots and close-ups of both actors, intensifying the spectators' affective involvement and the level of tension but not entering the child's perspective through internal focalization. Neither the shots on Mariano nor the reverse shots on Pablo correspond to their relative position; rather they are shot from a *neutral* spot at a right angle to either actor. The spectator fears for Pablo, but not with Pablo. Pablo's head is lowered, in a position that physically reflects his fear and subjugation to paternal rule. His mother (possibly serving as a surrogate for the spectator) looks on horrified—unable or unwilling to intervene in the escalating conflict.[15] After Pablo finally lashes out defiantly and spits at his father's face, the ensuing explosion of violence is tremendous, and this one act of agency by the child is harshly punished. Mariano hunts a fleeing Pablo down through the house, punching and kicking him with the full force of his adult strength even after he has knocked him down. The camera is relentless (in an excess of shots, framings, and reframings, alternating handheld with steady camera), seeking out Pablo's small writhing body to show the full impact of every blow. The perspective adopted by the camera is high angle, from adult height, aligning itself with either Mariano or an adult observer. The shots in this lengthy scene are quick and fragmented, alternating between the close-ups of Mariano's arms and feet and the movements of Pablo's body as he is repeatedly struck. Diegetic sound is constituted by Mariano's cursing and Pablo's moans, syncopated with the thumping of the blows. This excess of violence comes as a shock to the spectator, standing in sharp contrast with the previous *veiled* depiction. But while the scene might arouse the sympathy of the adult spectator (arguably without engaging empathy), in no way does it challenge adult perspectives in the discourse of child abuse and its representation; nor has it rendered Pablo's experience as more knowable from within his (the child's) own subjectivity. According to Lury's distinction between *seeing* and *showing*, Mañas has *shown* to us the effects of abuse, but we have neither *seen* nor *felt* them from Pablo's POV (cinematically or psychologically). This is not to deny the value of the scene, which does engage the spectator affectively but strictly from a concerned adult's standpoint, not from the child's perspective.

The beating scene's gratuitous, graphic nature, it might be argued, was unnecessary to establish the pattern of abuse that the film denounces and might have been left, like the first incident, offscreen or perhaps placed at the level and perspective of the child as the internal focalizer of the abuse. Its excess might be interpreted, in the worst case, as a move normalizing sadistic aggression as a justifiable form of parental discipline, which just "gets out of hand." The fact that Pablo is shown as powerless, while Mariano victimizes him with impunity, reveals a degree of hierarchical perversity inherent in the scene's filmic structure.

On the other hand, Pablo's vulnerable fragility quite possibly serves to trigger an affective response stemming from the spectators' protective instincts. Mañas calls forth the spectator's sense of ethics, facing him or her with the dilemma of whether he would intervene to save Pablo. In this sense, the violence might function via its shock value to puncture through spectator indifference.[16] But this affective and sympathetic approach leaves the child out of the realm of agency, at the mercy of the adults. It enhances the child's otherness by rendering him as a pitiable victim. As in *Rodrigo D*, the spectator is called to *testimoniar* (witness) the traumatic event; but unlike *Rodrigo D*, the adult spectator is not brought into alignment with the adolescents through POV and internal focalization. In *El Bola*, the spectator is a concerned yet distant observer because the child is not a *seeing*, active focalizer, only the *seen*, passive focalized subject.

Nowhere is the ethics of representation more confrontational than in the last scene of the film. In an extreme close-up revealing his bruised face, Pablo lists the litany of physical and psychological abuse, including the drinking of his own urine. Paul Begin notes that this filmic moment where the victim holds direct eye contact with the viewer functions as a device that breaks with classical Hollywood narrative and denies the spectator the possibility to be just a fly on the wall. For Begin, these are "powerful moments that transgress the boundaries which normally separate the victim and the voyeur" (273).[17] I agree with Begin but would point out that the adult spectator remains fully ensconced within the adult world, as he now takes the position of the sympathetic ear (and eye) to Pablo's plight, seeking a solution that will be determined and implemented by the same adult world that failed the child in the first place, perhaps even subjecting Pablo to laws that will return him back to the dysfunctional space of the abusive family, as the law dictates, and as "befits" a marginalized, voiceless subject.

CONCLUDING REMARKS: THE REDEEMING VALUE OF AMBIGUITY

Both *Rodrigo D: No futuro* and *El Bola* eschew the category of mere entertainment by engaging with pressing social questions of adolescent violence and domestic child abuse. The cinematic styles and techniques chosen to depict these extreme situations have been challenged by critics, at different times, either for being too focused on abjection and violence or for not being sufficiently direct and lacking political commitment. More importantly, both films can also be taken to task for their success or failure in rendering (intelligible) the *otherness* of children to adult spectators. Here the methods of the two films differ by dint of the camera's alignment. In *Rodrigo D*, the spectator often sees what the adolescents see. In *El Bola*, the spectator just sees the children. Only *Rodrigo D* relies on the children as internal focalizers, facilitating a closing of the gap between the adult world and that of the child characters. Does the adult spectator manage to align his or her subjectivity with the marginalized focalizing /focalized child characters in either film? The answer remains ambiguous nor is it clear whether it is desirable to fully colonize the experience and subjectivity of children. This seems to gesture toward the advantages of an open, unresolved, and ambiguous text. Perhaps, what we can say about both films, and *especially* about *Rodrigo D*, is that they create a space for understanding children, taking into account that "in an effort to be open to children's worlds, and in order to make (friendlier) worlds for them, we need to undo ourselves, and the adult geographies of the world, or at least loosen them, by tugging away at the tight, ossified and ossifying knots of adult being, space and knowledge" (Jones 211). *Rodrigo D* manages to go further than *El Bola* in this "undoing" of the adult world through its use of the internal focalizer. The elusive ambiguity and the ethical dilemmas posed by the filmic representation of adolescents and children in situations of violence and poverty, as well as the political stakes involved, ensure a heated debate for years to come. The use of the child as internal focalizer might provide one an entry point for that debate to consider not just how the child is *seen* but what the child *sees* and *feels*.

NOTES

1. The following question might arise: can the child's subject position even be presented as such, and is the spectator able to approach such a complex subjectivity? Naomi Sokoloff states on this regard that "no adult [. . .] can speak authoritatively in the name of childhood or in a child's voice, for none can fully enter and represent the consciousness of children. As a result fictive portrayals of childhood often tell us less about the nature and behavior of children than about images and values imposed on children by grown-up narrators" (239).
2. The title is a synthesis citing Vittorio De Sica's neorealist film *Umberto D* (1952) and the Sex Pistols's "God Save the Queen" refrain: "No future for you, no future for me" from their hit album *Never Mind the Bollocks, Here's the Sex Pistols* (1977).
3. While I am fully aware of the fact that film form is in part determined by the economic and historical factors of production and distribution (obviously different in Spain and Colombia), I chose to lay aside those considerations, as both directors have made very deliberate stylistic and aesthetic choices that go beyond these limitations.
4. My use of the word *abject*, here and elsewhere in the essay, is not in line with Julia Kristeva's understanding of the term; instead, I draw on its common usage dictionary definition, as seen, for instance, in the *Merriam-Webster Online*: "1. sunk to or existing in a low state or condition [. . .] 2a. cast down in spirit [. . .] 2b. showing hopelessness."
5. As Rodgers states, "The youth gangs and cartels have developed a strong symbiotic relationship, contributing to the proliferation of both. By 1990 there were no fewer than 120 youth gangs in Medellín, [. . .] mostly located in the poor northeastern part of the city. They involved approximately 3,000 youth, averaging 16 years old" (7).
6. The text reads: "Dedicada a la memoria de John Galvis, Jackson Gallegos, Leonardo Sánchez y Francisco Marin, actores que sucumbieron sin cumplir los 20 años, a la absurda violencia de Medellín, para que sus imágenes vivan por lo menos el término normal de una persona" (Dedicated to the memory of John Galvis, Jackson Gallegos, Leonardo Sánchez and Francisco Marin, actors who perished in Medellín's absurd violence, before reaching the age of 20, so at least their images might live the duration of a normal life; Gaviria).
7. I understand the problem of considering a generic or "universal" spectator (without race, without gender, etc.). Since I want to consider the possibility of closing the gap between adult and child subjectivities I posit an adult, middle-class spectator—clearly a simplification given the many other types of viewing positions.
8. By commoditization, also known as commodification, I am referring to the Marxist political economic concept of the transformation of goods and services—or in this case, human beings—into a commodity that can be bought or sold and has a given exchange value (*Capital* 41–96).

Margolin, Uri. "Focalization. Where Do We Go from Here?" *Point of View, Perspective, Focalization: Modeling Mediation in Narrative.* Ed. Peter Hühn, Wolf Schmid, and Jörg Schönert. Berlin; New York: Walter de Gruyter, 2009. 41–58.

Rodgers, Dennis. *Youth Gangs and Violence in Latin America and the Caribbean: A Literature Survey.* Washington, DC: World Bank, 1999. Web. 20 Apr. 2011. <http://www.ansarilawfirm.com/docs/Youth-Gangs-and-Violence-in-Latin-America.pdf>.

Rodrigo D: No futuro. Dir. Víctor Gaviria. Perf. Ramiro Meneses, Carlos Mario Restrepo, Jackson Idrian Gallego. Chicago: Facets Video, 2004. Digital videodisc.

Ruffinelli, Jorge. *Víctor Gaviria: Los márgenes, al centro; las películas, las ideas sobre cine, la poesía, los ensayos, los relatos, las crónicas.* Madrid: Casa de América, 2004.

Sokoloff, Naomi B. "Interpretation: Cynthia Ozick's *Cannibal Galaxy.*" *Prooftexts* 6.3 (Sept. 1986): 239–57.

Suárez, Juana. "Rafagazos de imágenes: Jóvenes y violencia en relatos fílmicos de Medellín." *Bad Subjects* 61 (Sept. 2002): n. pag. Web. 20 Apr. 2011. <http://bad.eserver.org/issues/2002/61/suarez.html>.

Triana-Toribio, Núria. *Spanish National Cinema.* London: Routledge, 2003.

CHAPTER 9

ROADS TO EMANCIPATION

SENTIMENTAL EDUCATION IN *VIVA CUBA*

ROSANA DÍAZ-ZAMBRANA
TRANSLATED BY CLINT HENDRIX

> We know nothing of childhood, and with our mistaken notions the further we advance the further we go astray. The wisest writers devote themselves to what a man ought to know without asking what a child is capable of learning. They are always looking for the man in the child without considering what he is before he becomes a man
> —Jean-Jacques Rousseau, *Émile*

> Education will always have to be a compromise between indoctrination and freedom.
> —Ala Alryyes, *Original Subjects*

> When do people grow up?
> —Malú, *Viva Cuba*

Recent Hispanic-Caribbean cinema shows a keen interest in exploring reality from the decentralized and contradictory position of the child as subject.[1] In the case of Cuba, films like *Life Is to Whistle* (Fernando Pérez 1998), *Havana Suite* (Fernando Pérez 2003), *The Silly Age* (Pavel Giroud 2006), or *Habanastation* (Ian Padrón 2011) feature a child—at times as a supporting character and at other times as a protagonist—as a dramatic resource to make conjectures about the political and sociocultural manifestations of the country, allocating to this young age a complex allegorical weight.[2] This resorting to child characters on the silver screen offers an unconventional vision—and, at times, a transgressive one—to the filmic narrative by producing alternative readings centering on the notions of identity, nation, diaspora, and self-knowledge in times of crisis.

Let us consider the 2005 film *Viva Cuba* from director Juan Carlos Cremata Malberti. This celebrated production and recipient of international awards, including the Grand Prix Écrans Juniors in the Cannes Film Festival given by a jury of children, reintroduces the filmic language of poetic simplicity and the animation techniques of infantile cinematography that broke new ground in *Nada* (*Nothing*), his 2002 *opera prima*. This story, without precedent in Cuban cinematography, continues with the topic of emigration and the image of the split nation that has become one of the defining themes to be found in almost every Cuban film after the nineties (Chanan 379). Therefore, even when the director of *Viva Cuba* warns us that "whoever views this film in terms of Castroism or anti-Castroism will understand nothing" (Vincent), it is possible to point out political references to emigration, above all the difficulty of returning for those who decided to leave the country, as well as references to the disagreements between supporters and opponents of the revolution and its politics and to the economic problems of those who love their country but are unable to go abroad. While children do not adhere to a political discourse per se, they live under the inescapable influence of domestic and institutional indoctrination.

Following Henry Jenkins's reflection about "what the figure of the child means to adults," Emma Wilson explains that "keeping children outside the political, the conception or fantasy of childhood innocence works further to shore up a sense of the distinction and distance between adults and children" and "this fantasy in itself has been seen in part responsible for the very disempowerment of the child" (331). However, with the focalization of the child in *Viva Cuba*, we see his or her restitution—through the proximity and subjectivity of the camera—his astonished gaze, and also his agency to rearm history and offer new strategies to navigate the repercussions of politics and ideology from a viewpoint rarely visited by filmmakers. In her essay "The Child in Film and Television," Karen Lury asserts, "An important aspect of the child-as-agent is that the child encourages us, as cliché as it is, to *see* the world differently" (307). The "unregulated gaze, timeless and ahistorical" (Lury 307) that the child possesses in his fascinating sensorial discovery of the (super)natural world in *Viva Cuba*—ocean waves, shooting stars, water spirits—is what makes the expansion of the political realm to the human realm possible, and even more importantly what enables the realm of the child to make an impact on the realm of the adult.

In *Viva Cuba*, Malú and Jorgito, a couple of ten-year-old children, are neighbors, study in the same class in school, and share games and arguments until their friendship is threatened when Malú's mother decides to emigrate from Cuba in an attempt to escape the complications of everyday life there. The two children then improvise a plan to set out in search of Malú's father to convince him not to approve her mother's plan so that their world as they know it remains unperturbed. After some unusual adventures and rites of passage typical of the road movie and formation novel genres, Malú and Jorgito achieve their goal only to find themselves in a conflict between their families, which serves as an emotional climax on one hand, and on the other, as a verification of the tie that binds them. In the final scenes, their mutual affection and solidarity leads them from their arguing parents to a desperate embrace as they face the ocean, literally at land's end and unable to run any further.

Driven by their desire to be together, the children embark on a journey that makes possible the creation of a *distinct* space where rebellion and the crossing of borders are privileged. This dramatic progression leads them to a figurative emancipation from the world of adults and the affirmation of spiritual/emotional values such as unconditional friendship, loyalty, and love. This displacement from the center (from the capital Havana and home) bears witness to the tensions and apparent contradictions inherent in their age and in the subtle changes that are operating in the child subject faced with the strangeness of the new space/time coordinates encountered on their journey.

This fluid stage between childhood and adolescence is evidenced by the dose of adventure and the potential risk to which the journey and confrontation with the unknown give rise. The stated distancing from the sphere of the familiar sets off a chain of conflicts that challenge the rules of the adult social group and the very parameters of the friendship between the children. In this essay I discuss this particular representation and evolution of children by means of the episodic structure of travel through Cuban geography. I argue that the principal transformation that Malú and Jorgito undergo is in their emotional awakening and sentimental education, giving rise to another stage of maturity and disillusionment that is solidified when they reunite with their respective families at the end of their voyage.

CHILD EDUCATION: BETWEEN INSTITUTION AND EXPERIENCE

Considering the political and historic juncture of the release of *Viva Cuba*, the special attention paid to this transitory group of children and youths as future agents of social change is rather fortuitous. In fact, a number of authors of Latin American literary works turn to childhood on a rhetorical level equating the child's potentiality with that of the nation, or drawing an analogy between the parent-child relationship, and the nation and its constituents (Browning 5).

The sociocultural and national transformation that childhood suggests is facilitated by what, in the words of Rosario Castellanos, is the liminal nature of children and their symbolic receptivity with respect to their circumstances and the phenomena that surround them. For Castellanos childhood is "a moment of void, in which the cultural content of adults has not yet spilled over: this void makes the child available, receptive, situated on the brink of imminence. Anything can happen to him/her, any adventure can find its protagonist in him/her, any phenomenon can manifest itself in him/her, without finding organized and effective resistance" (qtd. in Zamudio 130).

If on one hand this "void" makes a child "available," and consequentially vulnerable, it also makes him or her possible conductor of ideological and cultural turns and apertures without many restrictions. This receptivity of the child subject is intrinsic to the processes of initiation, self-realization, and subsequent social integration. That is to say, this intermediate stage between what is and what should be will enable the child to negotiate situations and regulations with greater freedom and less prejudice.

In accordance with the phases inherent to the literary genre of child formation and maturation—Bildungsroman—the child is subject to a multifaceted education that involves an emotional, social, and moral learning that is not exempt from pain and suffering. In his study of Bildungsromans, François Jost shows that an individual's holistic education is not found in a doctrine, book, or school, but rather in the experience of the world, and it is the lessons resulting from one's adventures in the world that will crystalize his or her character (99). In *Viva Cuba*, various basic components of the formation novel are brought together: childhood, the conflict of generations, provinciality, the larger society, self-education, alienation, ordeal by love, and the search for a working philosophy (Buckley 18). This subject matter oscillates between conflict and revelation making use of a frame of gradual preparation and instruction.

Because the child subject "is introduced into a web of dependency and interdictions constituted by school and family" (Jeftanovic), throughout the film there is an emphasis on accentuating the limitations and the external guidelines to which (s)he is exposed in his or her coming-of-age. In his study of child pedagogy, Luis Arturo Lemus draws a distinction between intentional or systematic education and cosmic or unsystematic education (56–57). The former is expressed in a spontaneous and unconscious way while in the latter there is intent to influence the child through educative action. This is to suggest that the fundamental attributes of education that favor the consolidation of personality derive from a bipartite instruction that includes informal and institutional components. In *Viva Cuba*, we witness both modes of education governed by the schematic teachings that school provides along with the rites accompanying it, the most improvisational practices reinforced by play and imagination.

It is worth mentioning that the aforementioned educational approaches contribute to fostering in children the values that establish the development of skills and qualities necessary for the process of individualization and decision making. One example of this is seen in the sequence that opens the film featuring kids playing "good guys" and "bad guys." The children simulate an armed conflict between Cubans (the good guys) and Spaniards (the bad guys). This game reveals the ideology transmitted by adults (both at school and at home) set into motion through the recreational activity. Just at that moment, Malú arrives inopportunely, and she interrupts the game by imposing her wish to be the queen of Spain. The low-angle shot of Malú highlights her prominence and foreshadows the force of change that she will play in Jorgito's formative trajectory.

Later we see Malú at school furtively writing Jorgito's name in the pages of her book, only to be reprimanded by her teacher later. In the subsequent scene, a teacher reviews the parts of the human body using an embarrassed Jorgito as a model in front of the class. We also see Jorgito and Malú rehearsing dance steps under the strict tutelage of their instructor. These are only a few of the scenes that demonstrate the importance of child education in differing degrees, spaces, and contexts, thus emphasizing the interconnection and superimposition of the education received at school (public) and sentimental education (private).

It is in this way that the affective and conflictive relationship between Jorgito and Malú is presented: separated by social class, their religious beliefs, and their political positions (or that of their families), but united in games, scholastic activities, and the natural affinity they feel for one another. However, the adult regime threatens the friends' relationship while it projects on them the fear of the social transgression that they are constantly committing with their friendship. Each mother views the other's child as the cause of corruption and bad habits. As a result, *Viva Cuba* calls into question the ability to communicate not only between parents and children but also between adults.

The plot thickens when, stemming from the death of her grandmother, Malú's mother tries to speed up her departure with her daughter from Cuba to meet up with her new husband, but not without first seeking authorization from Malú's father who lives on the other end of the island. The scene depicting the children seated on a roof with a panoramic view of the city visually announces to the viewer the role of protagonists that the children will play in the course of the story and adventure. It is in this exclusive place (free from adults) of privileged perception that, at Jorgito's suggestion, the two decide to set out for Punta de Maisí to prevent the father's signature that would authorize Malú's mother to take her out of Cuba. The children, therefore, exhibit in their puerile reasoning a way of confronting adversity with a practical solution, albeit a ridiculous one from an adult perspective. This defiant and optimistic attitude echoes one of the characteristics that Miguel Salmerón points out in the formation novel: *utopianism*, or the knowledge that solving one's problems, has as a precondition creating a framework for its resolution (10).

Before departing, the children write their vows of friendship on a piece of paper and bury them in a box underground. Immediately thereafter, Malú asks a question suggesting that her buried secret involves her wish to be an adult, an impatience shared by Jorgito as well. Even at the outset of the film one of Jorgito's friends gives him away by verbalizing what Jorgito is unable to recognize about himself: "I believe that you are in love with her [Malú]." Such difficulty in grasping and deciphering internal feelings coupled with the mysteries of the world around him will later form part of the friction between Jorgito and Malú and of the typical developmental process of sentimental education wherein the hero experiences a sudden existential conflict.

Themes that are at once philosophical and problematic like adulthood, time, the concept of foreigner, marriage, love, and death all form part of the dialogue about the human condition and emotional development that casually surfaces in the protagonists of *Viva Cuba*. "At what age do people marry?," "When do people grow up?," and "How long until the year 2030?" are some of Malú and Jorgito's rhetorical questions that corroborate the natural uncertainty and curiosity of a childhood on the verge of adolescence. Faced with doubt about origin and maturing, fantasy emerges to explain phenomena that are mysterious for a child's horizons and developing cognitive abilities. For Andrea Jeftanovic, the imagination of a child's mind produces contradictory accounts, greater experimentation in language, and ideological and cultural subversions. The presence of a magical and superstitious language capable of bringing things to life constitutes an intrinsic element of the "gap between imagining and reasoning" (Jeftanovic) of childhood mentality. This could explain the "real" apparition that gives life to the popular Cuban myth of the *güije*, a black character associated with water that roams around naked terrorizing people. This encounter between the children and the güije confirms the realization of fears driven by the fantasy and susceptibility endemic to childhood. In the film, this fear is used as just another example of the moralizing mechanisms used by adults to educate, indoctrinate, correct, and orient juvenile behavior.

Acting as stimulus to fantasy, play allows children to experience freedom through subversive practices while also granting them the ability to make believe they are grown-ups. According to Sigmund Freud, it is precisely the wish to act like grown-ups that play promotes: "It is clear that in their play children repeat everything that has made a great impression on them in real life, and that in doing so they abreact the strength of the impression and, as one might put it, make themselves master of the situation. But on the other hand it is obvious that all their play is influenced by a wish that dominates them the whole time—the wish to be grown-up and to be able to do what grown-up people do" (11).

As a prototypical activity of childhood that bolsters abilities and refines conduct and habits, play serves as a decisive function in *Viva Cuba* that provides the dynamic suitable for masking and acting out alternative roles that activate and materialize their hidden desires.

In a society where official education and familial tradition place limits on gender roles and where "girls play with girls," and "boys should play ball," the interaction between Jorgito and Malú defies constraints, so much so that Jorgito even dresses up as a girl as a ruse to trick adults and further advance their journey toward their ultimate goal. Although the children are, in part, "corrupted" by institutional and familial discourses, childhood permits them to maneuver and adapt to their circumstances and trials. The role change involved in many of these games serves to rearticulate gender and power relations. Even when Jorgito emphatically says, "Listen to me, I'm the boss," attempting to mimic the masculine authority exemplified by his father, Malú never backs down; instead, she firmly imposes her will when she takes advantage of the opportunity to sing on a public stage in front of television cameras despite Jorgito's objection: "Why do you always have to be in charge, Malú?" Jorgito even redefines the codes of masculinity imposed by the paternal model. For instance, he decides to go for a swim in his underwear in Varadero, disregarding that his father had warned him that it wasn't proper. This porosity in otherwise rigid traditions provided by being young gives the children access to gray areas where ambiguity is privileged.

It is important to note how the visual discourse in *Viva Cuba* reinforces the aforesaid focalization of the child and links the sentimental relationship and learning of the children. Among the filmic resources employed, the lowering of the shot below eye level, the low-angle shots, and the children's gaze at the camera stand out, as when Jorgito looks into the lens while acting like a horse in front of the class. The recurrence of extreme close-ups and close-ups of their heads and facial expressions following changes in emotion—whether small or substantial—and the reactions of each child to these changes help the viewer to glimpse the world from another perspective by delving into child subjectivity and the affective meaning of these dramatic moments. Some of these close-ups shift from Malú to Jorgito and vice versa in a cinematic attempt to document the effect each child has on the other in what visually becomes an emotional tuning of immediate action and reaction; take, for instance, the tight shots of Malú and Jorgito exchanging gazes to inspect one another when all of the school children line up to salute the flag. The powerful language of these shots is even clearer in the sequence shot at the end of the film to be considered later in which the camera is redirected to capture the children in a prolonged medium close-up that marks the strength of their pact and the symbolic dissolution of their childhood.

With the repeated use of overhead shots, for instance, of the sequences when the children appear seated at the base of a palm tree in the middle of a vast landscape, of when they bury their friendship vows, or during their journey in the ox cart through the dense Cuban countryside, the camera angle—and consequentially the viewer—assumes a higher position. This position of the lens renders the children smaller, which could be a reminder of the immense space as of yet unconquered by the children and the contrast with what could be described in many ways as a narrow and limited adult perspective.

A Children's Road Movie: New Geographies and Alliances

Viva Cuba presents an inventory of the beauty of the flora and fauna of the national landscape, spanning from the capital to the east via Matanzas, Varadero, Trinidad, Sancti Spíritus, Camagüey, and even Punta de Maisí, thus distinguishing itself from productions that privilege Havana as synonymous with *Cuban-ness*. As opposed to the emblematic Cuban road movie *Guantanamera* (Tomás Gutiérrez Alea 1995) and the "static" journey in *Lista de espera* (*The Waiting* List; Juan Carlos Tabío 2000), *Viva Cuba* testifies to the ease of mobility—be it by train, bus, automobile, boat, cart, or motorcycle—in Cuba, despite the economic consequences of the Special Period.[3]

The distancing from frames of reference and the solitude of the road make Malú and Jorgito improvise survival strategies, which at times provoke the rising conflict between them and at other times allow them to get even closer in their effort to overcome their obstacles together. With a hint of mockery, they will prove to be more ingenious and effective than the adults they encounter who surrender to their youthful charm. It is from here that the picaresque qualities of road movies will emerge: the children will have to rely on the means of transportation within their reach, resort to their own devices, and take advantage of the assistance of others en route to their destination, be it physical (Punta de Maisí) or metaphorical (maturity). Such processes in which identity is constituted are not as evident without the separation from familiar spaces that the journey makes possible. When referring to children, Carl Jung signals this necessity of abandonment: "'Child' means something evolving towards independence. This it cannot do without detaching itself from its origins: abandonment is therefore a necessary condition, not just a concomitant symptom" (142).

Malú and Jorgito are linked by an unusual friendship. In his book *Driving Visions*, David Laderman maintains that road movies exploit the coupled character structure that "appears mostly in two versions, romance or friendship; yet often it furnishes narrative tension between the two people traveling together" (17). This is due to the possibility of dialogue and dramatic conflict that the couple structure provides (Cohan and Hark 8). One of the great merits of *Viva Cuba* derives precisely from the verbal counterpoint established between Malú and Jorgito in which they confirm their personality, worldview, and will to change. From the filmic perspective, the use of two-shots emphasizes this double development and the simultaneous evolution of their sentimental education.

With respect to the cinematic narrative of the road movie, Laderman suggests that it is two-pronged: "The road movie's generic core is constituted more precisely by a tension between rebellion and conformity [. . .] The genre's deliberate rebellious impulse is conveyed primarily through two narrative pretexts: the quest road movie and the outlaw road movie" (19–20). In *Viva Cuba*, there is a fusion of both tendencies: the search for Malú's father and the police pursuit of the two fugitive children. It is the children's disobedience or, rather, nonconformity that will prove to be the motive for their escapade and allow the dramatic "knots" of their changing selves and circumstances to be untangled. Even while it exemplifies one of the fundamental driving forces behind the road genre in which "an embrace of the journey [is considered] as a means of cultural critique" (Laderman 1), the journey in *Viva Cuba* entails much more with regard to the socioemotional progression of the children and their relation to the world that epitomize the typical scheme of a Bildungsroman.

The long shots during the journey, particularly of the children walking, produce a coming and going effect, referring the spectator to the idea of displacement and the dual road toward experiential/cognitive and geographical/sentimental education. It is because of this interior and exterior interconnection that the Bildungsroman can be described as an "odyssey of selfhood in which the internal machinations of the self are foregrounded" (McWilliams 12). According to the distinction Salmerón draws between the novel of formation and the novel of peripeteia, in the former what happens is accidental or modal, and it is the character who is fundamental while the latter focuses not on what can be derived from what is narrated but on the narration itself (11). We can, no doubt, extend this character-happening maneuvering to *Viva Cuba*, as its story of formation does not exclude the peripeteia tied to the voyage. Nevertheless, the interior formation (emotions) that the children experience in *Viva Cuba* in many ways takes precedence over the exterior and anecdotal (action).

On one level, fleeing from home testifies to an act of solidarity between the children; on another, it becomes an act of rebellion in which they abandon the space of friction and hostility where their presence is ignored and/or marginalized. In both homes, the frustration of daily life in Cuba prevails over the well-being of parent-child relationships. In Malú's case, her father has not looked after her since she was six years old, and Jorgito's parents unabashedly vent their frustrations in front of their child. From the beginning of the film, the adults (especially the mothers) are limited to the domestic sphere; from there, they reprimand their children, bemoan their troubles on the phone, and complain about their neighbors. Until the children's departure, both families disregard their wishes and unilaterally impose their authority. It is only when the police search begins that the mothers put aside their prejudices and unite in their worry and love for their children.

Malú and Jorgito escape from their home life into exterior spaces, receiving a sudden autonomy and possibility to dream. We see them walking around the streets of Havana coming and going to school or their usual games in preparatory walks that precede the journey that awaits them. According to Andrea Jeftanovic, the use of child narrators is possible when the child figure is different from the rest of the subjects in his or her society, or when (s)he becomes recognizable or visible. In fact, it is not until the children run away and break with their daily routines that they stand out from their families and the rest of the country.

Among the themes common in road movies is the expression of uneasiness with respect to consumerist, capitalist society: the authoritarian patriarchal order and the disintegration of family and community (Polh 59). Both children unconsciously flee from authoritarian order and in doing so unleash a family crisis that adds another component to the preexisting dysfunction. As a result of the oppression of the protagonists in road movies, family serves as a metonymy of the society; it represents stability, collectivity, and limits to individual development. Consequently, the journey as stimulus for the reconfiguration of the subject creates an opening to forbidden and not yet domesticated zones of personality. It is in the mesh of these conditions and sociocultural determinants that the subject is forged; moreover, it is stipulated within the concept of *Bildung* itself that "there can be no formation outside of society [. . .] The truth and propriety of a formation are determined insofar as objective and commonly human perspectives are valued" (Salmerón 34).

Later, in one of the most defining scenes of the film, there is a confrontation between the children in which "the truths" about themselves and their families are shouted out with the express purpose of hurting one another's feelings. To an extent, this moment would appear to cause them to discover the feelings of love (potential desire?) that they feel for one another. In this allegorical "breakup" of their friendship, there is a masking of the phases of maturation and failure that usually characterize the passing from one stage to the next. It is in this moment that the cinematographic tone and rhythm of the setting change. After the fight, an ox skull appears in the foreground with an image of the children behind it with their heads bowed from hunger and thirst. The glass enclosing the portrait of Malú's grandmother that she has carried throughout the trip is now broken, Malú sheds her first tears and Jorgito gets sick and loses his voice. The children appear more disoriented and upset than they have been up to this point. A sky full of dark clouds and a torrential downpour accompany the melancholic tone of this uncoupled part of their trip. Here we see a demarcation separating the protagonists along the lines of their shared experiences and lost innocence. It is only when another young character, in what could be considered the guiding principle of road trips, offers them the advice "without friends you will get nowhere" that Malú and Jorgito reestablish the bond of friendship that had been broken.

If we draw a connection between the story of formation and the formation of the hero, György Lukács's ideas in *Teoría de la novela* are quite apropos. The hero of a novel is characterized by a "strangeness of the world" in which the story is told of the figure who departs to learn about himself and seeks out adventure in order to be proven (356). For Lukács, the hero's story will share with the story of sentimental education the sense of disillusionment and the failure of the adventure. How does the story of formation manage to reconcile the hero's clashes with the world? While *Viva Cuba*, on one hand, reflects both the utopic proposal of the child subject's attempt to correct the impositions of adults and the accompanying cementing of his personality and core values, the abrupt emotional awakening is invaded by the disconcerting reality of emigration, separation, and the imminent abandonment of one's first great love. This change is represented metaphorically through the final obstacles as the hardships of the journey begin to take their toll: physical weakness (sickness, hunger, and thirst) and mental weakness (fear and pessimism).

That being said, the voyage will culminate in lucidity or what Jerome Buckley calls "some ultimate coherence," which corroborates the quantum leap of the children into being companions and visionaries, validating the spiritual growth, learning, and peripeteia of the journey across the so-called threshold of conscience. However, what should be a reunion with their respective families becomes a series of complaints and contained violence, thus confirming the impending loss of childhood paradise. It is precisely in this moment that the children recognize in the complicity of each other's gaze that the "coherence of the world" is affirmed in the unique and impenetrable bond they created. Here ends the liberating saga as the characters are confronted with the reality of their subjugation to familial oppression: Malú's one-way trip abroad and Jorgito's submission to the implacable authoritarianism of his father. Malú and Jorgito, in what could be deemed an epiphanic decision, willingly separate from their families for a moment and join together in a hug before a turbulent sea, which appears to parallel their affection in an embrace of the characters. Childhood as a "dynamic, in itself, of losses" (Jeftanovic) suffers in this moment the transferal to a conscience marred with deception and failure. Consequently, the primary conflict should be resolved with a revelation that comes from within a character since "the central conflict in nearly every other Bildungsroman is likewise personal in origin: the problem lies within the hero himself" (Buckley 22). Recent criticism emphasizes that in a Bildungsroman the true ending resides in the indefinite self-formation of the hero and not in the hero's positive overcoming of the world (Gómez Viu 109). As such, an end is put to the hope of finding harmony in the world and to the idea of the ego as culmination of the evolution of the hero, just as we see at the end of *Viva Cuba* with the disconnect the children endure upon meeting up with their families. The discontinuity of childhood and the entry into another stage of lost unity are thus confirmed, as borne out with the sound of the characters' fighting being substituted by a somber soundtrack reminiscent of a death rite.

If we return to the types of spontaneous and formal education to which the children are subjected throughout the film, the graduation dance—for which they were rehearsing prior to their departure—would appear to represent closure to a cycle of institutional and public education. It is not by chance that the first thing Jorgito asks Malú upon finding out about her possible trip abroad is, "So, you're not going to dance in the ceremony at the end of the year?" The last embrace—part of the vow of eternal friendship—will now acquire a symbolic dimension that would seem to materialize the seal of sentimental and private education between Malú and Jorgito. In other words, the embrace profiles the emotional maturity that has been consecrated as the culmination of their journey and that would assume the place of an intimate and alternate graduation on the fringes of institutional and/or familial power structures. Similarly, the sea evokes the escape from an oppressive space to one that, in many ways, is emancipatory. It is beginning and end, gain and loss. The ocean that stretches out before them "in line with the general symbolism of water (. . .) symbolizes the joining of all the possibilities within an existential plane" (Cirlot 344). Just as the embrace establishes the continuity of their alliance and a horizon of possibilities, the open sea foretells closure to—or perhaps, as many have wanted to read this final scene, the death of—the state of equilibrium and security of the future.

In summary, *Viva Cuba* fuses with great skill the story of sentimental formation with the adventures and turns of the road movie, allowing its young protagonists (at once astute and loquacious, curious, and determined) to project a new Cuba, inviting through play and creativity a rereading of the practices of everyday interaction, of political legislation, and promoting a dialogue about how to perceive and confront life. The lucid discernment that the children acquire in their voyage—embodied in the emotional maturity of their "infinite embrace"—references one of the themes that contemporary Cuban cinema reintroduces and polemicizes: greater than the possibility of happiness, the will to be happy, in spite of the obstacles, and under the protection of solidarity, love, and friendship. Walking without a map but with a sound inner compass, with their gesture of loyalty and affection the children teach adults by showing them a road to hope, much like the song they sing on the school bus with a courageous and dynamic innocence: "Smile at life . . . being happy doesn't cost a thing."

Notes

1. In the Dominican Republic, the religious drama *Prisionera* (Federico Segarra 1995) has as its main character a pregnant teen, and the first horror film *Andrea* (Rogert Bencosme 2005) features a child who is possessed by an evil spirit. From Puerto Rico, the teen comedies *Casi casi* (Jaime Vallés y Tony Valles 2006) and *Party Time: The Movie* (Juanma Fernández-Paris 2009) stand out. Additionally, there are productions for and about children that combine humor with ecological adventures such as *Las estrellas del estuario* (Sonia Fritz 2009) and *Aventura verde* (Abdiel Colberg 2009). Local cinematography has turned attention away from films about urban violence and toward those portraying amusing situations, thus presenting an alternate depiction of children and adolescents.
2. *Viva Cuba* has become a pioneer in film not only because it was made for children with children but also because it has established itself as the first Cuban production made without the backing of the Cuban Institute of Cinematographic Art and Industry (Instituto Cubano de Arte e Industria Cinematográficos or ICAIC), thus marking "an important turn toward alternative cinematic production on the island" (Stock, "Abriendo caminos para el cine cubano" 265).
3. A period of crisis in Cuba in the 1990s stemming from the fall of the Communist Bloc, when economic politics were redesigned and daily life was altered by the scarcity of products and services. Some of the direct consequences were the lack of raw materials, fuel, food, medicine, transportation, and capital.

Works Cited

Browning, Richard L. *Childhood and the Nation in Latin American Literature.* New York: Lang, 2001.

Buckley, Jerome H. *Season of Youth: The Bildungsroman from Dickens to Golding.* Cambridge: Harvard UP, 1974.

Chanan, Michael. "La migración en el cine cubano." *Cinema paraíso.* Ed. Rosana Díaz-Zambrana and Patricia Tomé. San Juan: Isla Negra, 2010. 379–85.

Cirlot, Juan Eduardo. *Diccionario de símbolos.* Madrid: Siruela, 2005.

Cohan, Steven, and Ina Rae Hark. *The Road Movie Book.* New York: Routledge, 2001.

Freud, Sigmund. *Beyond the Pleasure Principle.* Trans. Jenseits des Lust-Prinzips. New York: Norton, 1975.

Gómez Viu, Carmen. "El *Bildungsroman* y la novela de formación femenina hispanoamericana contemporánea." *EPOS* 25 (2009): 107–17.

Jeftanovic, Andrea. "Una mirada cultural y literaria a esa 'perspectiva menor': Infancia, significados y artificios." Web. 20 Nov. 2010. <http://andreajeftanovic.jimdo.com/escritos-académicos/>

Jost, François. "La Tradition du Bildungsroman." *Comparative Literature* 21 (Spring 1969): 97–115.

Jung, Carl. *Psyche and Symbol.* Ed. Violet S. de Laszlo. Trans. R. F. C. Hull. Princeton: Princeton UP, 1991.

Laderman, David. *Driving Visions: Exploring the Road Movie*. Austin: U of Texas P, 2002.
Larrosa, Jorge. *Trayectos, escrituras, metamorfosis: (La idea de formación en la novela)*. Barcelona: Promociones y Publicaciones Universitarias, 1994.
Lemus, Luis Arturo. *Pedagogía: Temas fundamentales*. Buenos Aires: Kapelusz, 1969.
Lukács, György. *Teoría de la novela*. Barcelona: EDHASA, 1971.
Lury, Karen. "The Child in Film and Television." *Screen* 46.3 (2005): 307–14.
McWilliams, Ellen. *Margaret Atwood and the Female Bildungsroman*. Burlington: Ashgate, 2009.
Podalsky, Laura. *The Politics of Affect and Emotion in Contemporary Latin American Cinema: Argentina, Brazil, Cuba, and Mexico*. New York: Palgrave Macmillan, 2011.
Polh, Burkhard. "Rutas transnacionales: La road movie en el cine español." *Hispanic Research Journal* 8.1 (2007): 53–68.
Salmerón, Miguel. *La novela de formación y peripecia*. Madrid: Machado Libros, 2002.
Seminet, Georgia. "A Post-Revolutionary Childhood: Nostalgia and Collective Memory in *Viva Cuba*." *Studies in Hispanic Cinemas* 8.2 (2011): 189–202.
Stock, Ann Marie. "Abriendo caminos para el cine cubano." *Cuba: Cinéma et Révolution*. Ed. Julie Amiot-Guillouet and Nancy Berthier. Lyon: Le Grimh, 2006. 263–71.
———. *On Location in Cuba: Street Filmmaking during Times of Transition*. Chapel Hill: U of North Carolina P, 2009.
Vincent, Mauricio. "*Viva Cuba*, un filme sobre la aventura de la emigración." *El País* 26 May 2006: n. pag. Web. 15 Jan. 2011 <http://www.elpais.com/articulo/cine/Viva/Cuba/filme/aventura/emigracion/elpcinpor/20060526elpepicin_9/Tes>.
Viva Cuba. Dir. Juan Carlos Cremata Malberti. Perf. Malú Tarrau Borche, Jorge Miló, Luisa María Jiménez, Larisa Vega, Alberto Pujols and Abel Rodríguez. Epicentre Films, 2005. Digital videodisc.
Wilson, Emma. "Children, Emotion and Viewing in Contemporary European Film." *Screen* 46.3 (2005): 329–40.
Zamudio, Luz Elena. "Los personajes infantiles en *Balún-Canán*." *Escribir la infancia: Narradoras mexicanas contemporáneas*. Ed. Nora Pasternac, Ana Rosa Domenella, and Luzelena Gutiérrez de Velasco. México: El Colegio de México, 1996. 127–44.

PART III

GENDER IDENTITY

CHAPTER 10

Constructing Ethical Attention in Lucía Puenzo's *XXY*

Cinematic Strategy, Intersubjectivity, and Intersexuality

Jeffrey Zamostny

Argentine filmmaker Lucía Puenzo's movie *XXY* (2007) stands apart from a long line of other fictional and philosophical works concerned with intersexed characters. In contrast to works that use "the hermaphrodite" as a trope for an original unity of the sexes, decadence, or degeneration, the film focuses on the lived experience of a concrete intersexed adolescent raised as a girl.[1] By tracing five days in the life of 15-year-old Alex and her family on a sparsely populated Uruguayan island, Puenzo constructs a complex vision of an intersexed character portrayed not as a metaphor but as a material being in relation with others.[2] Throughout this process, the director propagates ideals that have been defended by intersex activists in Argentina and the United States. *XXY* disputes the need for genital surgeries at birth, objects to the naturalization of culturally contingent sexual binaries, and contends that intersexed individuals should be allowed to decide the destiny of their bodies for themselves.

At the same time, the film's aesthetic and social programs exceed the imperatives of activism by generating a nuanced, open-ended narrative that evades teleological demands for unabated progress toward political goals. In what follows, I trace how Puenzo deploys narrative and cinematic strategies both to draw ethical attention to the ideals defended by the intersex cause and to illustrate the intense struggles faced by adolescents who put the principles of intersex activism into practice in their daily lives. Puenzo's tactics generate a rich network of comparisons and contrasts between the film's protagonists. Their gazes, words, and actions, together with their metonymic association with aesthetically pleasing visual motives, converge to distinguish between static and dynamic characters. While the former cling tenaciously to sexual binaries and hope to "normalize" Alex as a female, the latter begin to form relationships with Alex predicated on respect for intersexual difference. Although Puenzo's cinematic language creates a positive vision of this second group of protagonists, it also reveals the obstacles that prevent even them from engaging in mutually respectful relationships with Alex. The result is a densely textured film that points to both the necessity and difficulty of modifying the cultural construction of sex so that intersexed people can live as such while maintaining satisfying bonds with others.

XXY AND INTERSEX ACTIVISM

The close association between *XXY* and intersex activist movements in Argentina and the United States is made clear by the movie's official website, which is a paratextual apparatus that offers insight into how the film's creators intended for their work to be perceived on the cultural market.[3] In a press review included on the site, Mauro Cabral claims that *XXY* represents "la primera vez que el discurso anti-normalización es expuesta tan claramente y en un medio tan masivo [como el cine]" (the first time the anti-normalization discourse has been presented so clearly and in a medium as pervasive as film). Identified on the website as an intersex researcher and activist, Cabral has emerged in recent years as a spokesperson for intersex activism both in Argentina and internationally.[4] As such, he participates in an activist movement that took shape in the 1990s when a generation of medically "normalized" intersexed individuals became increasingly aware of the costs of their childhood surgeries (Karkazis 236–90).

According to anthropologist Katrina Karkazis, the agenda of this movement includes both short- and long-term goals. On the one hand, intersex activists advocate for immediate change to the ways in which doctors and parents treat infants born with genitals that cannot be classified along a clear-cut male-female binary. Most activists challenge the necessity of surgical intervention at birth in cases in which an infant's health is not at stake. They defend the right of intersexed individuals to make decisions regarding their own bodies later in life. On the other hand, the intersex movement aims to gradually erode the culturally constructed naturalization of a binary sex system that renders intersexed bodies illegible and undesirable. It promotes "the acceptance, dignity, and humane treatment for those with gender-atypical bodies in an effort to challenge ideology, practices, and consciousness" (Karkazis 8). In contrast to medical practices that attempt to resolve the "problem" of intersexuality by surgically manipulating individual intersexed bodies, intersex activism seeks to expand medical and social conceptions of which bodies qualify as "natural" or "normal." The purpose is to avoid gratuitous medical procedures by redefining intersexuality as a benign natural variation for the majority of intersexed individuals.

XXY's website encourages interested viewers to learn more about intersex activism by reading three articles by Cabral and fellow activist Diana Maffía included on the site.[5] The essays reiterate the intersex ideals outlined above and point to activism's international scope. Cabral and Maffía cite a range of scholars and activists from Latin America and the United States, including Judith Butler. Their claim that "el sexo anatómico mismo, su propia presunta dicotomía, son producto de una lectura ideológica" (anatomical sex and its ostensible dichotomy are themselves products of an ideological construction) draws on Butler's argument in *Gender Trouble* (1990) against a strict separation between sex as something natural or biological and gender as a cultural construction (8–10).

Butler's famous book and the broad ideals of the intersex movement can be seen as the theoretical base on which Puenzo constructs a pro-intersex filmic narrative. *XXY* engages both the immediate and long-term goals of contemporary intersex activism. The protagonists must confront the question of whether 15-year-old Alex should continue taking medicine and undergoing surgeries to prolong her development as a female. The action begins with the decision of Alex's mother (Suli) to invite the surgeon Ramiro and his wife and son (Erika and Álvaro) to her family's home on a rural Uruguayan island. Ramiro's objective is to evaluate the feasibility of an operation on Alex. While Ramiro, Erika, and Suli push for surgery, Alex and her father Kraken are wary of medical intervention. Alex's resistance to the proposed operation and the departure of Ramiro's family without having scheduled the surgery make Alex's case an individual triumph of intersex activism's struggle against medical "normalization."

The film's most explicit statement against such intervention appears when Kraken visits Scherer, an intersexed individual who was raised as a girl and later decided to live as a man. Since Kraken goes to Scherer for advice about how to treat Alex, the film sets him up as an expert whose personal experience affords him the privilege of making authoritative statements about intersexuality. Scherer unequivocally denounces surgery at birth by renaming "normalización" (normalization) as "castración" (castration). Ultimately, his negative appraisal of medical operations on intersexed children influences Kraken's decision to accept Alex as both "hijo" (son) and "hija" (daughter) at the end of the movie.

In addition to defending Alex's right to choose for or against medical operations, *XXY* also participates in the activist project to destabilize culturally determined sexual dichotomies. Although Scherer elects to integrate himself into such binaries as a man—he has established what he calls "la familia tipo" (the prototypical family) with a wife and an adopted child—other characters and motives move beyond the male-female framework. Puenzo's camera pauses frequently on hermaphroditic plants and animals—eels, goldfish, marine plants with both carpels and stamens—so as to suggest that intersexuality is a ubiquitous natural phenomenon.[6] Even humans who appear to fall easily into the male-female dichotomy have certain "intersexual" tendencies, as suggested by a shot of Erika in bed with Ramiro. As Erika rubs beauty cream into her face, Ramiro reaches over to help her, and then rubs the excess cream onto his own cheeks. Whereas Ramiro is portrayed elsewhere as the film's most zealous defender of medical intervention and the male-female binary, this scene makes clear that Ramiro himself sometimes unwittingly blurs gender and sexual dichotomies. Indeed, Ramiro's fear of ambiguity within himself may motivate his need to consolidate sexual differentiation in others through surgery.

Moreover, the range of Ramiro's professional activities points to ways in which operations on intersexed individuals exist on a continuum with many other practices that construct sex on the body. In a scene set in the island's marine biology museum, a lateral traveling captures Alex and Álvaro walking alongside the hanging skeletons of whales and other sea creatures. In this context, Alex's questions about Ramiro's breast enlargement surgeries associate femininity-enhancing operations with death. In response to her claim that Ramiro must have enlarged thousands of breasts, Álvaro argues that "mi papá hace tetas y narices por plata, pero a él en realidad le interesan otras cosas," including "deformidades" (my dad does boob and nose jobs for money, but in reality he is interested in other things, including deformities). Álvaro establishes a connection between operations on intersexed individuals like Alex and cosmetic surgery: both form part of the cultural construction of biological sex—particularly by male physicians—to the extent that they modify bodies with the aim of approximating cultural fantasies of what it means to be female. Álvaro's reference to money further suggests that the discursive and corporal constitution of sex is a lucrative business with a vested interest in preserving binary sex systems.

Likewise, Alex's subsequent reinterpretation of Ramiro's surgeries as a form of slaughter—for Alex, Ramiro "rebana cuerpos" (slices up bodies)—implies that the cultural *construction* of the male-female dichotomy is actually a violent *destruction* of naturally occurring physical variations between humans. The film's moves to both illustrate and undermine the ways in which sexual difference is channeled by culture into a restrictive dual framework strongly support the objectives of intersex activism.

Ethical Attention and the Limits of Intersubjectivity

XXY would probably be a less engaging film if its sole aims were to buttress activist discourses and to indulge in a politically correct celebration of the ideals set forth by the intersex movement. What is most compelling about Puenzo's work is its aesthetically subtle use of narrative and cinematic strategies to simultaneously draw ethical attention to the goals of intersex activism and to contest excessively optimistic visions of social progress. My examination of these strategies in the following sections builds on film critic Jane Stadler's study of ethics at the movies in *Pulling Focus* (2008), and feminist psychoanalyst Jessica Benjamin's descriptions of intrapsychic and intersubjective relations in books such as *Like Subjects, Love Objects* (1995) and *Shadow of the Other* (1997).

For Stadler, ethical attention is a "perceptual capacity [. . .] characterized by concern for the specific needs and vulnerabilities of a unique individual or situation, within a concrete and particular ethical context" (206). In film, this type of perception may be exercised by diegetic characters, extradiegetic spectators, or the cinematic apparatus itself, by means of the techniques it deploys to construct particular visions of characters and their situations. Stadler focuses on how narrative action, characterization, camera angles and point of view, and montage generate ethical attention, the final goal of which is a "detailed, just, and caring awareness that enables an ethical agent to respond more appropriately to the unique requirements of a situation than application of general ethical rules, values, or principles would, on their own, allow" (206). In *XXY*, the production of awareness of this kind centers on the creation of respect for Alex's intersexual embodiment and personal autonomy. Puenzo's cinematic language distinguishes between dynamic characters that begin to adopt a contextually informed and ethically attentive attitude of care vis-à-vis Alex's difference, and static characters that consistently apply traditional sexual schemes to Alex's case and therefore attempt to integrate her into a male-female dichotomy. The characters in this second group fail to adopt an ethically attentive stance toward Alex, and instead practice other "modes of perception" (Stadler 208). These "forms of cinematic vision," including "voyeurism and objectification," establish hierarchies between the viewer and the viewed, active agents and passive objects, and the powerful and the dominated, all of which are foreign to the more egalitarian inflections of ethical attention (Stadler 216).[7] In *XXY*, the most asymmetrical gazes are clinical looks that inspect Alex's body in order to detect her intersexual difference with the aim of drawing it into the fold of "normal" biological variation.

One way to summarize Stadler's distinction between ethical attention and other modes of perception is to relate it to Benjamin's psychoanalytic work on intersubjective and intrapsychic relations. Benjamin significantly revises traditional models of psychoanalysis that imagine the individual as a subject whose mind treats others primarily as objects useful for its own development and gratification (*Like Subjects* 30). She argues that "the mind works through both the relation to the other as an object of identification/projection *and* the relation to the other as an independent outside subject" (6; emphasis added). The first operation results in intrapsychic relations in which individuals view others as "fantasy object[s]," whether "derogated or ideal" (19). Voyeurism is one type of look associated with these relations. In the second operation, on the contrary, people practice ethical attention and establish intersubjective relations by mutually recognizing and respecting each others' autonomy, similarities, and irreducible differences.

Coincidentally, Benjamin's most recent work acknowledges the difficulty of maintaining intersubjective relations and argues that the very condition for intersubjectivity is the periodic breakdown of mutual recognition through the disavowal of radical alterity. In other words, intersubjective relations regularly fail when individuals assume that they can fully know one another (*Shadow* xviii). *XXY* gives credence to Benjamin's theories, for the bonds between Alex and the people around her constantly oscillate between the poles of intrapsychic and intersubjective relations. While the film's static characters view Alex as an object, more dynamic figures experience occasional—and ephemeral—epiphanies of intersubjective connection with her.[8]

Kraken and Ramiro: A Paradigmatic Pair

The pair comprising Kraken and Ramiro vividly illustrates the differences between the characters in *XXY* who practice ethical attention and evolve toward intersubjective relations with Alex, and those who do not. The contrast between the two men is all the more powerful since they have much in common. Both Kraken and Ramiro are middle-aged, white, married men and fathers of sexually burgeoning adolescents. As scientists, they are equally interested in anatomy and sex, although Kraken works on sea creatures and Ramiro on humans. Most importantly, their scientific endeavors lead them to cultivate a similarly clinical gaze, aimed at determining the biological sex of either humans or animals. Puenzo captures this look in a series of close-up images and dialogues that converge on a cluster of related motives, including photographs, drawings, scientific texts, and flesh. While Kraken progressively abandons his clinically distanced mode of perception, Ramiro's gaze remains unchanged throughout *XXY*.

Ramiro's direct interactions with Alex over the five days that he spends at her home are minimal. Therefore, his knowledge of Alex derives primarily from his contact with medical records and photographs. The film's first shots of Ramiro are framed from Álvaro's point of view. As the boy spies on his father from the backseat of their car on the ferry, the camera reveals that Ramiro is reading Kraken's book *Orígenes del sexo* along with some other documents. A brief glimpse of a photograph of Alex suggests that the papers are her medical history. Ramiro immediately hides the photograph from Álvaro's gaze, as though to cut off access to privileged information over which Ramiro has sole ownership. This connection between knowledge and power appears once more on another occasion when the surgeon examines medical documents. After applying Erika's cream to his face in the scene described above, Ramiro returns his attention to the file he had been studying earlier. A close-up from his point of view shows that he is looking at what must be Alex's ultrasound and drawing and labeling her genitals. Ramiro reduces Alex to her sexual organs, objects over which he hopes to exert biomedical control with his pen—whose tracings render visible his clinical gaze—and his scalpel.

As Margaret Frohlich notes in a discussion of cutting in *XXY*, allusions to the blade of the surgical instrument are prominent in the only scene in which Ramiro has intimate face-to-face contact with Alex (165). On the morning of his second day on the island, Alex encounters Ramiro alone in the kitchen, where he is slicing a piece of sausage with a large knife. When Alex opens the refrigerator to retrieve a bottle of milk, Ramiro pauses to examine her. In one of the most overtly sexual gazes in the film, the camera follows Ramiro's look as it scans Alex's body from bottom to top. The invasive gaze is not lost on Alex, who turns the tables on Ramiro by asking him an uncomfortably direct erotic question: "¿Te gusta?" (Do you like it?). Alex's clarification that she is asking not about her body but about her house barely diminishes the scene's sexual tension. Her next question—"¿Abrir cuerpos te gusta?" (Do you like to open bodies?)—solidifies the analogy between Ramiro's cutting of the phallic-shaped sausage, possible future operations on Alex's body, and sexual violation. Overall, this scene illustrates Alex's resistance to Ramiro's vision of her as a piece of flesh on which he can exercise erotic and medicalized violence.

The connection between Ramiro's clinical objectification of Alex and sexual aggression remains strong throughout *XXY* and finally coalesces in Ramiro's response to the sexual assault against Alex. The film establishes a continuum between the surgeon's clinical gaze and the more obviously hostile looks of the three adolescent rapists. In the rape scene, the principal assailant assures Alex that he wants only to "ver, nada más" (see, nothing else). Like Ramiro, the boys are obsessed with observing Alex's genitals in order to subordinate her to their sexual domination. The affinity between Ramiro and the boys is sealed when he defends them from Kraken's fury at the dock. Kraken's reaction is damning, for he accuses Ramiro of being "igual que ellos. Peor que ellos" (the same as them. Worse than them). The following day, Ramiro departs from the island with his family without having reached an ethical understanding of Alex as an autonomous individual with the right to live in an intersexed body.

Kraken's claim that Ramiro is like the rapists represents a significant reversal of a similar line earlier in *XXY*. As Alex and Álvaro watch Kraken operating on an injured sea turtle in his laboratory, Alex concludes that "al final tu papá y el mío son el mismo" (in the end your dad and my dad are the same), since both manipulate living flesh. The following shot of Kraken's look of disapproval indicates that Alex's words are too harsh. His goals as scientist are different from those of Ramiro insofar as he does not hope to make money from surgery. On the contrary, he wants to save a creature that would likely die without his intervention. Yet Alex's observation rings true to the extent that Kraken, like Ramiro, does exercise a clinical gaze aimed at fixing sex along a male-female binary toward the beginning of the film.

Initially introduced from Suli's point of view, when she observes him in the marine biology museum, Kraken's earliest action in *XXY* consists of opening a sea turtle in order to identify its sex. Incidentally, his determination that the turtle is an "hembra" (female) is the first spoken word in the movie. This scene marks the start of an extended metonymic relation between turtles and Alex. Puenzo has indicated in an interview that she included the reptiles in the film because it is impossible to determine their sex without opening their shells, much as Alex's sex remains ambiguous until people like Ramiro or the rapists pry into her medical records or forcibly remove her clothing.[9] Just as Kraken pronounces the turtle a female, he and Suli have chosen to raise Alex as a girl. Later on, Alex's discomfort about Kraken's operation on the injured turtle may reflect her fear of surgery on her own body. Finally, the rapists leave a pile of broken turtle shells on the beach outside Alex's house just before they undress Alex in the assault. The effect of the turtle imagery throughout associates Alex with an endangered species constantly at risk of falling into dangerous nets, whether of fishermen or the cultural norms of a society that cannot accept intersexual difference.

Kraken's job tracking the migratory routes of turtles and determining their sex is linked to his wider interest in questions of biology and sex, which is in turn related to his preoccupation with Alex's intersexuality. As mentioned, Kraken is the author of a scientific manual on sexual evolution titled *Orígenes del sexo*. This book has more importance in the film than its few brief appearances might indicate. When a medium shot shows Alex reading from the manual in her bed, viewers are left to speculate about why she has the book. The passage read aloud by Alex is a clue: "En todos los vertebrados, incluso en el ser humano, el sexo femenino es el primario en un sentido evolutivo y embriológico" (In all vertebrates, including the human being, the female sex comes first from an evolutionary and embryological standpoint). The sentence on which Alex has become fixated—she has marked it with a feather and keeps the book under her pillow—suggests that she interprets the volume as an attempt by her father to help her understand sexual differentiation and to justify his decision to raise her as a girl. Alex's dismissal of the rest of the book signals her resistance to scientific discourses that uphold male-female sexual schemes.

Although his identification of the sea turtle as hembra and his scientific manual suggest that Kraken adopts a clinical gaze early in *XXY*, his development during the five days of the narrative leads him to affirm that Alex is perfect just as she is, to renounce his own clinical gaze, and to reject the medical look imposed by Ramiro. Symbolically charged speech and images gauge the degree of Kraken's evolution. While he inaugurates the film's dialogue by identifying the turtle as an hembra, by the end he calls Alex both hijo and hija. And while he initially gave Alex his book on sexual evolution, he takes the volume back when Alex returns it as a sign that her own developmental path will not follow the route marked out by a sexual binary.

In the end, Kraken's acceptance of Alex's decision to live as an intersexed individual is the result of his ethical attention to her needs and his efforts to establish an intersubjective relationship with his child in which he treats her not as an object but as an autonomous subject whose differences demand recognition and respect. In the film's final scene, Alex wraps Kraken's arm around her shoulder as though to accept her father's attempts at intersubjectivity. The relative success of mutual recognition between Alex and Kraken contrasts with the breakdown of intersubjective relations between Alex and a second dynamic character who strives for an ethically attentive understanding of Alex's intersexuality: Álvaro.

Álvaro and Intersubjective Breakdown

The most salient element of Álvaro's characterization in the first half of *XXY* are his headphones, which almost never leave his ears or neck. Symbolic of his desire to block out his fellow human beings, the headphones indicate the ambivalence of Álvaro's initial situation. On the one hand, he enjoys a stable and socioeconomically privileged family life. At the same time, he feels estranged from Erika and Ramiro. His distance from his father stems from his intense admiration for Ramiro's professional success, and from Ramiro's disappointment that his son has not proven himself sufficiently masculine. In a scene strategically placed just before Kraken accepts Alex's decision not to seek surgery, Ramiro harshly informs Álvaro that he has no talent and that "tenía miedo que fueras puto" (I was afraid you were a faggot). Unlike Kraken, Ramiro forecloses any possibility of establishing an intersubjective relationship with his son by assuming that he can fully know and name Álvaro's sexuality before Álvaro can self-identify. Just as Ramiro seeks to "normalize" Alex in order to disavow any kind of sexual ambiguity in himself, he labels Álvaro an abject "puto" in an intrapsychic attempt to project his own fear of homosexuality onto another. Whether or not Álvaro actually *is* homosexual is a moot point, since he eventually falls in love with Alex. His relationship with an individual with both male and female genitals effectively confounds the bounds of hetero- and homosexuality.

Incidentally, Álvaro must pass through an intense period of evolution before he can begin to establish a loving, ethically attentive relationship with Alex, and even after he begins to do so, there are numerous impediments to the preservation of intersubjectivity between the two adolescents. In the first third of *XXY*, Álvaro's prime objective is to uncover Alex's mystery and to determine why his father was examining her medical record in the car on the ferry. In order to do so, Álvaro adopts an objectifying gaze similar to that of Ramiro. Puenzo's camera insistently adopts Álvaro's point of view to show how he goes about exposing the details of Alex's personal life. The camera aligns itself with Álvaro's gaze when he first sees Alex under the porch, when he examines photographs of Alex displayed in the house, when he invasively enters Alex's bedroom, and when he sees her medicines. Like Ramiro's perusal of Alex's medical records, Álvaro's unrestrained gazes over her photographs and belongings transform Alex into an object of analysis.

Similarly, Ramiro's drawings of Alex's genitals are mirrored by Álvaro's own drawings throughout *XXY*. In a scene on the beach, a close-up shows Álvaro poking a beetle with a pen so as to hold it in place while he draws it. When Alex asks Álvaro what he is doing, he replies that he has "un bichito raro. No lo toques" (a strange little insect. Don't touch it). Offended by his words, Alex asks, "¿Qué sabés vos de las especies de mi casa?" (What do you know about the species of my home?). As happened with the turtle, Alex implicitly identifies with the beetle. In the same way that Álvaro pins down the insect in order to bring it under his control through his drawing, he tries to get a handle on Alex through surveillance of her body, photos, and possessions. Rather than freeing the beetle, Alex maliciously smashes it into Álvaro's notebook in a move that reflects her self-destructive tendencies, as revealed by the opening images of the film in which she runs violently with a knife through the forest.

If Álvaro's objectification of Alex initially hinders the formation an intersubjective bond between the two adolescents, Alex's instrumental use of Álvaro is equally obstructive. Although Puenzo's camera aligns itself more closely with Álvaro than Alex, when the boy first arrives at Alex's home, the camera alternates between the two perspectives. Thus Álvaro's gaze on Alex under the porch is met by her similarly penetrating look. The camera also adopts Alex's point of view when she watches Álvaro urinating the following morning. Alex's voyeuristic looks reveal her desire to use the boy as a sex object. After squashing the insect on the beach, she admits that she wants to have intercourse with Álvaro because she does not plan to fall in love with him. Later, when the two adolescents do have sex, Alex is quite coercive and Álvaro does not anticipate being penetrated.

This sexual encounter marks a turning point in the relationship between Alex and Álvaro. Forced to come to terms with what has happened, the latter must repudiate his tendency to view Alex as an object, and begin to relate to her as an active subject capable of changing his own self-understanding. In an attempt to learn more about Alex as a complex human being, Álvaro again enters Alex's bedroom. His objective this time is not to determine what is "wrong" with Alex, but to comprehend her feelings. The artwork in Alex's diary aids him in this endeavor and contrasts with the other sketches in *XXY*. While Ramiro and Álvaro's drawings are scientific images of Alex's genitals and the beetle, Alex's expressionistic art offers Álvaro a window into her troubled subjective world. Close-ups of the diary reveal disturbing sketches of intersexed children being hung and beheaded. In one, a comic-like blurb shows a figure reminiscent of Alex hanging upside down and screaming "Help!" The drawing testifies to Alex's desperate need for intersubjective contact with others who will not overlook or stigmatize her intersexual difference.

In response, Álvaro tries unsuccessfully to bond with Alex for the remainder of his time at her home. The clearest symbol of the change in his attitude toward Alex is his decision at the end of the film to wear the chain that she had given him prior to the sex scene. At one point, Alex offers him a necklace with a tag used to track the migration routes of sea turtles. She explains that the tag on Álvaro's chain belongs to a turtle from the same family as the one whose tag is on her own necklace. While Álvaro declines to wear the chain at the time, he decides to put it on the morning of his last day with Alex. In a medium shot, he shows the tag to Alex, as if to confirm that his desire now makes him part of her family.

Alex's final response is devastating, for she refuses to acknowledge Álvaro's evolution. She pulls away defensively and interrogates him: "¿Qué te da más lástima? ¿No verme más, o no haberla visto?" (What pains you most? Not seeing me anymore, or not having seen my dick?). In response to the boy's confused silence, Alex asks if he wants to see her genitals, and then pulls down her pants to reveal them. Alex's question—"¿Quieres ver?" (Do you want to see?)—echoes her rapist's claim that he "quier[e] ver" (wants to see) her private parts. In the wake of her trauma, Alex attributes false motives to Álvaro, confuses him with her aggressors, and fails to recognize his subjective autonomy.[10] She internalizes others' objectification of her body and offers herself as a target for Álvaro's gaze. Tragically, the sequence's final shot does not make clear whether the boy looks at Alex's genitals. For most of the shot, Álvaro refuses to lower his gaze. Yet just when Ramiro interrupts the scene to guide his son to the ferry, Álvaro's eyes look downward. The implication is a failure of intersubjective relations in the moment when the boy would most like to empathize with Alex. A final image capturing Alex's troubled expression and tear-filled eyes indicates that she realizes too late that Álvaro is not the same as her rapists.

Between Isolation and Intersubjectivity: An Open Ending

The final breakdown of intersubjective connection between Álvaro and Alex, together with the difficulty of such contact between the boy and his father, is but one example of estrangement between subjects in *XXY*. Just as Álvaro's headphones signify his efforts to block out the world, the other characters' island home foregrounds their personal isolation. Despite living in close quarters for five days, the characters inhabit distinct subjective spaces, only tenuously linked to other subjectivities through glances and terse conversations. Within this context, moments of mutual recognition stand out as epiphanies, as when Alex removes Álvaro's headphones so that she too can listen to his songs. The contact proves ephemeral, as Alex miscalculates Álvaro's intentions at the end of the film. The final scenes thus leave Alex suspended between isolation from the boy and a new sense of proximity to Suli and especially Kraken. A final pan over the open sea emphasizes the questions raised by the equally open ending about Alex's future as both an intersexed individual who has chosen to reject surgery and an adolescent traumatized by her first sexual experiences.

XXY's ambiguous conclusion hampers any interpretation of the movie as a clear-cut espousal of ideals upheld by contemporary intersex activism. Although dialogue, visual motives, and the perspectives adopted by the camera portray dynamic protagonists in a positive light and draw attention to their increasing acceptance of Alex's decisions about her body, constant failures of intersubjectivity suggest that overcoming medical pressure to undergo surgery will not immediately resolve the difficulties faced by intersexed adolescents. Consequently, *XXY* sets up ethical attention and intersubjectivity as goals whose attainment is subject to perpetual deferral to the future.[11] Actually achieving such aims is far less important than continuously striving for mutual recognition and respect between subjects, whether intersexed or otherwise. The film's open ending leaves viewers to decide whether they will join in that striving.

Notes

1. See Gary Williams (xiv–xx) for the use of "the hermaphrodite" as a trope in nineteenth-century European and US literature and philosophy.
2. I recognize the limitations of using gendered pronouns when referring to intersexed people, yet I retain them so as to avoid using dehumanizing neuter words like "it." See Julia Epstein's discussion of this issue (105).
3. As this article goes to press, it has come to my attention that the official website first used to market *XXY* is no longer available on the Internet. Margaret Frohlich notes the disappearance and observes that a newer webpage omits most of the original information about the film (162). The articles by Mauro Cabral and Diana Maffía listed in my bibliography were available on the old official website.
4. Cabral belongs to the Observatorio Internacional Intersexualidad y Derechos Humanos and to Mulabi: Espacio Latinoamericano de Sexualidad y Derechos. His writings appear in volumes published in the United States. See his essay in *Transgender Rights*.
5. See "Como la que más," "Pensar la intersexualidad, hoy," and "Los sexos: ¿Son o se hacen?" under "Diagnóstico de Alex" at http://www.puenzo.com/xxylapelicula/main.html.
6. Frohlich's work on *XXY* explores positive and negative effects of the film's insistent linkage of nature and intersexuality. On the one hand, "*XXY*'s representation of an idealized natural realm where liminality belongs, and need not be corrected, contests the reduction of certain types of variance to the abnormal and the unnatural within medical and juridical discourse" (164). At the same time, the film runs the risk of prioritizing "nature over agency" and "[l]inking intersexed people with a romanticized biodiversity" (161, 166).
7. A strand of feminist criticism on the classic Hollywood film notes that power imbalances in voyeurism often correspond to a male or masculinized gaze over the female sex object. See Laura Mulvey and E. Ann Kaplan. One problem with these theories for *XXY* is that the film's intersexed protagonist confounds easy distinctions between male and female gazes. When Puenzo's camera adopts Alex's point of view, is the look male or female?
8. Benjamin's feminist psychoanalysis offers a solution to the impasse faced by feminist film theory that runs up against "subject-object" structures in more traditional psychoanalysis (Kaplan 135). Her ideas on intersubjectivity offer firm theoretical backing for E. Ann Kaplan's suggestions about the possibility of "*mutual* gazing" in film (135). Other scholars who have used the term *intersubjectivity* in discussions of cinema (see George Butte, Tarja Laine, and Jane Stadler) turn to phenomenological usages of the term in Jean-Paul Sartre and Maurice Merleau-Ponty in order to evade psychoanalysis altogether. Although Merleau-Ponty's thoughts on the topic are similar to those of Benjamin's, the advantage of the latter's framework is that it sustains a psychoanalytic interest in sex and gender lacking in phenomenological discourse.
9. See the interview with Puenzo at http://www.youtube.com/watch?v=sYg7Ak4JuAA&NR=1. Sophie Mayer records additional statements by Puenzo on *XXY* in "Family Business."

10. For an analysis of *XXY* through the lens of contemporary trauma theory, see Bécquer Medak-Seguín.
11. I draw here on Jacques Derrida, for whom justice and democracy exist in an infinitely deferred future and are "impossible [...] *in the present*" (16, 23).

Works Cited

Benjamin, Jessica. *Like Subjects, Love Objects: Essays on Recognition and Sexual Difference*. New Haven: Yale UP, 1995.

———. *Shadow of the Other: Intersubjectivity and Gender in Psychoanalysis*. New York: Routledge, 1997.

Butler, Judith. *Gender Trouble: Feminism and the Subversion of Identity*. 2nd ed. New York: Routledge, 1990.

Butte, George. *I Know That You Know That I Know: Narrating Subjects from Moll Flanders to Marnie*. Columbus: Ohio State UP, 2004.

Cabral, Mauro. "Como la que más." *XXY: La película*. Web. 20 Feb. 2010 <http://www.puenzo.com.xxylapelicula/main.html>.

———. "Pensar la intersexualidad, hoy." *XXY: La película*. Web. 20 Feb. 2010 <http://www.puenzo.com/xxylapelicula/main.html>.

Cabral, Mauro, and Paula Viturro. "(Trans)sexual Citizenship in Contemporary Argentina." *Transgender Rights*. Ed. Paisley Currah, Richard M. Juang, and Shannon Minter. Minneapolis: U of Minnesota P, 2006. 262–73.

Derrida, Jacques. "Force of Law: The 'Mystical Formation of Authority.'" *Deconstruction and the Possibility of Justice*. Ed. Drucilla Cornell, Michel Rosenfeld, and David Gray Carlson. New York: Routledge, 1992. 3–67.

Epstein, Julia. *Altered Conditions: Disease, Medicine, and Storytelling*. New York: Routledge, 1995.

Frohlich, Margaret. "What of Unnatural Bodies?: The Discourse of Nature in Lucía Puenzo's *XXY* and *El niño pez/The Fish Child*." *Studies in Hispanic Cinemas* 8.2 (2011): 159-74.

Kaplan, E. Ann. "Is the Gaze Male?" *Feminism and Film*. Ed. E. Ann Kaplan. Oxford: Oxford UP, 2000. 119–38.

Karkazis, Katrina Alicia. *Fixing Sex: Intersex, Medical Authority, and Lived Experience*. Durham: Duke UP, 2008.

Laine, Tarja. *Shame and Desire: Emotion, Intersubjectivity, Cinema*. Bruxelles: Lang, 2007.

Maffía, Diana, and Mauro Cabral. "Los sexos: ¿Son o se hacen?" *XXY: La película*. Web. 20 Feb. 2010 <http://www.puenzo.com/xxylapelicula/main.html>.

Mayer, Sophie. "Family Business." *Sight and Sound* 18.6 (2008): 14.

Medak-Seguín, Bécquer. "Hacia una noción de lo traumático queer: *XXY* de Lucía Puenzo." *Nomenclatura: aproximaciones a los estudios hispánicos* 1.1 (2011): 1-23. Web. 13 Mar. 2012 <http://uknowledge.uky.edu/cgi/viewcontent.cgi?article=1001&context=naeh>.

Mulvey, Laura. "Visual Pleasure and Narrative Cinema." *Feminism and Film*. Ed. E. Ann Kaplan. Oxford: Oxford UP, 2000. 34–47.

Puenzo, Lucía. "*XXY* Director Lucía Puenzo Conducts Q&A, NY Premier (Part 3)." *YouTube*. Web. 5 Mar. 2010. <http://www.youtube.com/watch?v=sYg7Ak 4JuAA&NR=1>.

Stadler, Jane. *Pulling Focus: Intersubjective Experience, Narrative Film, and Ethics*. New York: Continuum, 2008.

Williams, Gary. "Speaking with the Voices of Others." *The Hermaphrodite*. By Julia Ward Howe. Ed. Gary Williams. Lincoln: U of Nebraska P, 2004. ix–xliv.

XXY. Dir. Lucía Puenzo. Perf. Inés Efron, Ricardo Darín, and Martín Piroyansky. Film Movement, 2007. Digital videodisc.

CHAPTER 11

CINEMATIC PORTRAYALS OF TEEN GIRLS IN BRAZIL'S URBAN PERIPHERIES

REALIST AND SUBJECTIVIST APPROACHES TO ADOLESCENT DREAMS AND FANTASY IN *SONHOS ROUBADOS* AND *NINA*

JACK DRAPER

While many famous Brazilian films featuring poverty and crime tend to focus more on the perspective of teen boys (such as *Cidade de Deus* [*City of God*] and *Cidade dos homens* [*City of Men*], some provide an alternative focus on the desires and dreams of teen girls—as well as their nightmares. Sandra Werneck's *Sonhos roubados* (*Stolen Dreams* 2010) takes a realist perspective on the everyday lives of three teen girls living in the favelas, or urban slums of Rio de Janeiro. Werneck portrays many serious problems related to urban poverty: child abuse, the drug trade, and related violence and prostitution. However, she makes a special effort to demonstrate that her protagonists, amid this lawless landscape of dangerous obstacles, continue to pursue the dreams they have for a more normal life and to try to care for their nascent families as well. Yet it should be understood that realism is not the only stylistic approach taken by Brazilian filmmakers when dealing with teen girls in a setting of urban poverty. Heitor Dahlia's *Nina* (2004), described by the director as a loose adaptation of Fyodor Dostoevsky's *Crime and Punishment*, takes a much more subjective approach. The film overall focuses on the mind-set and emotional state of its protagonist Nina (Guta Stresser), exploring this teenaged girl's passion for her manga-inspired art and gothic subculture as well as her often tenuous grip on reality.[1]

In this introductory section, we can briefly consider each film more specifically to emphasize their unique perspectives on teen girls' lives and situate them generally within Brazilian cinematic history. Werneck's *Sonhos roubados*, for one, can clearly be situated within the context of the many recent filmic portrayals of Rio's favelas. These films include *Cidade de Deus* (2002) and the related film *Cidade dos homens* (2007) as well as *Última parada 174* (*Last Stop 174*; 2008), *Linha de passé* (*Life Is What You Make It*; 2008), *Tropa de elite* (*Elite Squad*; 2007) and *Tropa de elite 2* (2010) among others. Many of these popular films feature male children as characters. Often this masculine dominance of the screen is a symptom of the cinematic focus on violent conflicts between gangs and police perpetrated primarily by men and boys, but even in films such as *Cidade dos homens* and *Linha de passe* that do not dwell on these violent conflicts, the boys are central characters while girls play supporting roles if any. Werneck herself has criticized this situation, stating, "O cinema brasileiro sempre falou dos meninos, como em 'Cidade dos Homens', 'Cidade de Deus'. As meninas, quando aparecem, são sempre como coadjuvantes amorosas, você nunca sabe qual é o universo delas" (Brazilian cinema always spoke of the boys, like in *Cidade dos homens*, *Cidade de Deus*. The girls, when they appear, are always in romantic supporting roles, you never know what their world is; Ezabella).

Werneck has sought to represent more woman-centered narratives in many of her films, including most recently her documentary *Meninas* (*Teen Mothers*; 2006), on teen mothers from Rio's favelas. The more recent *Sonhos roubados* is a fictional film based on Eliane Trindade's *As meninas da esquina*. *Sonhos* focuses on the testimonials of three of the girls from Trindade's book. These films provide us with an epistemological standpoint and an emotional perspective of girls in Brazilian slums that are often marginalized in Brazilian cinema and in the society as a whole. Nevertheless, the portrayal of the girls' thoughts and actions in these films are inscribed within the generic framework of an urban realist drama or documentary featuring a male, adult-centered, violent environment. These elements define what I refer to as the dominant "realist approach" of contemporary Brazilian cinema's portrayals of the popular classes. *Meninas* and *Sonhos roubados* effectively move beyond the typical male-centered narratives of the realist approach but maintain their adult-centered conventions. The girls of these films negotiate the dangers and pleasures of the favela, but nevertheless Werneck is less successful than Dhalia at producing a child-centered narrative that could recognize her subjects'/characters' specific standpoints as girls. For example, little attempt is made to structure the narrative according to the internal, subjective logic of the girls' world via scores, editing, cinematography or art direction.

Nina, on the other hand, departs from what we could call the hegemonic strain of urban realism in order to focus on a far more intimist and subjective, psychological portrait of its eponymous protagonist. Director Dhalia calls it "um mergulho para dentro, para o lado mais escuro do ser humano" (a journey within, to the darker side of the human being; Dhalia, DVD extras). In addition to directing, Dhalia cowrote the screenplay and with this film establishes himself as a filmmaker who wishes to test the boundaries of the conventional genres of Brazilian cinema. Fabiano Gullane, one of the two producers behind the film, along with lead actress Guta Stresser, claim that it took courage to make the film since it has neither Brazilian folklore nor regionalism, but rather it sticks to a universal story of psychological alienation akin to that of Dostoevsky's protagonist Raskolnikov (Dhalia, DVD extras). *Nina* was shot on location in several rather unremarkable urban landscapes of São Paulo; the interior scenes were largely filmed in an old factory converted to represent a gloomy yet nondescript apartment building that Nina calls home. Nina's obsessions, delusions, and fantasies take center stage and are often depicted using manga-style artwork, which is her favorite pastime. The film's portrayal of a girl's traumatized and paranoid subjectivity problematizes the apparent directorial goal in many urban realist dramas of providing easy access to a child's unique standpoint epistemology. That is, the film appropriately emphasizes the gap between adult knowledge and the other, differential logic of how a child understands the world.

THEORETICAL BACKGROUND: IMAGINING THE MULTIPLE OTHERNESS OF LATIN AMERICAN GIRLS

As I focus on the perspectives of teen girls portrayed in these films, my analysis of their alterity is informed by the exploration of "otherness" in the geography of chilhood (Jones; Cloke and Jones). Insight regarding this alterity can also be found in feminist-Marxian standpoint theory (Hartsock; Jaggar), thanks to both its critical focus on epistemologies of gender and class as well as its more general understanding of what I term *multiple otherness*. While considering girls' standpoints in girl-centered narratives, it is necessary to recognize the specificity of poor Latin American girls' epistemological difference. Categories such as childhood, social class, integration in a developing economy, and especially gender and sexuality combine to mark the lives of these characters. The level of engagement with these various facets of a poor Latin American girl's standpoint determines a film's ability to imagine multiple otherness. Thus we can focus on four different areas of otherness with respect to lower-class Brazilian girls that are variously addressed by *Sonhos roubados* and *Nina* in order to initiate a consideration of the films' ability to represent the protagonists' specific standpoint epistemologies.[2]

To begin, we can consider the otherness of childhood itself. As younger and older teenagers, the girls in these two films represent various adolescent stages that range from early puberty to near adulthood. While all these girls are sexually active and thus to some degree resemble adults in their sexuality, many themes arise in the filmic narratives that are common to pre- and postpubescent childhood. Here, I will analyze these themes and related standpoints from the theoretical perspective of the otherness of childhood vis-à-vis adulthood. Owain Jones argues that "the idea of otherness is a way of 'un-knowing' which allows children space and autonomy [and] acknowledges limits" (199). Applying this understanding of childhood to film studies, then, signifies the question, to what degree does a given film acknowledge and thematize the otherness of childhood and the limits of adult experiences and perspectives with respect to that otherness?

In this sense, otherness can serve as a guiding principle in the construction of a filmic narrative that refuses to "colonize," homogenize, and thus familiarize the space of childhood for the adult viewer. The best that can be hoped for is that the adult filmmaker achieves "a kind of inter-subjectivity between child and adult self" (Jones 209). In a similar vein, Emma Wilson describes the strand of child-centered contemporary cinema as "[. . .] contend[ing] more closely with children's distress and sensation, emotional or physical, testifying to child experience, both painful and pleasurable, offering its imprint, yet also envisaging child autonomy, subjectivity, survival" (106). In a filmmaker's attempt to reach such an intersubjective representation of the child, there are common characteristics of childhood that can be explored, including children's play. Jones describes play as "future-orientated, wil[l]fully [. . .] perverse experimental practice which is always opening into the new" (208). Both *Nina* and *Sonhos roubados* feature the playfulness of their protagonists in various ways and thus can be revealingly analyzed in this light. However, I argue below that *Nina*'s intimist, subjective approach is better suited to imagining the imprint of a whole range of painful and pleasurable child experiences.

Another aspect of childhood's otherness featured to varying degrees in these films is its relative disorder with respect to the adult world. Paul Cloke and Owain Jones argue that "children are able to disorder the street as adult space when they transgress spatial and/or temporal boundaries and thereby enter a more liminal, hybrid, inbetween [sic] world" (312). These disordered spaces should not be understood as a "mere disruption" to the ordered space of the adult world, but rather "as territories for becoming other," thus affirming the child's autonomy and unique epistemology (313). The space of the street is featured in both of the urban dramas analyzed below, and to varying degrees the protagonists disrupt this space and other spaces often dominated by adults in order to participate in public life on their own terms. In addition, Cloke and Jones argue that these disordered spaces of childhood tend to be morally coded by adults and are subject, from the adult viewpoint, "both to romanticism and to the risk of unchecked desire" (312). Werneck and Dhalia both make apparent efforts to avoid such moral coding of these disordered spaces in their respective films; however, Dhalia is ultimately more successful with his concentrated focus on the psychological standpoint of his protagonist. While Werneck tries to avoid passing judgment on her characters, she is influenced by the memoirs that are the basis of the *Sonhos roubados* screenplay to dramatize various social problems. These include an array of violence and abuse suffered by girls in Brazil's favelas that could be coded as "the risk of unchecked desire." This broad overview of social ills faced by girls in Brazil's favelas is important but not always the best mechanism for portraying how the girls perceive their own world.

Continuing on to the remaining three forms of otherness of Latin American girls, we shall see that they are well represented by the narratives of both films. For instance, in second place let us consider the otherness of social class, which should be considered within the context of Brazil as a large but still (unevenly) developing economy. The otherness established within this context is the difference between these girls' lives and the ideal childhood as imagined from the perspective of the dominant capitalist economies in the United States and Europe. Tobias Hecht describes this contrast as that between wealthy countries and the wealthy elite in Latin America on the one hand (who highly differentiate the lifestyles of children from that of adults) and the popular classes in Latin America on the other, among whom child labor is often an economic necessity. Among the wealthier classes and countries, idyllic notions of childhood innocence and freedom from economic burdens tend to predominate. Yet these notions tend to influence considerations of childhood as a whole even in Latin America. As Hecht argues, "Surprisingly few studies of childhood in contemporary Latin America consider the possibility that there may be multiple forms of childhood coexisting and competing with one another at a single moment and that the terms and limits of these socially constructed notions are partially set by children themselves" (247).

Films such as *Nina* and *Sonhos roubados* help to reveal the existence of multiple forms of childhood. In both films the children themselves play a large role in defining how dreams, desires, and fears characterize their actions and experiences in childhood. Characters such as Nina of the eponymous film and Daiane (Amanda Diniz) of *Sonhos roubados* feel free to alternate between playful, disorderly behaviors that disrupt the adult world and the day-to-day efforts of survival in a context of poverty and social decay. These girls can also be influenced by middle-class visions of childhood as demonstrated by Daiane's obsessive desire to have a debutante party or *quinceañera* when she turns 15.

In addition, perhaps an even more obvious form of otherness demonstrated in these two films is that of gender. Nina often subverts traditional gender roles and takes a dominant position in her playful moments (an attitude succinctly exemplified by a T-shirt she wears, which boldly proclaims, in English, "Suck My Dick"). The girls of *Sonhos roubados*, while somewhat more normative in terms of their gendered behavior and relationships with men, frequently participate in social bonding activities and maintain a mutual solidarity in the mode of the girl-oriented coming-of-age genre. Mary Celeste Kearney describes this "girl power" genre as one that arose in the United States in the 1990s and "incorporate[s] contemporary feminist themes, especially the need for girls to develop confidence, assertiveness, and self-respect apart from boys and through same-sex relationships" (125). The three protagonists of *Sonhos roubados* exhibit various forms of girl-power solidarity that gives them the strength to survive life in the favela. In fact, the treatment of these girls' friendships is perhaps the area of the film closest to romanticizing childhood relationships—though the influence of these friendships could never really be deemed normative in any sense. This romanticized picture of female friendship certainly sends a strong message about a certain need for girl-power solidarity in the favela, however it is something that separates the film somewhat from *Nina* in which the protagonist's feelings of alienation and mistrust are shown to extend to several women and girls in her life as well. Even so, Nina's relationships with women in general seem to be far more stable and supportive than those she has with men.

The question of sexual relationships brings us to a fourth iteration of these young protagonists' otherness. According to Lee Edelman's theory of reproductive futurity, the figure of *the child* often serves in cinema to represent not only the future but also the specific future of the heteronormative (i.e., hegemonic, conventional, and heterosexual) family. Thus threats to the child are often manipulated to gain ideological support for protecting not just the future in the abstract but a heteronormative future. *Nina* and *Sonhos roubados*, however, do not traffic in hegemonic narratives of futurity with respect to sexuality. The only future that seems somewhat certain in either of these films with respect to gender (though not necessarily sexual) relations is one of homosocial solidarity between the three girls in *Sonhos roubados*. Overall, both of these films question the heteronormative futurism that is often projected on the figure of the child. In *Sonhos roubados*, the oldest girl Jéssica already has a young daughter, while the younger Sabrina (Kika Farias) becomes pregnant and will soon have a child, yet neither of them is shown to be entering into stable, heterosexual relationships or even prioritizing this step as necessary for their children. Nor does the film's narrative give any kind of central focus or valorization to such a quest to reestablish the nuclear family. The youngest child, Daiane, is shown to be far from normative in her sex life, which is characterized entirely by sexual abuse at the hands of her uncle and prostitution. It is through her two older friends and a surrogate, single mother character that Daiane receives emotional support and ultimately the ability to turn her abusive uncle in to the police. However, there is no evidence of same-sex desire in this film as all of the romances and couples portrayed are heterosexual. *Nina* goes a bit further in a nonnormative direction in this regard with its protagonist and one of her friends, since the film clearly evidences her girlfriend's sexual interest in Nina. Nina is shown to be at least somewhat interested in this girlfriend as she kisses her at a rave dance party. Yet this film does not romanticize a possible lesbian relationship for Nina either, since she is shown to literally run away from the penetrating (and possibly judgmental) gaze of the girl who seems to love her most at the film's end.

Multiple Otherness in Cinematic Portrayals of Girls: *Sonhos Roubados* and the Realist Approach

In the following two sections, I analyze *Sonhos roubados* and *Nina* with respect to their filmic styles and come to some conclusions about how effectively these divergent approaches portray the multiple otherness of poor Latin American girls' experiences and epistemologies. The three main characters of *Sonhos roubados*—in order of descending age—are Jéssica, Sabrina, and Daiane. Jéssica is a 17-year-old single mother who has only part-time custody of her 3-year-old daughter due to a past stint in prison. Jéssica's own mother was a prostitute who died five years earlier of AIDS. Her primary occupation and source of income seems to be prostitution as well, although she does attend school at least some of the time with the other two girls. She is also seen to be somewhat protective of her younger friends, demonstrating a certain commitment to "girl power" by sheltering Daiane, to a degree, from prostitution and lending money to Sabrina.

Jéssica also develops a romance with a man in prison in a story line that is directly taken from one of the real testimonials although romanticized somewhat in its filmic translation. Nevertheless, this relationship is one of the clear examples of how this film does not follow the logic of reproductive futurity. The prisoner Ricardo (played by rapper MV Bill) proposes marriage to Jéssica but she refuses, doubting that they have a realistic chance at a future together. Ricardo also talks about his dream of getting out of prison and taking Jéssica and her daughter out of the favela to go live on a farm, a dream that Jéssica rejects outright since she is "daqui do asfalto [from here on the asphalt]" and does not wish to leave the city. At the same time, she does not break off the relationship and introduces Ricardo to her daughter near the end of the film. Therefore, the ambiguities and difficulties of this far-from-ideal long-distance relationship, accepted and represented by Werneck, do not allow for the establishment of a heteronormative familial unit.

A scene that Jéssica shares with Daiane and Sabrina toward the middle of the film gives us a better picture of her relationship with the two younger girls as well as a sense of her friends' desires and mind-sets. After the two older girls bring Daiane along on a date with two johns, the three girls go to a deserted city beach and share an intimate moment as they strip down to their underwear, lie on the beach, and begin to share a joint. Jéssica proposes that they each share something they really want out of life as they take a drag. She herself goes first, stating that she really wants to get a stylish pair of pants and wants her grandfather, in whose house she lives, to recover from his apparent respiratory illness. Then Daiane takes a drag and expresses her wish for a memorable fifteenth birthday party, including a waltz with her absentee father, a machinist who lives elsewhere in the favela. Daiane's mother, like Jéssica's, is dead and she lives with her aunt and uncle in an environment that becomes increasingly abusive. She wants to reconnect with her father, as symbolized by the desire to dance with him, but he tries to maintain his distance when she repeatedly visits him at his workshop. Another "girl power" plotline in the film is developed as Daiane meets the owner of a hair salon, named Dolores (Marieta Severo), who helps pressure her father to both fund and attend Daiane's fifteenth-birthday dance. It is this character that becomes a surrogate mother or auntlike figure to Daiane and ultimately helps her find the courage to denounce her uncle for sexual abuse to the police.

Both the scene on the beach, where Daiane expresses her desires to her girlfriends, and the way she goes about pursuing and achieving some of those desires match up well with Kearney's definition of cinematic girl power—namely, the development of girl characters' "confidence, assertiveness, and self-respect" through same-sex relationships (125).

Other scenes further develop the potential for empowerment, which can be found in relationships between females. For example, Daiane describes how her older friend Jéssica protected her from getting beaten up by another girl at school. Even as Jéssica and Sabrina engage in prostitution with Daiane nearby or in the same room, they attempt to minimize her exposure to the johns themselves. They treat her as a younger sister who needs to be protected, perhaps assuming that she does not need to get involved in prostitution because she has an apparently stable home where she lives with her aunt and uncle. Daiane does not seem to want to dispel this impression because she never shares with her two peers that her uncle is sexually abusing her—rather, it is with the surrogate mother figure, Dolores, that she finally feels comfortable enough to talk. This confessional closeness can be further explained by the fact that Dolores herself tells Daiane that she once gave birth to a girl when she was a teenager, but that the baby was given up for adoption and she never saw her again. Therefore, there is a reciprocal sense that Daiane is a surrogate daughter figure for Dolores. Additionally, Daiane senses that her aunt would not accept her denunciation of her uncle, and in fact her aunt later refuses to believe Daiane's accusations of abuse. It is not until Daiane feels she has someone to replace her aunt as a surrogate mother that she feels comfortable enough to talk about her uncle's sexual advances. Taken as a whole, Daiane's various same-sex relationships, both with older peers and with a motherly figure, allow her to achieve a greater level of confidence and self-respect and to assert her desires and directly challenge some of her worst fears.

Sabrina (aged between Daiane and Jéssica) at 15 also finds strength among other females. When she takes her drag at the beach, she emphasizes her desire to kiss and be kissed by her new boyfriend, a drug kingpin named Wesley (Guilherme Duarte). While their passionate affair lasts, these two lovers seem happy together and Wesley provides Sabrina with an apartment to live in. Yet when Sabrina announces she is pregnant with his baby and wishes to have the child, some of her gangster boyfriend's misogynistic tendencies are exposed. He angrily orders her to have an abortion or he will cut off all contact with her, refusing to contemplate her wishes or discuss the matter further. When Sabrina eventually decides to refuse his ultimatum and have the baby in any case, we see the solidarity of her friend Jéssica as she gives her money to help make ends meet after Wesley kicks her out of the apartment. Again, the "girl power" afforded by homosocial relationships is emphasized, and one gets the sense that it is these social networks of girls and women that is the key to their own survival and that of their young children.

Throughout these scenes Werneck encapsulates the otherness of girlhood in the girls' intimate conversation. At the beach in particular, the three friends are shown to turn urban space into a "territory for becoming other." As noted, Cloke and Jones describe this transitory reterritorialization of urban space as a common activity of children, often stemming from their preference for disorder and playfulness. The girls' discussion of their desires for the future happens within a playful context of relaxing with each other on the deserted, urban beach and smoking a joint. Here, we can recall Jones's definition of play as "future-orientated" and "always opening into the new" to confirm the function of this moment of togetherness in their lives as a way of thinking about the future and imagining how they might shape it to match their own needs and desires.

The beach scene also shows us a private moment between the three girls in which their dialogue is indicative of the limitations of the urban-realist stylistic approach. At this moment, all of the girls have easy access to their own emotions and desires; consequently, the viewer is given this same access through the girls' clear, conscious expression of their emotions. There does not seem to be a concept of the heterogeneity of the girls' epistemological standpoints with respect to those of the filmmaker and the film's audience. Within the universe of Werneck's film, knowing the girls' stories and what they say they want out of life is presented as a full understanding of their psychological-emotional perspectives. Thus to a certain extent the film enacts what Jones would call a "colonization" of the emotional and ideological space of childhood on behalf of the adult audience. We are not allowed an *epistemological or perspectival* sense of the otherness of these girls' experiences and related cognitions and emotions, especially with respect to their status as children. This "other" epistemology is what the subjective, more psychologically complex portrait of *Nina* contributes to the project of representing poor girls in Latin America on film.

Multiple Otherness in Cinematic Portrayals of Girls: *Nina* and the Subjectivist Approach

Before entering into a close analysis of Dhalia's subjectivist approach in *Nina*, we should consider in greater detail the character of the film's eponymous protagonist. Much like the situation of the girls of *Sonhos roubados*, Nina's parents seem to be largely absent from her life. We are only given a hint as to the whereabouts of her mother through a photograph that she looks at. She has been more or less left to her own devices while her mother presumably has gone away to live with the man in the photo. Nina eventually tears the man out of the photo, evidencing some kind of resentment or anger toward him for whatever he did to her and/or her mother. One can already begin to see here that we are not being given all the answers regarding Nina's past. Another photo seen briefly in Nina's room depicts a small girl wearing a white dress—again, there is no dialogue or voice-over regarding this photo but it is a hint about her past history as well as her current psychological state.

Similar to the girl in the picture, Nina finds herself in a state of isolation much of the time. In place of her mother or other family, Nina boards in an apartment with her landlady, a horrible old woman named Dona Eulália, whose matter-of-fact sadistic attitude is captured in a memorable performance by Myriam Muniz. Among other humiliating treatments meted out to Nina, Eulália steals money sent to her by her absentee parents, thus assuring she remains in a state of poverty and hunger. Eulália is shown to treat her cat far better than Nina, and accordingly in a moment of desperation at one point, Nina eats the cat's food since it is the only food in the house not locked away from her by Eulália. In general, Eulália is represented as a sadist, the kind of person who likes to catch insects in a glass jar and study them as they die, as we see her do in one striking scene. The insect Eulália catches happens to be a wasp, and assuming that it symbolizes Nina's position, the viewer can see that she is not entirely passive and has the ability to sting her captor.

In fact, it is in her responses to her landlady's coldness and cruelty that we get a sense of Nina's ironic playfulness, which is well captured by Jones's description of play as "willfully perverse experimental practice." In revenge for Eulália's refusal to share any food with her or let her have the money sent to her by her parents, Nina covers Eulália's soap with pubic hair and urinates in a cup and serves it to the landlady as tea. Later, she takes her playful vengefulness even further, stealing Eulália's cat and releasing it in another part of the city. While Eulália is presented as an absolute sadist, Nina's play oftentimes seems like a tongue-in-cheek experimentation with cruelty. This playful cruelty is also evidenced in her interactions with a blind man Nina meets in the street (an unnamed character played by Wagner Moura). In fact the only time Nina has sex in the film is with this character shortly after meeting him, but she also taunts and teases the man in various ways. For example, knowing that his apartment is exactly organized so that he can easily find everything without sight, when leaving she laughingly throws his entire CD collection on the floor and tosses the furniture around to disrupt his orderly life. This is of course a clear example of a child disordering an adult space through play. Overall, scenes like these also give one the impression that Nina is playing with the idea of what kind of adult she might become, perhaps not wanting to dominate others but considering whether it might be a necessity to assert her will and defend her own self-esteem.

Thus Nina relies on an attitude of playfulness to help her psychologically deal with abusive treatment and even consensual sex with a relative stranger. By avoiding taking seriously her dangerous interactions with (potentially) violent or abusive adults, Nina evades what Vicky Lebeau calls "the erasure of the child, the death of the child, in the realization of adult desire" (131). This character's playful behavior demonstrates once again the essential otherness of the child's standpoint with a worldview that places much more emphasis on play. One final example of Nina's play qua "willfully perverse experimental practice" is her involvement in a goth subculture in São Paulo. By its very nature, this subculture subversively appropriates or flirts with images of death and mortality, accordingly we frequently see such images represented in Nina's manga artwork throughout the film.

Nevertheless Nina seems to go beyond the realm of playfulness to imagine murdering her landlady through her passion of manga artwork. In fact, much of her fiercest anger is sublimated and channeled into gruesome imagery of stabbing Eulália to death. These black-and-white manga images are intercut with live action shots of Nina to give us a sense that they represent her increasingly disturbed emotional state. At the start of the film in a voice-over from Nina herself, we are also introduced to her Raskolnikov-like ideology in which certain "extraordinary" people are essentially above the law or normative morality.[3] On the other hand, her general behavior in much of the film is really only to play with the idea of murdering her landlady. She imagines Eulália's death the same way that anyone taking on a goth identity or becoming part of such a subculture (as Nina does through clothing, make-up, art, social gatherings, recreational drugs, and choice of friends) is playing with the idea of being "alternative" or rebellious through a countercultural performance. Nina's membership in an exclusive gothic subculture props up her fantasies of being "extraordinary." In fact, in a conversation early in the film with one of her fellow travelers, Nina asks, "Are you extraordinary?" Her friend laughs off the question but seems to understand the desire behind it. Certainly this friend from the goth subculture does not wish to be ordinary herself. However much her imaginings of killing Eulália are a fantasy to begin with, as Nina becomes increasingly dissociative and hallucinatory in the latter part of the film, she develops strong feelings of guilt and paranoia about being caught for the crime of murder. As a result Nina appears to suffocate Eulália with a plastic bag, yet the reality of this action is called into question later when a doctor concludes that Eulália has simply died of a heart attack. Ultimately the investigating police officer does not believe Nina's confession that she did indeed kill her landlady.

On the other hand, Dhalia equips himself well to represent the "more liminal, hybrid, in-between world" of childhood because the logic of his film corresponds to this world more effectively than the works of Werneck and other directors following the urban-realist paradigm (Cloke and Jones 312). Dhalia represents the diverse playfulness of childhood with great skill, a playfulness that cannot easily be grasped from an adult perspective—after all, part of Nina's playful imaginings involve murdering the adult she lives with. Another key feature of the logic of Dhalia's film in this regard is that it is not mostly or even primarily based in dialogue. Thus the film is in keeping with Lebeau's insight that "the small child tends to be discovered at the limit of what words can be called upon to tell, or to mean" (16). The greater focus on the visual, on an imaginary or perceptual logic, actually serves to bring the film closer to the epistemological otherness of childhood.

Although Nina herself is not an infant but an adolescent, certainly a large portion of her interior world is expressed via imagery and not words. Thus Dhalia takes the extra step of embracing fully the otherness of childhood experiences and standpoints not captured in language. A significant example of such a step is the representation of Nina's nightmare involving the whipping of the white horse. This scene is witnessed by the girl in the white dress, who should be considered closely because she constitutes an important figure in Nina's subconscious. In general, this girl (who is probably six or seven years old and could certainly pass for a younger Nina) appears over and over again in Nina's dreams, nightmares, and hallucinations, apparently symbolizing a key traumatic event in her past. In the nightmare, a beautiful white horse is surrounded by a crowd of people, who laugh uproariously as they savagely whip the horse while the little girl in the white dress looks on with an impassive gaze. When Nina first has this nightmare, she says in a pained whisper, "Paizinho! [Daddy!]." So there is some kind of psychological association for Nina between this scene of abuse and her past experience with her family, particularly her father. This relationship remains ambiguous and may indicate past abuse or simply that Nina feels the absence of her father most keenly in a moment of terror and therefore calls out for him in her sleep. In any case, the fact that she says "Daddy," assuming the voice of little girl here as we see the image of the girl in the white dress, combined with the fact that a photo of this girl is in Nina's room, all strongly suggest that the girl is Nina. Furthermore, white commonly connotes purity and innocence, particularly when associated with a child, but in this case it establishes a link between the girl and the white horse. Thus in Nina's subconscious mind, her ego is linked both to an innocent inner child who is a passive spectator and also to the horse that she witnesses being victimized.

Through these dream images associated with childhood, we see Nina has insecurities regarding her own agency and a fear of abuse. Through the mostly visual information of the white girl/horse scene, some kind of traumatic event is suggested as the kernel of Nina's alienation; yet we are not afforded a transparent, verbal explanation of this trauma. In particular, we do not see Nina in any significant confessional scene where she reveals all of her desires and fears such as those between the girls in *Sonhos roubados*. At the root of these distinctions between the two films lies a larger difference—namely, that Werneck operates under the assumption that her girl protagonists' lives have been more or less fully penetrated by the adult world and therefore can easily be accessed from a standpoint within that world. On the other hand, Dhalia more provocatively charts what a "disruption to the ordered striations of adult spaces" might look like (Cloke and Jones 313).

Beyond the scenario with the little girl and the white horse, Dhalia presents us with a whole series of manga animations, dreams, nightmares, and hallucinatory apparitions that do not allow for an unproblematic colonization of Nina's standpoint by an adult audience *for* an adult narrative. One other key series of scenes in this regard is constructed by Dhalia with frequent recourse to a peephole shot. Nina's gaze through the peephole of her front door follows in the long tradition of so-called "keyhole shots" in that it thematizes the voyeuristic side of the protagonist's psyche.[4] The peephole shot's limitation and slight warping of the field of vision also help to symbolize the general position of the audience vis-à-vis her standpoint—we are required to experience the world as best we can on the terms set by Nina's viewpoint, and by extension, within the framework of her epistemology and emotional-psychological disposition toward the world. Through the peephole of her apartment's front door, Nina sees a variety of strange and disturbing characters that almost all seem to represent some kind of threat to her increasingly paranoid state of mind. Generally speaking, Nina's voyeurism is not motivated by sexual desire but rather by curiosity and to some degree a fear of entering into the scene beyond the door.

Conclusion: On Absent(ing) Mothers and Representing Girls

Fritz Lang once stated in an interview that the message of his classic film *M* (1931) was not the conviction of the child murderer at the end of the film but rather a warning to mothers that they should keep better watch over their children (Lebeau 166). We can recall Edelman's concept of reproductive futurity here to see once again in Lang's message how the mortal threat to the figure of the child is invoked ideologically to defend the heteronormative, nuclear family. On the contrary, Lang's wife at the time, Thea von Harbou, posed the important class critique of such a message, asking how any woman working outside of the home could possibly maintain constant vigilance over her children. In *Sonhos roubados* and *Nina*, two Brazilian filmmakers feature the stories and perspectives of four poor girls whose mothers (and fathers) are more or less absent from their lives. The girls' mothers in *Sonhos roubados* are dead, victim to a mixture of prostitution, unprotected sex, and drug abuse, while Nina's mother seems to have abandoned her, perhaps under the malign influence of the man Nina tears out of the photograph she has of her mother (probably the mother's partner or husband). One gets a sense from the two films of mothers in the Brazilian urban peripheries who are continually displaced and absent, making it near impossible for them to "keep watch" as the discourse of reproductive futurity would require. The urban, relatively unprotected environments of Rio de Janeiro and São Paulo's favelas and working-class neighborhoods, however, are not shown to be inevitably destructive and fatal for the films' adolescent protagonists. To a surprisingly large extent, they are able to adapt to this environment and make it their own, at least temporarily, through imaginative play and homosocial solidarity.

The films do not presume to tell Brazilian mothers to keep better watch over their children but instead attempt to represent the lives and perspectives of these children themselves. They can both be considered to contribute to the strand of child-centered contemporary cinema described by Emma Wilson. Having acknowledged this focus on the children per se, of course, we have also seen in this chapter the substantial distinction in stylistic approach of the two films, amounting to two different logics with respect to representations of the otherness of poor Latin American girls. All things considered, Heitor Dhalia's film resolutely positions the viewer within the epistemological and emotional standpoint of its protagonist, coming closer to the imprint of child experience that Emma Wilson describes than Sandra Werneck's more conventional realism.[5] While both films are invaluable and unique in their focus not only on the lives and desires of poor youth but also on those of girls in particular, I hope to have demonstrated here some of the advantages of Dhalia's less common approach. It is a filmic logic that could lend insight to future filmic representations of poor and working-class girls in Latin America's cities—and the otherness of their standpoints.

NOTES

1. Here I refer to the famous genre of meticulously drawn Japanese comic books that often feature violent scenes—some involving a focus on bladed weapons such as knives, as can be seen in *Nina*'s take on the genre.
2. I take the concept of standpoint epistemology from standpoint theory to refer to the specific logic of knowing the world inherent in a given perspective or standpoint. In this chapter, I outline various forms of otherness that I deem inherent to the standpoint of Latin American girls and that collectively approximate this group's standpoint epistemology.
3. The character Raskolnikov also has his own diary/journal that is a basis of part of *Crime and Punishment* (Dostoevsky). In Dhalia's film, the equivalent seems to be Nina's artwork. Though at the film's close, it is quickly revealed that she also possesses a written journal that may mirror the murderous imaginings of her drawings.
4. Lebeau points out that the keyhole shot has a long history that can be traced back to the Victorian era and the popular "through-the-keyhole" films of the 1890s and 1900s (104–5). These films tended to thematize voyeurism and placed the audience in the position of the voyeur looking through a keyhole in a door to someone's bedroom or other private space.
5. Since Wilson argues that women directors have special access to "young female experience," the example of Heitor Dhalia demonstrates that the ability to imagine the specificity of a child's experience is in no way limited to female directors (118). Werneck's oeuvre taken as a whole, though, combined with that of many other female directors in Brazil (such as Tata Amaral, Sandra Kogut, and Lúcia Murat) certainly suggests that, in general, women filmmakers have explored female experience more than their male counterparts.

WORKS CITED

Cloke, Paul, and Owain Jones. "'Unclaimed Territory': Childhood and Disordered Space(s)." *Social and Cultural Geography* 6.3 (2005): 311–33.

Dhalia, Heitor, dir. *Nina*. Perf. Guta Stresser. Gullane Filmes/Columbia Tristar do Brasil, 2004. Digital videodisc.

Dostoevsky, Fyodor. *Crime and Punishment: A Novel in Six Parts with Epilogue.* Trans. Richard Pevear and Larissa Volokhonsky. New York: Vintage Books, 1993.
Edelman, Lee. *No Future: Queer Theory and the Death Drive.* Durham: Duke UP, 2004.
Ezabella, Fernanda. "Em 'Sonhos Roubados', Sandra Werneck filma garotas de periferia." *Folha Ilustrada* 23 Apr. 2010. Web. 8 July 2010 <http://www1.folha.uol.com.br/folha/ilustrada/ult90u724722.shtml>.
Hartsock, Nancy. *Money, Sex, and Power.* New York: Longman, 1983.
Hecht, Tobias, Ed. *Minor Omissions: Children in Latin American History and Society.* Madison, WI: University of Wisconsin Press, 2002.
Jaggar, Alison. "Love and Knowledge: Emotion in Feminist Epistemology." *Emotions: A Cultural Studies Reader.* Ed. Jennifer Harding and E. Deidre Pribram. New York: Routledge, 2009. 50–68.
Jones, Owain. "'True Geography Quickly Forgotten, Giving Away to an Adult-Imagined Universe.' Approaching the Otherness of Childhood." *Children's Geographies* 6.2 (May 2008): 195–212.
Kearney, Mary Celeste. "Girlfriends and Girl Power: Female Adolescence in Contemporary U.S. Cinema." *Sugar, Spice and Everything Nice: Cinemas of Girlhood.* Ed. Frances Gateward and Murray Pomerance. Detroit: Wayne State UP, 2002: 125–42.
Lebeau, Vicky. *Childhood and Cinema.* London: Reaktion, 2008.
Trindade, Eliane. *As meninas da esquina: Diários dos sonhos, dores e aventuras de seis adolescentes do Brasil.* Rio de Janeiro: Record, 2010.
Werneck, Sandra, dir. *Sonhos roubados.* Perf. Nanda Costa, Amanda Diniz, and Kika Farias. Cineluz/Estúdios Mega/Labocine/Europa Filmes, 2010.
Wilson, Emma. "Women Filming Children." *Nottingham French Studies* 45.3 (2006): 105–18.

CHAPTER 12

No Longer Young

Childhood, Family, and Trauma in *Las Mantenidas sin Sueños*

Beatriz Urraca

A look at recent Latin American film through the eyes of its child and adolescent protagonists provides a bleak view of family relationships and a panorama of lost innocence in the face of extreme poverty, street violence, and political turmoil. The filmographies and cinematographies of Brazil and Colombia, for example, have produced multiple examples of a genre that exposes the stark consequences of orphanhood, drugs, and urban violence among street youths[1] and harshly criticize societies that fail to provide the most basic support network for their youngest and most vulnerable members.[2] While street children and slum life are as much a reality in large Argentine urban centers as in Medellín or Rio de Janeiro, few among Argentina's contemporary filmmakers have chosen to focus on this aspect of childhood, with the notable exception of *Villa* (Slum; 2008). Its director, Ezio Massa, cites social activism as the motivation for his depiction of orphaned children in a Buenos Aires shantytown located less than two miles from the city's National Congress building.[3] The vast majority of recent Argentine films, however, portray children or adolescents as inseparable from the traditional middle-class nuclear family structure, with plots that revolve around the difficulties youths encounter when that family ideal is absent or damaged. Films about adolescents, for example, tend to address the threat that sexual awakening poses for the family, as in Lucrecia Martel's *La niña santa* (*The Holy Girl*; 2004), Albertina Carri's *Geminis* (2005), and Lucía Puenzo's *XXY* (2007) and *El niño pez* (*The Fish Child*; 2009).

A second group, which is representative of an approach to the figure of the child as the central victim of the Dirty War, includes Marcelo Piñeyro's *Kamchatka* (2002) and Fabián Hofman's *Te extraño* (I Miss You; 2010). The young protagonists are not kidnapped yet suffer the disintegration of their families when their parents or siblings disappear as a result of state-sponsored violence. These directors seek to return to the child a focus that had been diluted in the family melodrama of the 1980s, as epitomized by Luis Puenzo's *La historia oficial* (*The Official Story*; 1985), which revolves around the illegal placement of the daughter of disappeared parents within a family with ties to the military regime but does not attempt to represent the child's own point of view. A third thematic line, exemplified by Alejandro Agresti's *Valentín* (2002) and Vera Fogwill's and Martín Desalvo's *Las mantenidas sin sueños* (*Kept and Dreamless*; 2005), characterizes children as precocious urchins skilled at caring for themselves and for the weak or dysfunctional adults in their families. Other recent films, such as Celina Murga's *Una semana solos* (*A Week Alone*; 2007) and Sofía Mora's *La hora de la siesta* (*The Hour of the Nap*; 2009), represent the painful transitions and discoveries experienced by groups of children left to their own devices while adults are temporarily absent; the fact that the children in these films break their families' rules presupposes that there are families to return to and rules to disobey. Finally, Albertina Carri's *La rabia* (*Anger*; 2008) goes into a deeper exploration of the dark side of children's emotional processing of their parents' oppressively violent and sexually charged environment.

In all these films, as well as in many others in which children play supporting roles,[4] childhood is construed as part of a familial milieu under siege from multiple threats—Dirty War disappearances, illnesses, drug addictions, prison, illicit sexual affairs, self-centeredness—that result in the parents' inability or unwillingness to protect their offspring and cause the children to endure the trauma of abandonment. Grandparents, parents, and siblings may misbehave, leave, or disappear temporarily or permanently, but they constitute a presence—and a potential—in films that resist portraying young children as completely bereft of a family context.[5] Taken as a group, these depictions of children as part of very visible yet dysfunctional families serve as an implicit denunciation of Argentine society's failure to proffer a viable model of the family and, by extension, of the nation.[6]

The coupling of childhood trauma with social critique of the family is at the center of *Las mantenidas sin sueños*, a film whose child protagonist lives in the midst of a disturbing situation of ongoing parental neglect and occasional abuse.[7] At age nine, Eugenia (Lucía Snieg) is a character old enough to articulate her feelings and emotions convincingly but still preadolescent, creating a set of circumstances that allow the plot to evolve into an untimely coming-of-age denouement. The film's strength lies in characterization through dialogue and mise-en-scène with an uncomplicated plot that focuses on the depiction of the sordid lives led by Eugenia and her mother, Florencia (Vera Fogwill), a young, pregnant drug addict. As they struggle to stay afloat with no money to pay the bills, a cast of neighbors, friends, and acquaintances drift in and out of their apartment in search of drugs, sex, or company. In the midst of this dismal environment, Eugenia idealizes her absentee father, Martín (Gastón Pauls), whose occasional phone calls and gifts brighten her otherwise dire existence until he takes her to live with him in the film's version of a fairy-tale ending.

Though the family relationships depicted in this film are fractured, and Eugenia essentially functions as an orphan despite the fact that she has living parents, the story also foregrounds the importance of extended familial ties for the child's development, while offering a reflection on the psychological effects caused by the breakdown of those relationships. Ultimately, filmmakers Fogwill and Desalvo present the family as both the cause of trauma and the key to recovery. This is portrayed through a profound and intricate exploration of the complexity of mother-daughter bonds complemented by subplots that focus on the resolution of strained relationships between previous generations. This examination of the foundations of familial relationships leads to a happy ending that reunites the child with her long-absent father and paternal grandmother, two characters who have themselves been reunited after a long separation. The ending also brings reconciliation to Florencia and her own mother, Sara (Mirta Busnelli), as both women set aside their ongoing conflict over money and values to focus on the arrival of a new baby who will give them a second chance to become better parents.

This article analyzes the narrative and filmic strategies employed in encoding the mind-set of the child protagonist, her articulation of self-altering traumatic events, and her socialization as part of a family composed of maladjusted female or feminized characters. Though this analysis relies on psychological and psychiatric studies of trauma in actual children, it does so with the understanding that mental access to a child represented in fiction is impossible, and that such studies can only illuminate the degree of realism in what is essentially an adult construction determined by the preconceptions, idealizations, and unreliable memories of the scriptwriter, director, other adult actors, and even an audience presumed to be adult.

Children in cinema very rarely represent themselves, and this has led several researchers to address the implications of examining the techniques employed in any fictional representation of childhood. Kathy M. Jackson has convincingly argued that

> children have no say regarding their own portrayals in film. They do not write the script, direct the scenes, set up the shots, design the costumes, or edit the final product. The only role that they have in films is that of actor, and most often they are simply expected to mimic the director's actions and words, thereby allowing very little of what it feels like to be a child to enter into their performances. This is not likely to change; thus, images of children in film will continue to bear the adult's stamp and perception. (188)

In the same vein, Karen Lury asks, "How can children's subjectivity, their emotions, their experiences and their thoughts be represented on screen?" (10), and concludes that "by watching films that represent and employ children I have had the opportunity to explore a different point of view . . . [that] reveal[s] the strangeness of the world in which they live" (14). The appeal of Lury's approach is that it allows for an examination of a film from a perspective that attempts to set itself up as "other" to that of ostensibly adult characters and creators, while acknowledging that films about children are often, as André Bazin said of *Los olvidados* (*The Young and the Damned*), "a value judgment on . . . adult characters" (211).[8] While believing in the impossibility of representing children in fiction, Susan Honeyman's approach, to which I subscribe in this chapter, is to "concentrate on techniques that authors have used to depict childhood in spite of their awareness of the impossibility of verifying their accuracy" (6). Therefore, the premise behind this analysis of the film is that "to study 'the child' is to limit one's focus to a child-figure, indicating awareness of social constructedness" (10).

Las mantenidas sin sueños deliberately attempts to place the subjectivity of the child at the forefront of the narrative, but the only pretension that the film may in any way relate to real-life children comes from the filmmakers' choice of Lucía Snieg, a first-time actor, to play the role of Eugenia. Concerned that the use of nonprofessionals in the New Argentine Cinema might jeopardize the actor's craft, screenwriter and codirector Vera Fogwill had cast experienced actors in all the roles except this one because "las niñas-actrices estaban muy teñidas, porque en un nene los vicios se colocan muy rápido" (child actors were very spoiled, because in children vices become entrenched very quickly; Burstein). Although some of the adult roles in the film were written for specific actors, Snieg was selected personally by Fogwill after a long casting process. This was followed by a yearlong process of developing a rapport between her and Snieg that would be based on terms similar to the relationship between Florencia and Eugenia. For example, Fogwill had other adults in the crew establish discipline and limits, and begged the child's parents not to let her study the script at home so that her performance would be more natural (Soto). She also hired an assistant whose responsibilities included making sure no one on the set was too affectionate to Snieg, in order to maintain consistency with the vulnerable nature of her character (Commiso).

As Lury argues, using a nonprofessional child actor is a common strategy, often considered to be a key to the success of the performance given that "audiences are less likely to feel manipulated if they believe that the child actor is genuine or (a) natural" (150). Lury likens the child actor to a prop: "The acting is not something done by the child, instead the child's behaviour is read as a performance because it is situated in a particular, meaningful context" (162). In fact, in *Las mantenidas sin sueños* the child's subjectivity is revealed more consistently through the context devised by an adult team—especially the script—than through Snieg's otherwise stellar performance. To this effect, the filmmakers employ a traditional third-person perspective, devoid of point-of-view shots or voice-over narration in a portrayal of Eugenia that depends as much on her interactions with the adult characters as it does on her own presence. Snieg shares equal screen time with Fogwill, as they alternate the roles of helpless child and responsible adult (or responsible child and helpless adult). Indeed, the immature behavior of the adult characters in the film calls into question the very concepts of childhood and adulthood as stable categories and assigns them the status of temporary roles instead. Within the story, Eugenia and her preoccupations appear to be marginal to the other characters, yet she is central to the viewer, whose character identification is steered toward the child because of her victim status,[9] and who thus projects on the young character the anxieties and fears about trauma that she is presupposed to feel.

The events depicted in the film can be considered traumatic according to Linda Chernus's definition of the term as "an assault on the self." She argues that trauma "refers not to an external event in itself, but rather to its internal and subjective meaning to the individual, one that in some way is so difficult to integrate that it induces a fragmentation in the structure of the self" to which children are particularly vulnerable (449–51). Furthermore, the plot chronicles incidents and situations that would cause a child to suffer what is known as complex psychological trauma, which according to Julian Ford results "from exposure to severe stressors that are [1] repetitive or prolonged, [2] involve harm or abandonment by caregivers or other ostensibly responsible adults, and [3] occur at developmentally vulnerable times in the victim's life" (13). Judith Mishne singles out the alteration of a parent through substance abuse as something experienced as abandonment and that leads the child to experience psychic loss (480–81). An absentee father and a drug-addicted, alternately violent, and guilt-ridden mother place Eugenia in the position of needing to care for herself as well as for Florencia. She is a child straddling the boundary with adolescence in an environment where her most basic needs are not being met, and where she witnesses adult behaviors involving sex and drugs that are, in the director's own words, "realmente espeluznantes" (really horrifying; Burstein).

Eugenia struggles to maintain a front of normalcy, organizing her behavior around keeping the secret of her family's poverty and her mother's inability to function. Meanwhile, Florencia drifts in and out of consciousness, her grandmother stops sending money, her neighbor Olga (Edda Díaz)—otherwise a source of affection—overmedicates herself, and the only signs of her father are sporadic phone calls and mailed gifts. The first few scenes in which Eugenia appears are illustrative of her determination to stick to a routine as her world crumbles around her: a series of brightly lit long to medium shots depict her as she begins her day with a burst of efficiency, making her bed, cleaning herself up, making her own breakfast, and dressing for school. This requires ample resourcefulness, the first indication that something is not quite right in her household: she heats up the iron on the gas cooker because the electricity has been cut off for lack of payment and brushes her teeth with soap because there is no toothpaste. Throughout the film, she is presented as having an eccentric personality, yet one designed to appear adorable in order to appeal to the viewer's sympathies: the camera repeatedly lingers on close-ups of her different-colored socks, her dialogue lines often imitate popular philosophy adages, and she is shown taking devices apart so she can learn their mechanisms and be prepared to fix them when they stop working. All this helps Eugenia assert her individuality, make sense of her chaotic world, articulate her feelings, and relate to the inconsistent conduct of the adults who surround her. Bessel van der Kolk identifies these behaviors as survival strategies in cases where the child's trauma emanates from within the family. They can also be interpreted as indicators of a "lack of continuous sense of self" (230), which reinforces Chernus's idea, previously presented, that trauma causes a fragmentation of the self, and lends support to the hypothesis that Eugenia exhibits many of the characteristics typical of trauma victims.

As Leigh Gilmore has pointed out, "the relation between trauma and representation, and especially language, is at the center of claims about trauma as a category" (6). The script of *Las mantenidas sin sueños* draws from the book *Máximas y aforismos* (Maxims and aphorisms), a gift sent by Eugenia's father, to ascribe to the child speech patterns that are incongruous with her nine years of age; with a wink at Quino's popular cartoon character Mafalda, Eugenia expresses an ability to glimpse the adult world with more lucidity than the adults themselves. But rather than give the child character a voice, quotations such as Nietzsche's "no existen fenómenos morales, sólo una interpretación moral de los fenómenos" (moral phenomena do not exist, only a moral interpretation of phenomena), though spoken by Eugenia, highlight the constructed nature of appropriated discourse. They also remind us that this film does not construct childhood in opposition to adulthood but rather as a version of it. Though Eugenia appears quite capable of engaging adults in debate, an in-depth look at her dialogue lines reveals that only her outbursts of frustration sound realistic for her age.[10] Of course, the child's philosophical-sounding lines were written—or appropriated—by an adult scriptwriter, but within the fictional world of the film they also originate in an adult-authored book. This strategy appears to defeat the purpose of hiring a first-time actor to play the role, stifling any spontaneity Snieg might have brought to her performance. But because it is not used consistently, the contrast between those utterances indicative of abstract reasoning and her more age-appropriate lines underscores the fragmentation of the traumatized child character's self. It also illustrates her internal struggle to express her "true" personality while trying to fit in a community of adult women and to defend herself from her mother's abuses by presenting a controlled, adult-sounding persona.

In *Las mantenidas sin sueños*, everyone philosophizes too much, and characterization is heavily dependent on the stilted dialogue that stems from the heavy dose of anticapitalist ideology that informs it. Eugenia is no exception; besides deriving from the book, her lines also echo the existential soliloquies that other characters declaim throughout the film to construct their own fictions of self-victimization in a series of dramatic scenes reminiscent of live theater. Her grandmother Sara for example, expresses her disappointment with contemporary society's failure to deliver on the hopes built up by hippies and militants in the 1960s. Florencia's friend Celina (Mía Maestro) rejects her conventional yet empty life entirely planned by others, lamenting, "Me convirtieron en un proyecto sin vida" (They turned me into a lifeless project). Florencia herself continuously rants against capitalism; at times she does so in her own voice and at times in Eugenia's, because many of the child's expressions seem to have been scripted by Florencia who, not coincidentally, is played by this film's real-life scriptwriter. For instance, when Eugenia receives a rare birthday party invitation, knowing that she cannot afford a gift, the child herself declares, "El regalo es un invento capitalista para que la gente gaste plata que no tiene" (Gifts are a capitalist invention so that people will spend money they do not have). Similarly, when she expresses her wish to see the sea, her mother prompts her: "Eso de ir a conocer es un invento ¿de qué?" (That stuff about going to see a place is an invention, of what?) to which she replies, "De las compañías aéreas" (Of airlines).

These responses sound deliberately ironic and overly rehearsed. The wisdom expressed in Eugenia's utterances is not indicative of real maturity: speaking in words obviously put in her mouth by her mother is a defense mechanism that reinforces Florencia's twisted logic and thus helps her avoid conflict. But this is not sustainable. As Susan Honeyman argues, "Often child characters disrupt discourse by turning adults' presumptions of power and linguistic bullying back on them" (128). Thus Eugenia reproaches her mother: "De lo que me doy cuenta es de lo que te conviene que me dé cuenta . . . ¡Y no me mientas más!" (What I realize is what is convenient for you that I realize . . . And don't lie to me anymore!)

As Veronica M. Rojas and Tal N. Lee have pointed out, the traumatized child often "incorporates traits of the aggressive offender in an attempt to master the fear that aggressor induces" (250). For Eugenia, the purpose of these affected utterances is not so much to explain her circumstances as to sound them out and observe their effect on others, to exert a measure of control as she observes them losing control. In doing so, she often irritates adults because her fake-sounding words force them to face the grim reality behind the self-centered universes they inhabit and the distance between who they are and who they were supposed to become. In the central mother-daughter relationship of the film, there is a blurred line between a child who is growing up too fast and a mother who refuses to grow up at all. Right after Florencia pours a stash of cocaine down the toilet, afraid that Eugenia may have consumed some of it by mistake, the two engage in a rapid exchange of adult-child roles: the girl characterizes the gesture as "simbólico y poco creíble" (symbolic and not very believable), while Florencia's reaction betrays an unstable person who struggles between the child she wants to be and the responsible mother she is expected to be. This is expressed in her pleading "necesito que me creas" (I need you to believe me), after which she curls up in the fetal position, wailing "puedo, puedo, puedo, puedo llegar a estar mejor" (I can, I can, I can, I can become better). But she immediately follows this apparent regression with a classic motherly reproach: "No repitas palabras que escuchaste y que no sabés lo que significan" (Do not repeat words that you heard and don't know what they mean).

Inconsistencies in the parents' treatment of the children often lead to identity crises in the latter. Florencia's abrupt fluctuations between abusive or neglectful and affectionate force Eugenia's role in the film to alternate between age-appropriate behaviors and a take-charge attitude of wisdom beyond her years. Her self-assurance increases as her mother relinquishes control or responsibility, but it automatically diminishes whenever Florencia shows the slightest willingness to fulfill her motherly role and then the child reverts to acting like a nine-year-old. At times, such as in the scene when both suck their thumbs on either side of a closed door, their behaviors coincide. At other times, Eugenia's apparent maturity and nurturing gestures are reluctant responses to a mother who is herself acting like a child. As Kristina Pinto notes, "In cases where the family is the source of stress [. . .], children often adapt by assuming the maturity of a caregiver for siblings and sometimes parents, such that the stress serves as a developmental impetus [. . .], though admittedly one with possible psychological costs to the child (i.e., a sense of growing up before one's time)" (513).

The film emphasizes the similarities between Florencia and Eugenia in other ways besides speech patterns, such as the child's statement that her paternal grandmother "es como nosotras" (is like us), their personal styles, and the mise-en-scène, particularly set decor. Color plays an especially important role, with pink filters used in scenes where the filmmakers wanted to emphasize dramatic tension (Burstein); pinks and reds also predominate in all the characters' clothing and in the apartment's decorative murals and props. If Eugenia wears two different colored socks, her mother's fingernails are painted in different hues. Mother and daughter dress in similarly bright outfits, whose pinks and reds symbolize the strength of the blood bonds in the film. In some scenes Florencia even wears her daughter's clothes—and not the other way around, as might be expected, because the identification works both ways. But while Florencia may see herself in her daughter, as a connection to her own truncated childhood, Eugenia resists accepting her mother as a preview of her own future. By switching alliances at the end from mother and maternal grandmother to father and paternal grandmother, and starting her life afresh with them, the child also rejects the disturbed relationship between Florencia and Sara as a mirror of her own relationship with her mother.

With a comfortable middle-class adolescence cut short by an untimely pregnancy, Florencia views Eugenia as the child she would still like to be: "Cuando era chica como vos quería ser grande, y ahora te juro que quisiera ser de nuevo infinitamente chica" (When I was young like you I wanted to be older, and now I swear to you that I would like to be infinitely young again). Florencia was not born futureless, but her inability to move forward seems due to having been cheated of her past. She also refuses to get a job and, most pointedly, rejects her own mother's notion of a "proyecto de vida" (life project), of using the advantages of her own privileged childhood to become a productive member of society. The film offers no viable model of what that might mean, no evidence that the future may bring a better life, and this is apparent from the staging of outside shots in the deserted urban ruins of Buenos Aires's marginal neighborhoods. Florencia's apartment building is the only one left standing on her block: crumbling buildings, vacant lots, and streets completely devoid of passersby give the impression that the film's network of female relatives, neighbors, and acquaintances are the last survivors in a postapocalyptic world in which social institutions have ceased to function just as the family has ceased to function. These exterior locations, which recall the German post–World War II "rubble film,"[11] present a world literally and metaphorically in ruins. According to Antonio Traverso, "Poverty produces a war-like scenario" in which "the adult is too self-absorbed to notice the needs of the child" (180). The apparently shell-shocked characters react by gathering in Florencia's freshly painted pink living room in the climactic scene of the film, a 12-minute sequence shot for which the actors rehearsed separately, none of them knowing how the others were going to react. The result is a theatrical improvisation, which the director intended to transmit the lack of communication among the characters (Burstein), whose dialogue lines reinforce their isolation and self-centeredness as they expound on the shortcomings of their families in a moment of mass rejection of children by their parents and vice versa: "A las chicas las tuve que dejar en lo de mamá porque en este momento es como que no las soporto" (I had to leave the girls at my mother's because right now it seems that I cannot stand them), says Celina, while Santiago (Julián Krakov), Florencia's dealer and occasional lover, complains, "Mi vieja está imbancable" (My mother is unbearable). Meanwhile, they ignore Eugenia's presence at the edges of the frame as she answers the phone call that will change her life.

The film's cast consists of single, widowed, and about-to-be-divorced mothers and grandmothers on the one hand and passive, marginal, and feminized men on the other.[12] An overly made-up Gastón Pauls and a flabby, cross-dressed Julián Krakov provide the only visible male presence. It is also important to note the extradiegetic presence of Los Babasónicos, the all-male band who, playing with gender ambiguity, sing in the film's main track: "La vida me hizo mujer" ("Life made me a woman"). When asked about the significance of gender in the film, Fogwill replied, "Yo quería hacer una película femenina, pero no feminista, que es algo bastante diferente . . . Las mujeres en esta película ocupan lugares de hombre, por lo que tienen roles que no son los que les están supuestamente asignados."[13]

While I disagree that women in this film play male roles, it is quite obvious that the two male characters are presented as soft, dependent, and more concerned with their appearance than with providing for their families. Rather than follow the path of Hollywood "womanpower" films in which female characters exhibit "traits typically associated with masculinity" or "depict two or more females who gain confidence through and support in same-sex friendships" (Kearney 131), *Las mantenidas sin sueños* is underpinned by a poignant attack on the futility of the neoliberal ideal of the Argentine middle-class family as a transaction-based exchange in which caring for others is supposedly reciprocated. "Si quiero algo, doy algo" (If I want something, I give something), Sara announces, summing up the shared feeling that parenthood only brings disappointment because one never gets either the offspring or the parents of one's dreams. These comments, contextualized within a script that constantly rants against capitalism and within a mise-en-scène dominated by crumbling ruins and darkened interior sets refer the viewer to Argentina's 2001 crisis and to the national malaise produced by the collapse of an economic model that had been closely linked to the survival of the traditional middle-class family.

In this dismal environment, Eugenia's progress toward adolescence is anything but straightforward, which subverts the romantic idea that this development should follow a linear process. The film turns her journey into a Bildungsroman that proceeds in reverse, in search of a happy, carefree childhood that finds itself at odds with the untimely evolution of her body. At the end of *Las mantenidas sin sueños*, Eugenia's father and her paternal grandmother, Lola (Elsa Berenguer), meet her in the small provincial town where they have decided to settle after Lola was evicted from her home in Buenos Aires. With Florencia about to give birth to a new baby, Eugenia does not hesitate to grasp her chance at living with adults who seem to her prepared to take charge. Staying home would have meant an additional burden of responsibility: "Voy a tener una hermanita, así que pronto voy a ser abuela" (I'm going to have a little sister, so soon I'm going to be a grandmother), she writes to Martín, and continues, "Yo no quería. Ojalá que no nazca" (I didn't want her. I hope she's never born). The final scenes show father, daughter, and grandmother laughing and playing in a river. The handheld camera wielded by Martín sets these final scenes in opposition to the rest of the film, its unsteady, overexposed rendering of Eugenia playing in the water endowing the happily-ever-after ending with an aura that alludes to the child's fantasy about seeing the sea for the first time. Eugenia has escaped, transported—albeit by bus—to an alternative world of love and happiness from which she does not ultimately need to return home. Ironically, this "alternative" world is filmed with an amateur video camera; the immediacy of the natural light and direct sound suggest that her realized fantasy is less montaged, scripted, and staged than the rose-filtered life she led back in the city with her mother.

Unfortunately, just as her new life as a child in this "fantasy" world is about to begin, Eugenia gets her first period. Unprepared for the pain, the shock of the blood, and the revelation of its meaning by a grandmother she has just met, Eugenia reacts with anger and denial: "¡No quiero ser mujer . . . no quiero tener hijos!" (I don't want to be a woman . . . I don't want to have children!). At precisely the same time, back in the city, Florencia goes into labor screaming that she does not want to give birth again. The cross-cutting of the two scenes, which emphasizes the parallel action, suggests a strong mother-daughter bond as the two protagonists struggle simultaneously against unstoppable biological processes. The pathos of Eugenia's woman-child predicament is encapsulated in a long shot of her small figure walking down the street in her bloodstained white shorts, holding a cat in one hand and her father's hand in the other, entering a new stage of life without completely being able to let go of all ties to the previous one. As some researchers have suggested, the early onset of menarche is related to childhood stress (Pinto 514). Seen in the context of the traumatic experiences encountered by Eugenia in the earlier part of the film, the menstrual blood may be interpreted as a way of encoding in the body that which "cannot be assimilated into the mind" and is "recalled via bodily sensations rather than through words" (Robson 608). A further implication of this sign of biological maturity is that Eugenia will soon have to take charge of her new family as she did with the old: the viewer is aware—though she is not yet—that her grandmother is destitute, and her father is an immature 27-year-old who has never held a job and professes to live "responsibly on vacation," because he is keenly aware that life holds no opportunities for him: "¿Qué tipo de inserción podría intentar yo que no sepa desde antes que voy a fracasar? . . . Decidí fracasar contento" (What kind of endeavor could I attempt where I wouldn't know from the start that I was going to fail? . . . I decided to fail happy).

Las mantenidas sin sueños presents circumstances in which a child lacks a consistent relationship with a parent or caregiver. The bond between Eugenia and her mother deteriorates and is ultimately broken even as other blood relationships in the film become strengthened and neighbors, friends, and lovers get pushed aside. Eugenia would have had to go to extraordinary lengths to maintain any kind of idealization of Florencia, who is no heroine, preferring instead to romanticize a father whom she has known only sporadically and adopting an alter ego in which she herself becomes the mother she would have liked to have. In the end, as Eugenia distances herself from her mother and rejects all that womanhood represents—the possibility of motherhood, responsibility for others—her body rebels against her and brings her closer to Florencia in a shared moment of physical pain. The film explores the psychological tools utilized by a nine-year-old girl to survive trauma caused by parental abuse and neglect. Eugenia emerges at the end of the movie as a resilient child on the verge of a new stage of life, resisting the inexorable changes of her own body and advancing toward the only role she has ever known—that of woman and mother—even as her mind clings to childhood. Yet the ending is optimistic, as it grants Eugenia the only true act of power in the entire film: she throws a lump of mud at the camera lens and thus decides when it all ends cutting the last scene abruptly.

Notes

1. See for example Víctor Gaviria's *Rodrigo D: No futuro* (1990) and *La vendedora de rosas* (The Rose Seller; 1998), Fernando Meirelles and Kátia Lund's *Cidade de Deus* (*City of God*; 2002), and Joshua Marston's *María, llena eres de gracia* (*Maria Full of Grace*; 2004). In a study of the debt of recent Brazilian cinema to Italian neorealism, Antonio Traverso writes that films like these "represent childhood as a state that requires the negotiation of homelessness, violence, sexuality, and survival" (178). Among the many examples of this genre in world cinema, it is worth mentioning Luis Buñuel's *Los olvidados* (*The Young and the Damned*; 1950), a portrayal of abandoned children in Mexico City's slums, as a precursor.
2. This sentiment is behind Edgardo Dieleke's study of violence in Brazilian cinema, which relates *Cidade de Deus* to "a cinematography that reveals a search for identity, symbolized in the repeated narratives in which the protagonists appear as orphans, in search of an absent father." According to Dieleke, *Cidade de Deus* suggests "the experience of living in a country that has metaphorically abandoned its children" (71).
3. Massa made these comments during his presentation of the film at the 2009 International Festival of Human Rights Cinema in Buenos Aires.
4. See Lucrecia Martel's *La ciénaga* (*The Swamp*; 2001), Adrián Caetano's *Un oso rojo* (*Red Bear*; 2002), Alejandro Agresti's *Un mundo menos peor* (*A Less Bad World*; 2004), and Pablo Trapero's *Nacido y criado* (*Born and Bred*; 2006) and *Leonera* (*Lion's Den*; 2008).
5. As Traverso has pointed out, the exploration of "the weaknesses and strengths of the familial" and "the severed and yet still surviving ties between fathers and sons" rather than "the autonomous, parentless child" is a characteristic of Italian neorealism (179), an aesthetic trend that has had a great impact on Argentine cinema, particularly in the 1960s and again in the 1990s.
6. The child-as-victim theme has been studied in other geographical contexts to provide evidence of the doubtfulness of national projects. See for example Karen Lury (17).
7. *Las mantenidas sin sueños* is Vera Fogwill's first film as a director and writer; she also plays the lead adult character, Florencia. The daughter of Argentine writer and sociologist Rodolfo Fogwill, she is better known as an actress for her performances in Alejandro Agresti's films *El viento se llevó lo que* (*Wind with the Gone*; 1998) and *Buenos Aires Vice Versa* (1996), among others. Codirector and cowriter Martín Desalvo has worked mostly as a television director and producer. *Las mantenidas sin sueños* is his first full-length feature film.
8. See also Susan Honeyman (5) for a similar viewpoint referring to children in literature.
9. In her analysis of children in war films, Karen Lury points out that "animals and children are 'perfect victims,' since they are blameless" and their suffering "puts the viewer in a superior position. We are feeling sorry for those who cannot care for themselves and for those we believe should be cared for as some kind of universal right" (105–6).

10. Here I am thinking of Honeyman's assertion that "the concept of childhood serves as a *tabula rasa* for adult constructions, which seem all the more legitimate for their lack of opposition, as discursive boundaries already exclude possible counter-expressions from unspeaking or illiterate young still in the process of achieving the socialized means to power in adult ideologies—mastery of literate language" (2). Lury has also reflected on "the child's apparent inadequacy in relation to language" and its implications for fictional representation (7).
11. Referring to Brazilian films about orphans and homeless children, Traverso argues that ruins are testimony to the "permanent war on the individual by capitalism" (179). It is interesting to note the parallels, particularly as the characters of *Las mantenidas sin sueños* repeatedly rant against capitalism.
12. In a different interview, Fogwill comments that the film "trata sobre mujeres que se desdoblan, son sus propios hombres, sus propios maridos. El bigotito que le pinta la nena a la madre tiene un simbolismo" (is about women that unfold, that are their own men, their own husbands. The little mustache the child draws on the mother's face is symbolic; Soto). The in-depth analysis of gender roles is beyond the purview of this chapter, but it offers rich possibilities for further study.
13. (I wanted to make a feminine film, not a feminist one, which is something quite different . . . The women in this film occupy men's places, and therefore they have roles that are not those supposedly assigned to them; Burstein).

Works Cited

Bazin, André. "Cruelty and Love in *Los Olvidados*." *What Is Cinema?* 3 (1951): 209–12.

Burstein, Sergio. "Vera Fogwill. La mirada femenina." *¿Cómo? En L.A.* N.d. Web. 7 Jan. 2011. <http://www.comoenla.com>.

Chernus, Linda A. "'Separation/Abandonment/Isolation Trauma': An Application of Psychoanalytic Developmental Theory to Understanding Its Impact on Both Chimpanzee and Human Children." *Journal of Emotional Abuse* 8.4 (2008): 447–68.

Commiso, Sandra. "Las mujeres que buscan su lugar." *Clarín* 26 Apr. 2007. Web. 7 Jan. 2011. <http://edant.clarin.com/diario/2007/04/26/espectaculos/c-01011.htm>.

Dieleke, Edgardo. "*O sertão nao virou mar*. Images of Violence and the Position of the Spectator in Contemporary Brazilian Cinema." *Visual Synergies in Fiction and Documentary Film from Latin America*. Ed. Miriam Haddu and Joanna Page. New York, NY: Palgrave Macmillan, 2009. 67–84.

Ford, Julian D. "Defining and Understanding Complex Trauma and Complex Traumatic Stress Disorders." *Treating Complex Traumatic Stress Disorders: An Evidence-Based Guide*. Ed. Christine A. Courtois and Julian D. Ford. New York, NY: Guilford Press, 2009. 13–30.

Gilmore, Leigh. *The Limits of Autobiography: Trauma and Testimony*. Ithaca, NY: Cornell UP, 2001.

Haase, Donald. "Children, War, and the Imaginative Space of Fairy Tales." *The Lion and the Unicorn* 24 (2000): 260–377.
Honeyman, Susan. *Elusive Childhood: Impossible Representations in Modern Fiction.* Columbus, OH: Ohio State UP, 2005.
Jackson, Kathy M. *Images of Children in American Film: A Sociocultural Analysis.* Metuchen NJ: Scarecrow P, 1986.
Kearney, Mary Celeste. "Girlfriends and Girl Power: Female Adolescence in Contemporary U.S. Cinema." *Sugar, Spice, and Everything Nice: Cinemas of Girlhood.* Ed. Frances Gateward and Murray Pomerance. Detroit, MI: Wayne State UP, 2002. 125–42.
Mantenidas sin sueños, Las. Dir.Vera Fogwill and Martín Desalvo. Perf. Vera Fogwill, Gastón Pauls, and Lucía Snieg. Avalon Productions, 2005. Digital videodisc.
Lury, Karen. *The Child in Film: Tears, Fears and Fairy Tales.* New Brunswick: Rutgers UP, 2010.
Mishne, Judith. "The Grieving Child: Manifest and Hidden Losses in Childhood and Adolescence." *Child and Adolescent Social Work Journal* 9.6 (1992): 471–90.
Pinto, Kristina. "Growing Up Young: The Relationship between Childhood Stress and Coping with Early Puberty." *The Journal of Early Adolescence* 27 (2007): 509–44.
Robson, Kathryn. "Bodily Detours: Sarah Kofman's Narratives of Childhood Trauma." *The Modern Language Review* 99.3 (2004): 608–21.
Rojas, Veronica M., and Tal N. Lee. "Childhood vs. Adult PTSD." *Posttraumatic Stress Disorders in Children and Adolescents.* Ed. Raul R. Silva. New York, NY: Norton, 2004. 237–56.
Soto, Moira. "Mujeres con bigotes." *Página/12.com.* Página/12, 25 Apr. 2007. Web. 15 Mar. 2012. <http://www.pagina12.com.ar/diario/suplementos/las12/13-3307-2007-04-20.html>.
Traverso, Antonio. "Migrations of Cinema: Italian Neorealism and Brazilian Cinema." Ed. Laura E. Ruberto and Kristi M. Wilson. *Italian Neorealism and Global Cinema.* Detroit, MI: Wayne State UP, 2007. 165–86.
Van der Kolk, Bessel A. "The Developmental Impact of Childhood Trauma." *Understanding Trauma: Integrating Biological, Clinical, and Cultural Perspectives.* Ed. Laurence J. Kirmayer, Robert Lemelson, and Mark Barad. New York, NY: Cambridge UP, 2007. 224–41.

Notes on Contributors

Janis Breckenridge is associate professor of Spanish at Whitman College. She specializes in contemporary Latin American literature and film and is a former recipient of the Feministas Unidas Essay Prize for her study of experimental documentary film. Breckenridge's publications focus on cultural representations of the last dictatorship in Argentina, collective memory, and literary and visual testimony. This research culminated in the volume *Pushing the Boundaries of Latin American Testimony: Meta-morphoses and Migrations* (Palgrave Macmillan, 2012), coedited with Louise Detwiler. Breckenridge's most recent scholarship studies issues of social justice as depicted in graphic novels and comics.

Jack Draper is associate professor of Portuguese at the University of Missouri where he also serves as the Portuguese Language coordinator for the Romance Languages and Literatures Department. His general field of research is Latin American cultural studies and he specializes in Brazilian literature, music, cinema, and popular culture. His first monograph is *Forró and Redemptive Regionalism from the Brazilian Northeast: Popular Music in a Culture of Migration* (Lang, 2010). Select recent work includes "Forró's Wars of Maneuver and Position: Popular Northeastern Music, Critical Regionalism, and a Culture of Migration," in the *Latin American Research Review*, and "Renovation and Conservation in Brazilian Literature and Music" in the *Journal of Latin American Cultural Studies*.

Antonio Gómez L-Quiñones is associate professor of Spanish at Dartmouth College where he teaches Hispanic and Comparative Literature. He is the author of three books: *Borges y el Nazismo: Sur (1937–1946)* (Servicio de Publicaciones de la Universidad de Granada, 2004), *La guerra persistente: Memoria, violencia y utopía: Representaciones contemporáneas de la Guerra Civil Española* (Iberoamericana/Vervuert, 2006), and *La precariedad de la forma: Lo sublime en la literatura Española contemporánea* (Biblioteca Nueva, 2011). He has also coeedited *The Holocaust in Spanish Memory: Historical Perceptions and Cultural Discourses* (Leipzig University

Press, 2010) and a special issue of the *Vanderbilt Journal of Spanish and Luso-Hispanic Studies* (2009) on the cultures of war in the Iberian Peninsula. He has published more than fifty essays on Latin American and Spanish cinematography and literature.

Eduardo Ledesma is a doctoral candidate in the Department of Romance Languages and Literatures at Harvard University and will defend his dissertation on Luso-Hispanic experimental, avant-garde, and digital poetry in May 2012. He holds advanced degrees in both structural engineering and Hispanic and Lusophone literature. His current research focuses on contemporary Latin American and Iberian film, literature, and new media, with a special emphasis on digital poetry and narrative. In August 2012, he will be joining the Department of Spanish, Italian, and Portuguese at the University of Illinois at Urbana-Champaign as assistant professor of contemporary Latin American literatures and cultures.

Carolina Rocha is associate professor of Spanish at Southern Illinois University–Edwardsville. She specializes in contemporary Southern Cone literature and film. She is the editor, along with Hugo Hortiguera, of *Argentinean Cultural Production during the Neoliberal Years*. She is also the coeditor with Elizabeth Montes Garcés of *Violence in Contemporary Argentine Literature and Film* (University of Calgary Press, 2010) and coeditor of *New Trends in Argentine and Brazilian Cinema* (Intellect Press, 2011). Her articles on film and literature have appeared in *Hispania, Revista de estudios hispánicos, Bulletin of Spanish Studies, Studies in Latin American Popular Culture, Journal of Modern Jewish Studies*, and *Ciberletras*, among others. She has recently published *Masculinities in Contemporary Argentine Popular Cinema* (Palgrave, 2012).

Dan Russek is assistant professor of Spanish in the Department of Hispanic and Italian Studies at the University of Victoria (UVic). He is a native of Mexico and has taught at UVic since 2004. He completed his PhD in Comparative Literature, specializing in modern and contemporary Latin American literature and visual arts. His fields of research include the links between literature and the visual arts and media and urban studies and aesthetics. He is currently finishing a manuscript that explores the relations between twentieth-century Latin American literature and photography. His publications have appeared in *Revista canadiense de estudios Hispánicos, Hispanic Journal, Chasqui, Revista de literatura latinoamericana and mosaic*, among others.

Notes on Contributors

Ignacio M. Sánchez Prado is associate professor of Spanish and International and Area Studies at Washington University in St. Louis. His areas of research are Mexican literary, film, and cultural studies and the genealogies of Latin American humanism and the uses of canon theory and world literature theory in Latin American studies. He is the author of *El canon y sus formas: La reinvención de Harold Bloom y sus lecturas hispanoamericanas* (2002) and *Poesía para nada* (2005). His most recent book is *Naciones intelectuales: Las fundaciones de la modernidad literaria mexicana (1917–1959)* (2009), for which he was awarded the LASA Mexico Section's 2010 Humanities Book Prize. He also has edited and coedited eight collections of critical essays, the most recent of which is a collaboration with Mabel Moraña, *El lenguaje de las emociones: Afecto y cultura en América Latina* (Iberoamericana/Vervuert 2012).

Georgia Seminet is assistant professor of Spanish at St. Edward's University in Austin, Texas. Her area of concentration is modern Latin American fiction. Her current research centers on metaphors of globalization in contemporary Latin American literature and culture. She has previously published in *Revista de literatura mexicana contemporánea*, *Siglo XIX*, *Chasqui*, *Hispania*, and the *Journal for the Association of Humanities in Higher Education*. She is currently working on a manuscript tentatively titled *Delirium, Chaos, and Instability: Metaphors of Globalization in Latin American Narrative*.

Julia Tuñón is a full-time researcher at Direction of Historical Studies (DEH) and the National Institute of Anthropology and History (INAH). She has been awarded the Emilio García Riera Award given by the University of Guadalajara for her achievements in historical research and the Gabino Barreda Award given by the UNAM. She is the author of *Cuerpo y espíritu: Médicos en celuloide* (Pinacoteca, 2005); *Los rostros de un mito: Personajes femeninos en las películas de Emilio "Indio" Fernández* (CONACULTA, 2000; *Mexican Women: A Past Unveiled* (U of Texas P, 1999); *Mujeres en México: Recordando una historia* (CONACULTA, 1998); *Mujeres de luz y sombra en el cine mexicano: La construcción de una imagen (1939–1952)* (El Colegio de México, 1998); and *En su propio espejo: Entrevista con Emilio "Indio" Fernández* (Universidad Autónoma Metropolitana, 1988).

Beatriz Urraca is associate professor of Spanish at Widener University and co-chair of the film studies section of the Latin American Studies Association. A native of Spain, she received her PhD in Comparative Literature, specializing in nineteenth-century literary constructions of national identity in Argentina and the United States. Her current research focuses on contemporary Argentine independent cinema and her most recent articles on the films of Pablo Trapero, Adrián Caetano, Fabián Bielinsky, Rodrigo Moreno, Alejandro Agresti, and Verónica Chen have appeared in *New Trends in Argentine and Brazilian Cinema* (Intellect, 2011), *Representations of Violence in Contemporary Argentine Literature and Film* (University of Calgary, 2010), *Imagofagia*, and *Hispanic Research Journal*.

Rosana Díaz-Zambrana is associate professor of Spanish at Rollins College and a native of Puerto Rico. Her research focuses on modern Latin American literature, specifically contemporary Brazilian and Southern Cone narratives. She has published numerous essays on the motif of the journey in Latin American literature, popular culture, and film. In 2010, she coedited *Cinema paraíso: Representaciones e imágenes audiovisuales en el Caribe hispano*. Currently, she is coediting the first anthology on horror cinema in Latin America and the Caribbean.

Jeffrey Zamostny is assistant professor of Spanish at the University of West Georgia. His research focuses on modernity and (homo)sexualities in the mass culture of early twentieth-century Spain. In addition to having published essays in *Chasqui*, *Decimonónica*, and *MELUS*, he has served as editor of the journals *Nomenclatura: Aproximaciones a los estudios hispánicos* and *disClosure: Journal of Social Theory*.

Index

abuse, 7, 20, 109, 153, 159–65, 168n16, 205, 209, 225
  domestic abuse, 163
  sexual abuse, 211–13
  state violence, 8, 97
  women, 146n1
adulthood, 3, 5, 14, 21n6
  and citizenship, 118
  and class, 118, 121, 128
  and parental roles, 227
  representation in film, 161, 229
  and sexuality, 126–27, 208
  transition from childhood, 57–58, 87, 129
agency, 106, 110, 218
  and child focalizer, 85, 154, 160–64, 172
  and representation of childhood, 72
  and sexuality, 202n6
  symbols of, 142
Agresti, Alejandro, 10, 236n4, 236n7
  Valentín, 10, 29, 224
Aguilar, Fabrizio
  Paloma de papel, 10, 65
allegory, 16
  and childhood, 17, 65
  and citizenship formation, 122, 129
  and national identity, 70, 130n9
Árbenz, Jacobo, 17, 65–68, 74, 80n17
Argueta, Luis, 67–69
  silencio de Neto, El, 17, 63, 67–69, 71, 74–77, 79n10, 79n13
Armendáriz, Montxo
  Secretos del corazón, 11
Armiñán, Jaime
  nido, El, 8

Athié, Francisco
  Lolo, 146n1
Babenco, Héctor
  Pixote: A lei do mais Fraco, 8
Betriu, Francesc
  Réquiem por un campesino español, 9
Bildungsroman, 102, 121–22, 174, 180, 182, 234. *See also* coming-of-age
Biraben, Gastón
  Cautiva, 10
Borau, José
  Camada negra, 8
  Furtivos, 8
Boytler, Arcady
  mujer del puerto, La, 146n1
Buñuel, Luis, 6, 7, 8, 18, 35, 46n6, 135–40, 143, 146n1, 146n3, 147n4
  olvidados, Los, 6, 7, 8, 18, 135–36, 140, 143, 236n1

Caetano, Adrián, 1, 13, 242
  Francia, 13
  Pizza, birra, faso, 1, 13
capitalism, 130n8, 230, 233, 237n11
Carrera, Carlos
  Crimen del padre amaro, 124
Castilla, Sergio
  Gringuito, 11
Chávarri, Jaime, 8, 9
  A un dios desconocido, 8
  bicicletas son para el verano, Las, 9
child
  and culture, 5–6, 9
  definitions of, 3, 21n6, 50–51, 179

child (*continued*)
  development of, 19
  focalization, 3, 4, 7, 8, 18, 64–65, 77, 79n13, 83, 85, 104, 152–56, 160–65, 167n15, 172
  and gaze, 4, 7, 49, 51, 59, 86, 92, 108, 113n12, 161
  as protagonist, 20, 50, 64, 102–4, 110–11, 171
  and representation in film, 2, 4–6, 33, 64, 69, 103–6, 158–59, 226, 237n10
  as a subject, 22n23, 171, 174, 227
  See also childhood
childhood
  and abuse, 109, 153, 159–65, 168n16, 205, 209, 216–18, 225
  as allegory, 17, 57–58, 65, 66, 70, 76, 85, 174
  and class, 125–26
  and effects of military conflict, 49
  and exile, 11, 17, 33–34, 39–43, 46n1
  and family dysfunction, 224, 231
  and gender, 197–98, 211
  and identity, 39
  and infantilization, 125–26
  innocence, 51, 67–68, 70–72, 77, 83, 85–90, 95, 117, 120, 174
  and memory, 45, 46n6, 74–76, 79n10
  and modernity, 121–22
  and orphanhood, 135–39, 141, 145, 146n1
  and otherness, 207–10, 213, 216–17
  and poverty, 10, 152, 232
  and privilege, 73, 79n11
  relation with citizenship, 118–19, 121–22
  as romantic trope, 53
  and sexuality, 79n16, 117, 120
  transition to adulthood, 70, 87, 121, 129
  and trauma, 34–35, 228–30, 234
  and violence, 151, 158, 160–65, 167n10
  See also child
citizenship, 5, 18, 19, 118, 128, 130n3
  and allegory, 122
  and class, 118
  formation of, 129
  and gender, 119
  and innocence, 119
class, 2, 14, 17, 130n4, 130n8
  in Argentinian cinema, 233
  in Brazilian cinema, 206
  citizenship, 119
  class structure, 76
  divisions, 87–89, 96, 98n7, 122–23
  and gender, 73, 126, 207
  inequality, 73, 158
  lower class, 15, 87
  in Mexican cinema, 124–29, 145
  middle class, 16, 18, 102, 113n10, 120, 137, 145, 148n12
  orphanhood, 138–39
  otherness, 209
  social class, 14, 65, 73, 76, 175
  upper class, 65, 67–69, 74, 79n13, 86, 97
coming-of-age, 13, 16–18, 20, 64–70, 76–77, 90, 130n2, 138, 225
  as representation of political conflict, 97
  as social critique, 101
  See also Bildungsroman
Coton, Alan
  Soba, 18, 128
Cremata Malberti, Juan Carlos, and Iraida Malberti Cabrera
  Viva Cuba, 12, 15, 172
Cuarón, Alfonso
  Y tu mamá también, 13, 117, 118, 120–21
Cuarón, Jonás
  Año uña, 18, 119, 121–22
Cuerda, José Luis
  lengua de las mariposas, La, 1
culture, 3–6, 9–10, 15, 130n1, 130n2

and childhood, 50
and ethnicity, 40–41, 72
indigenous culture, 14
and orphanhood, 135
popular culture, 12
and sexuality, 193
subculture, 206, 126
and violence, 155
death
  as a narrative event, 55–58
  as a symbol, 37, 43, 89, 123, 155–58
Del Toro, Guillermo
  and childhood in film, 50
  espinazo del diablo, El, 11, 13
  and fairy tale, 54, 57, 60
  laberinto del fauno, El, 1, 11
  Spanish Civil War, 54
Desalvo, Martín
  mantenidas sin sueños, Las, 20, 224, 225, 236n7
Dhalia, Heitor
  Nina, 16, 20, 205–9, 214–20, 220n3, 220n5

education, 2, 19
  and *Bildungsroman,* 174
  and privilege, 74
  sentimental, 173, 175–76, 179–82
  systematic/unsystematic, 175, 183
Eimbcke, Fernando
  Lake Tahoe, 15, 18, 130n7, 135–37, 141–45, 148n10, 148n11
  Temporada de patos, 15, 18, 121, 135–41
epistemology
  of children, 207–9, 218, 220n2
  of fairy tales, 53–57
  moral, 59
  and otherness, 214
Erice, Víctor
  espíritu de la colmena, El, 7, 21n10, 46n11
ethical attention, 19, 189–90, 193–95, 198, 201

ethnicity, 17
  and child focalization, 65
  and ethnic divide, 72, 76, 78n6, 93–94
  and the Nepantla generation, 40
exile, 2
  and identity, 39–41
  and the Spanish Civil War, 33–35, 38, 46n1
  See also migration; Nepantla generation
family
  and class, 73–74
  dysfunction, 13, 20, 87, 140, 153, 159–60, 181, 224, 228–31
  heteronormativity, 19, 210–11
  as a metaphor, 6, 8, 17, 70, 73, 86, 96, 111, 224, 236n5
  and orphanhood, 141–43, 225
  structure of, 2, 137, 192, 233
  tension, 66–67
  and traditional values, 2, 71, 75, 118
  violence, 16, 153, 159, 165
Favio, Leonardo
  Crónica de un niño solo, 7
feminism, 16, 23n31
  cinematic girl power, 213–14
Finzi, Beadle
  Only When I Dance, 14
Fogwill, Vera
  mantenidas sin sueños, Las, 20, 224, 225, 236n7
Francoism, 22
  in *Pan's Labyrinth,* 57–59
Fukunaga, Cary
  Sin nombre, 10

Gamboa, Alejandro
  primera noche, La, 126
  segunda noche, La, 126
  ultima noche, La, 126, 130n10
García Ascot, Jomí
  balcón vacío, El, 17, 34

García Ruiz, Salvador
  Mensaka, 12, 21n3
Gaviria, Víctor, 159–60
  Rodrigo D: No futuro, 12, 151, 154–59, 167n9–11, 236n1
  vendedora de rosas, La, 9
gaze, 2–4, 20, 49, 91–92, 108, 178, 218
  as eye among the blind, 86–88
  innocence of, 7, 51, 96–97
  and intersexuality, 195–96, 199–200
  of the male director, 127, 202n7, 202n8
  of the spectator, 161
gender
  and citizenship, 119, 129
  construction of, 16, 19, 191
  and expectations/roles, 118, 177, 210, 233, 237n12
  intersexuality, 13–14, 16
  male/female dichotomy, 190, 192
  and narrative structure, 121–27
genre
  and child formation, 173–74
  and fairy tale genre, 20n2, 49, 53–56, 60, 61n8
  and girl power, 210
  and hybrid genre, 15
  and representation of children, 16, 153–54, 236n1
  and street urchin film, 8
González Iñárritu, Alejandro
  Amores perros, 1, 13, 122, 130n8, 146n1
González Rubio, Pedro
  Alamar, 15, 22n18
Gutiérrez Alea, Tomás
  Guantanamera, 178
Gutierrez Aragón, Manuel
  Camada negra, 8

Hamburger, Cao
  O ano em que meus pais sairam de férias, 14, 17, 83, 85, 92
Hofman, Fabián
  Te extraño, 224

identity
  and class, 122–23
  construction of, 39–41, 66, 102, 122
  of indigenous people, 75, 79n9
  national identity, 14, 70, 117
  in Spanish film, 11

Kogut, Sandra, 220
  Mutum, 13

Lazkano, Arantxa
  Urte ilunak/Los años oscuros, 11
León de Aranoa, Fernando
  Barrio, 11
Lichtmann, Gabriel
  Judíos en el espacio, 14
Littin, Miguel
  Alsino y el cóndor, 8
Llosa, Claudia
  Madeinusa, 14
Loriga, Ray
  pistola de mi hermano, La, 12
Luna, Bigas
  teta i la lluna, La, 11
Lund, Kátia
  Cidade de Deus, 236n1

Mandoki, Luis
  Voces inocentes, 10, 64
Mañas, Achero
  Bola, El, 13, 15, 151, 159–64, 167n14, 168n16
Marston, Joshua
  María llena eres de gracia, 9, 65, 236n1
Martel, Lucrecia
  ciénaga, La, 13, 236n1
  niña santa, La, 13, 223
Meirelles, Fernando
  Cidade de Deus, 9, 236n1
memory, 4, 15
  historical memory, 16, 42, 56, 69, 85
  as narrative theme, 38, 43
  politics of, 85, 96–97
  See also nostalgia

INDEX

metaphor
  of childhood, 44
  of class division, 87, 96, 98n7
  and fairy tales, 21n2
  of family, 42
  of Francoist regime, 22n19
  of the nation, 6, 66–67, 76–77
  and orphanhood, 135–36, 145
  of violence, 162
  See also allegory
migration, 10, 17, 39, 172
  and effects in adulthood, 34
  See also exile
Murga, Celina
  Una semana solos, 14, 224

Naranjo, Gerardo, 135
  Drama/Mex, 127–29
  Voy a explotar, 123
narrative, 16–17
  coming-of-age, 18, 20, 64, 119 (see also *Bildungsroman*)
  dual narrative, 54, 61n7
  ethical attention, 19, 189, 191, 193
  fairy tale, 54–56, 61n8
  focalization, 158, 162
  formation narrative, 119
  gendered narrative, 121, 127, 206–7
  historical narrative, 67–68
  personal narrative, 42, 45, 58
  road movie, 179
Nepantla generation, 35, 40–43, 45
nostalgia, 59, 68–77, 79n13. *See also* childhood: innocence; memory

Olivera, Héctor
  noche de los lápices, La, 9
Orphanhood
  definitions of, 136
  functional orphanhood, 139–40, 225
  in Mexican cinema, 135, 145n1
  as a trope, 18
Pérez, Fernando
  Havana Suite, 171
  Life Is to Whistle, 171

Piñeyro, Marcelo
  Kamchatka, 10
postmodern, 12
  childhood, 53, 148n7
  narrative, 61n8
  politics of nostalgia, 58, 139, 148n7
Puenzo, Lucía
  niño pez, El, 13, 223
  XXY, 13, 15, 19, 189
Puenzo, Luis
  Historia oficial, La, 224
purity, 58
  of childhood, 52
  children in cinema, 33
  in cinema, 7, 85
  the color white, 89, 218
  loss of, 90

road movie, 178–79, 181, 183
Rodríguez, Ismael
  Nosotros los pobres, 146n1
Rotberg, Dana
  Angel de fuego, 146n1

Salles, Walter
  Central do Brasil, 1
  Linha del passé, 14
Sariñana, Fernando
  Amar te duele, 10, 22
  Hasta morir, 124
  Niñas mal, 125–26
  Todo el poder, 124
Saura, Carlos
  Cría cuervos, 8
  Prima Angélica, La, 8
sexuality, 16, 18, 19
  of adolescents, 73, 79n16, 117, 126
  See also gender: intersexuality
Sistach, Maryse
  niña en la piedra, La, 146n1
  Perfume de violetas: Nadie te oye, 9
social norms, 104
  of women, 123, 126
Solomonoff, Julia
  último verano de la boyita, El, 13

Spanish Civil War, 1, 6, 9, 11, 17, 45, 49, 51, 54–60, 60n4
Stagnaro, Bruno
  Pizza, birra, faso, 1

Tabío, Juan Carlos
  Lista de espera, 178
Tagliavini, Gabriela
  Ladies' Night, 126
Thomas, Daniela
  and *Linha de passe,* 14
Tort, Gerardo
  De la calle, 146n1
trauma, 227, 228
  in childhood, 4, 224, 225, 230
  and coming of age, 123, 128, 129, 201
  and exile, 34
  and family, 225, 229
  and Guatemalan history, 76
  and loss of parents, 103
  and psychological trauma, 34–36, 45, 228
  witnessing of, 89
Trueba, David
  buena vida, La, 13

Uribe, Imanol
  viaje de Carol, El, 11

values, 2
  and adulthood, 88
  cultural values, 5, 40
  emotional values, 51
  and moral values, 57
violence, 1, 2–5, 8, 9, 16, 65, 89, 96, 101, 155
  and child focalizer, 8, 49, 152, 160
  and children in film, 151, 236
  and class, 122
  domestic violence, 16, 153, 159, 165
  and effects on childhood, 34, 85
  and emotional release, 143
  and gaze, 108, 196
  and gender, 9, 196, 209
  images of, 158
  representation of, 161, 162
  self-violence, 155
  and urban youth, 16, 137, 154–55, 167n10, 223

Werneck, Sandra, 16, 19, 205, 219
  Sonhos Roubados, 16, 19, 205
Winograd, Ariel
  Cara de queso, mi primer ghetto, 14

Yasín Gutiérrez, Ishtar
  camino, El, 10
child focalization, 64
youth, 1–3, 16, 118, 153
  as an audience, 5, 124
  casting of, 1, 124, 152
  and cinema of formation, 129, 138
  and citizenship, 122, 129
  and economy, 11, 148n7
  and family tension, 12, 223
  as focalizers, 157
  and gender, 12, 119, 129
  and globalization, 14
  manipulation of youth, 12, 89
  and memory, 42
  as metaphor, 59, 90, 118, 121, 122
  and national identity, 174
  and social class, 10, 119, 124, 129, 145, 158
  violence, 151, 154, 158, 223
  and vulnerability, 145

GPSR Compliance
The European Union's (EU) General Product Safety Regulation (GPSR) is a set of rules that requires consumer products to be safe and our obligations to ensure this.

If you have any concerns about our products, you can contact us on

ProductSafety@springernature.com

In case Publisher is established outside the EU, the EU authorized representative is:

Springer Nature Customer Service Center GmbH
Europaplatz 3
69115 Heidelberg, Germany

www.ingramcontent.com/pod-product-compliance
Lightning Source LLC
LaVergne TN
LVHW011812060526
838200LV00053B/3747